The overall summary report of the work of the OECD Ad Hoc Group on Transport and the Environment presented here in Part I was approved by the OECD Council for derestriction in June 1987.

It is accompanied by the reports of the three activities carried out by the Group concerning:

- The Impact of Road Transport on the Environment;
- The Assessment of Innovations in Urban Transport Management;
- The Assessment of Technical Changes to Reduce Air Pollution and Noise Emissions From Motor Vehicles.

The Ad Hoc Group on Transport and the Environment Committee recommended the derestriction of these three reports on the authority of the Secretary-General, who subsequently agreed.

Also Available

THE STATE OF THE ENVIRONMENT – 1985 (June 1985)
(97 85 04 1) ISBN 92-64-12713-5 272 pages £16.50 US$33.00 F165.00 DM73.00

OECD ENVIRONMENTAL DATE. COMPENDIUM 1987 (June 1987) bilingual
(97 87 05 3) ISBN 92-64-02960-5 366 pages £20.00 US$42.00 F200.00 DM86.00

FIGHTING NOISE. Strengthening Noise Abatement Policies (September 1986)
(97 86 01 1) ISBN 92-64-12827-1 146 pages £7.50 US$15.00 F75.00 DM33.00

ENVIRONMENTAL EFFECTS OF AUTOMOTIVE TRANSPORT. The OECD Compass Project (October 1986)
(97 86 03 1) ISBN 92-64-12862-X 172 pages £10.00 US$20.00 F100.00 DM44.00

Forthcoming

CITIES AND TRANSPORT

Prices charged at the OECD Bookshop.

THE OECD CATALOGUE OF PUBLICATIONS and supplements will be sent free of charge on request addressed either to OECD Publications Service, Sales and Distribution Division, 2, rue André-Pascal, 75775 PARIS CEDEX 16, or to the OECD Distributor in your country.

TRANSPORT AND THE ENVIRONMENT

ORGANISATION FOR ECONOMIC CO-OPERATION AND DEVELOPMENT

Pursuant to article 1 of the Convention signed in Paris on 14th December, 1960, and which came into force on 30th September, 1961, the Organisation for Economic Co-operation and Development (OECD) shall promote policies designed:

- to achieve the highest sustainable economic growth and employment and a rising standard of living in Member countries, while maintaining financial stability, and thus to contribute to the development of the world economy;
- to contribute to sound economic expansion in Member as well as non-member countries in the process of economic development; and
- to contribute to the expansion of world trade on a multilateral, non-discriminatory basis in accordance with international obligations.

The original Member countries of the OECD are Austria, Belgium, Canada, Denmark, France, the Federal Republic of Germany, Greece, Iceland, Ireland, Italy, Luxembourg, the Netherlands, Norway, Portugal, Spain, Sweden, Switzerland, Turkey, the United Kingdom and the United States. The following countries became Members subsequently through accession at the dates indicated hereafter: Japan (28th April, 1964), Finland (28th January, 1969), Australia (7th June, 1971) and New Zealand (29th May, 1973).

The Socialist Federal Republic of Yugoslavia takes part in some of the work of the OECD (agreement of 28th October, 1961).

Publié en français sous le titre :

TRANSPORTS
ET ENVIRONNEMENT

GENERAL OUTLINE

DETAILED TABLE OF CONTENTS

Part I

TRANSPORT AND ENVIRONMENT: AN OVERVIEW

Part II

THE IMPACTS OF ROAD TRANSPORT ON THE ENVIRONMENT

Part III

ASSESSMENT OF INNOVATIONS IN URBAN TRANSPORT MANAGEMENT

Part IV

ASSESSMENT OF TECHNICAL CHANGES TO REDUCE AIR POLLUTION AND NOISE EMISSIONS FROM MOTOR VEHICLES

Part I

TRANSPORT AND THE ENVIRONMENT: AN OVERVIEW

INTRODUCTION

Transport systems play a major role in the economic life of OECD countries and in the daily lives of their citizens. The production and use of transport infrastructures and mobile equipment have considerable weight in the economies of OECD countries: 4 to 8 per cent of GDP and 2 to 4 per cent of jobs. The balances of payments in Member countries are also strongly influenced by the international trade in transport equipment and "invisible" transport services. The purchase of transport services and personal transport equipment makes up a significant percentage of outlays by businesses and of household consumption expenditure (around 10 per cent in Europe, more in North America, less in Japan). A substantial share of tax revenues also goes towards public expenditure on transport, particularly for capital investment and service subsidy.

The negative effects of transport activities include accidents, congestion, air pollution and noise due to road transport, oil pollution by maritime transport, noise from aircraft, energy consumption and consumption of land and other natural resources for the production of vehicles and infrastructures. For instance, the non-internalised social costs of road transport were estimated to amount to about 5 per cent of GDP for OECD countries. In recent years public concern has increased in several OECD countries especially with respect to air pollution and noise from road transport.

The nature of the problems relating to the impact of transport on the environment is international for several reasons and goes far beyond the general need to harmonise environmental policies among OECD countries:

- Transport vehicles are products subject to international trade, and various standards and related regulations (e.g. noise standards and emissions standards) should not be used as non-tariff barriers to trade;
- Transport vehicles contribute to the emission of air pollutants which are transported across borders (e.g. NO_x) or contribute to global atmospheric pollution (CO_2);
- Transport vehicles themselves cross national borders and imply some harmonisation in fuel provision and in environmental standards.

The present part of the report is based on three documents:

- *The Impacts of Road Transport on the Environment* (Part II of this document), providing facts and figures concerning the road transport sector and its related noise and air pollution effects in OECD Member countries;
- *Assessment of Innovations in Urban Transport Management* (Part III of this document), itself based on case studies conducted by independent teams of experts in 10 different cities: Athens, Gothenburg, Hong Kong, London, Los Angeles, Munich, New York, Osaka, Paris and Singapore[1].
- "Assessment of Technical Changes to Reduce Air Pollution and Noise Emissions from Motor Vehicles" (Part IV of this document), reviewing regulations and standards, test procedures, exhaust emission and noise emission control technologies for gasoline-fuelled cars, diesel-fuelled cars, trucks, buses and two-wheeled motorized vehicles, fuel changes, and compliance with standards.

It focuses on road transport and the environment, and attempts:

- To consider air pollution and noise issues in relation to other major issues such as transport safety, energy consumption and congestion;
- To relate actions concerning motor vehicles to those concerning infrastructures and the use of motor vehicles and infrastructures;
- To take into account non-environmental objectives of transport systems; indeed the questions reviewed here have the most significant trade, industrial, technological, and energy implications, and therefore exemplify issues of integration of the environment in these sectors.

Chapter I

THE PROBLEM: ROAD TRANSPORT IMPACTS ON THE ENVIRONMENT

1. AIR POLLUTION

The most prevalent air pollutants emitted from transport sources include carbon monoxide (CO), lead (Pb), volatile organic compounds (VOCs), nitrogen oxides (NO_x), and particulate matter. They may cause the following direct and indirect effects:

- Health effects (irritation of respiratory, eye, or other systems; acute toxic systemic effects; mutagenic or carcinogenic action; adverse effects on defense mechanisms against infections);
- Environmental damage (material soiling; loss of agricultural productivity; acidification of soil and water; forest damage); or
- Nuisance (odour, decreased visibility).

Lastly, increasing concentrations of CO_2 in the atmosphere resulting from fossil fuel combustion (including traffic sources), and their possible climatic, economic and social impacts are also of some concern.

Success in attaining ambient air quality objectives has been limited. Only Japan and the United States have been able to attain better ambient air quality standards in the 80s compared to the 70s even though exceedances are still observed. In Europe, emission reduction policies for the transport sector have not been strong enough to achieve absolute environmental improvements. Only those countries that have already, for a considerable number of years, been enforcing the most stringent emission requirements per individual vehicle, have until now been able to reverse trends of rising pollution from the transport sector.

2. NOISE

The state of the noise environment and community exposure to noise seems to have remained relatively static in recent years. At national level, transport is by far the prime source of noise, ahead of building or industry, with road traffic being the chief offender. Aircraft noise is generally next in terms of overall population exposure in most countries, before rail transport and stationary sources.

While the situation overall does not seem to have worsened, there has certainly been no change for the better. It is no easy matter to gauge the extent to which the relative stabilisation of the problem in the last five to ten years can be ascribed to "scattered" noise abatement policies, general economic trends (the slowdown and even levelling off in economic growth may have given some respite) and technological progress. In the aviation industry, for example, in addition to international noise regulations, energy constraints have impelled constructors to develop aircraft with greater fuel efficiency which have also proved to be quieter.

There is evidence that past and current measures to impose stringent vehicle noise emission standards have brought results, though the full effects of such measures are only felt some ten to twenty years after their adoption. Moreover considerable efforts have been and are being made to equip existing infrastructures and housing by installing anti-noise screens and soundproofing especially in "black spot" areas (an Leq of above 65 dBA). Greater account is being and will be taken of noise abatement objectives at the design and construction stages.

All this, however, will not in itself greatly improve the quality of the environment with regard to noise. If trends are to be reversed, given the conclusions of the various studies on the future outlook, there is a clear need to strengthen these noise abatement policies in all areas in order to counter the almost certainly adverse trend, particularly as regards the extension of areas subject to moderate noise (what may be called the "grey areas", i.e. Leq levels between 55 and 65 dBA).

There are subjects of growing or new concern for the future state of the environment with regard to noise. These mainly relate to the emergence of new sources of noise (e.g. recreational vehicles, increasing use of diesel vehicles) and trends in the communities at risk (aging population and other demographic changes), multi-exposure to noise from several sources and the encroachment of noise into rural, tourist and unspoilt areas that have hitherto been spared.

SELECTED DATA ON TRANSPORT AND THE ENVIRONMENT
EARLY 1980s

	North America	OECD Europe	Japan	OECD	
TRANSPORT					
Road network length					
All roads	59%	25%	9%	100%	12 700 000 km
Motorways	67%	29%	3%	100%	115 000 km
Road vehicle stocks					
Motor vehicles in use	49%	36%	12%	100%	368 million vehicles
Passenger cars in use	48%	41%	9%	100%	292 million vehicles
Goods vehicles in use	57%	18%	22%	100%	73 million vehicles
Road traffic volumes					
All vehicles	57%	33%	8%	100%	5 212 million vehicle km
Passenger cars	55%	36%	7%	100%	3 940 million vehicle km
Goods vehicles	63%	22%	12%	100%	1 221 million vehicle km
AIR					
Total transport emissions as % of total emissions					
NOx	47%	51%	39%	48%	
CO	71%	81%	na	75%	
SOx	4%	3%	9%	3%	
Particulates	14%	8%	na	13%	
HC	39%	45%	na	40%	
NOISE					
Population exposed to high noise levels due to road transport (leq > 65 dBA)	19 million	53 million	36 million	110 million	

Source : OECD, *OECD Environmental Data,* Paris, 1987.
Note : More detailed data are given in the part on "The Impact of Road Transport".

Chapter II

IMPROVING THE ENVIRONMENT: ACTIONS RELATED TO VEHICLES

1. THE NEED FOR INTERNATIONAL CO-OPERATION

Most OECD countries have adopted regulations on motor vehicle exhaust and noise emissions. Existing regulations however are of differing degrees of stringency in Member countries and those countries which are the most advanced in motor vehicle air pollution abatement are not necessarily the most advanced in motor vehicle noise abatement:

- Countries which have adopted very stringent regulations on motor vehicle air pollution (United States, Japan, and in the near future, Scandanavia, Switzerland and Austria) or noise (Switzerland and Japan);
- Countries of the European Communities where the emission limits are for the time being less stringent and where these limits apply equally to all member countries; more stringent measures will be introduced at the beginning of October 1988; these standards can already be applied on a voluntary basis;
- Some OECD Member countries which, because of different levels of economic development and environment climate, have not adopted emission limits equivalent to the ones of the previous two groups.

Opinions differ as to the pace at which the progressive tightening of emission standards should occur and as to the priority to be allocated to the abatement of the different pollutants and nuisances produced by motor vehicles. National differences in the severity of the impact of air pollution (health effects, acid deposition, deterioration of lakes and forests, etc.), in the assimilative capacity of the environment and in public attitudes may call for different rates and timetables for tightening air pollution emission standards. In the same way, national differences in the degree of urbanisation and population density, as well as in the quality of housing and urban planning, may call for different noise emission standards and even for different sets of policy instruments altogether. However, although some air pollution problems are regional and even transfrontier – abatement strategies are different and international action against motor vehicle air pollution may be more necessary than against motor vehicle noise.

However, since motor vehicles are internationally traded goods, cross national boundaries (e.g. for tourism), and generate some pollutants and related damage across borders, international co-operation will continue to be needed; further choices and decisions regarding emissions from motor vehicles should concern both the estimated direct impacts of these emissions on human health and the indirect impacts (even if the latter are more complex and less well understood) of motor vehicles on people and on the environment.

2. TOWARDS A BETTER INTEGRATION OF REGULATIONS CONCERNING MOTOR VEHICLES

The question of how much and how soon to abate motor vehicle air pollution and noise has recently been and will remain the subject of debate, not only because perceptions of the severity of the problem vary from country to country, but also because of the industrial, trade, transport and energy implications of more stringent emission limits. What technologies should be adopted, how soon, and at what cost? And how can the need to reduce emission limits be reconciled with energy conservation and safety? These questions have been frequently debated in the EEC over the past three years, during which time the strengthening of EEC regulations (on air pollutants, lead in petrol and noise emissions) was under discussion. They have also been debated elsewhere at different times (in the early 70s in the United States and Japan, and more recently in the Scandinavian countries and Switzerland).

The importance of appropriate trade-offs between environmental improvement and other constraints must not be disregarded. However, it is now believed that the two goals, low emissions of air pollution and noise and low energy consumption, are not fundamentally incompatible; by using appropriate technologies (e.g. improved combustion, better aerodynamic design), efforts to achieve them can even be mutually reinforcing. As to cost, it appears that while unleaded fuel entails a small cost increase, other controls necessary to reduce air pollution and noise (fuel injection and computer control of the engine, reduced drag, etc.) can reduce the running and maintenance costs of vehicles, if not their price.

Whatever the solutions adopted, care will still have to be taken to give industry a chance to find the best and most efficient technologies and to allow sufficient lead time before adoption of those technologies. A balance will also have to be struck between environmental requirements on the one hand and safety, energy and economic constraints on the other.

3. STRICTER ENFORCEMENT OF REGULATIONS CONCERNING EMISSION STANDARDS AND VEHICLE MAINTENANCE

Evidence shows that in formulating emission standards not only new vehicles but also vehicles already in use must be considered, since it is the latter that are in fact responsible for pollution. Vehicles' performance with respect to the emission of pollutants and noise deteriorates over time. Enforcement of emission standards and maintenance of vehicles in use are therefore two key elements of any strategy aimed at reducing air pollution and noise from motor vehicles.

Furthermore, the behaviour of drivers substantially influences motor vehicle pollution emissions (for instance, through misfueling) and above all noise emissions (for instance, through deliberate modification of mufflers).

For reasons of costs and practicality, test procedures to check vehicles in use should be made simpler than the test procedures used for new vehicles. Procedures (which could include on-the-spot checks) must be inexpensive, rapid and easy to apply; in some countries it may be necessary to develop a specific network and staff to carry out these tests and thus ensure that vehicles in use comply with the standards imposed.

In addition, in order to promote durable technical solutions, special durability tests should be carried out on new vehicles. Regular tests of vehicles in use (which could be linked with safety tests) would be useful, even if the simplified test procedures did not provide for a wide range of operating conditions. Such regular tests would be an inducement to drivers to maintain their vehicles properly.

4. STANDARDS AND TECHNOLOGIES

Technologies to reduce air pollution and noise emissions by vehicles are quite different. Generally, however, one does not detract from the other; indeed, the two may be complementary.

The stringent *air pollution* standards enforced in the United States and Japan are achieved by the use of catalytic converters, especially 3-way catalytic converters, requiring the use of unleaded gasoline. (This in itself is of benefit to the environment, since lead is harmful to public health.) The cost per car of such a device and its accompanying equipment ranges from $250 to $750, i.e. a 4 to 20 per cent increase in the cost of the vehicle, with small, inexpensive cars having to bear the biggest cost increase in relative terms. Other advanced technologies are being developed, especially in Europe and Japan. The best known is the lean-burn engine, which would have the advantage of consuming less gasoline and emitting less pollution than present engines. However, if standards are to be as stringent as those enforced in the U.S. or Japan, or in the European Community as from 1988, the use of a simple two-way catalytic converter to complement the lean-burn engine may be necessary.

Neither diesel cars, trucks and buses or motorised two-wheeled vehicles have yet received as much attention as cars powered by gasoline engines. Since their use is becoming more widespread and NO_x and particulate emissions are increasing in consequence, more stringent standards in respect of them are also needed. Indeed, some countries such as the United States are now introducing such standards; the Commission of the European Communities has also made such a proposal.

The goals regarding *noise emissions* set at the OECD Conference on Noise Abatement Policies in 1980 – 75 dB(A) for cars and 80 dB(A) for heavy vehicles – have not yet been achieved, but two countries – Japan and Switzerland – have already adopted standards very close to these goals, and EEC standards for 1988 are also to be raised.

Various technologies (some of which are already being used) exist to reduce noise emissions, especially those of the noisiest vehicles, heavy lorries. To reach OECD goals set in 1980 the cost increases involved would generally be less than 5 per cent of the vehicle's price and even, for cars and buses, less than 3 per cent.

Now that engine noise and exhaust system noise are gradually being reduced, other sources of motor vehicle noise may become more noticeable, especially noise produced by the interaction between tyres and road surface and the low-frequency sounds emitted by certain types of vehicle. Efforts to reduce these two types of noise will have to be made, and regulations imposing limits on noise emission at highway speeds and on emission of low-frequency sounds may be required in the near future.

5. POLICY INSTRUMENTS

Emission standards are the policy instrument most widely used in OECD countries in dealing with motor vehicle air pollution and noise. By the end of this decade, most new vehicles in OECD countries will be subject to very stringent emission standards for both air pollution and noise. However, some significant differences will remain. The United States, Japan and the European Community will not see the full results of their decisions at the same time. Whereas the United States and Japan severely tightened their emission limits in the late 70s and early 80s, the EC will not have similar limits until the late 80s or early 90s. Moreover, the proposed EC limits will not be as stringent as the most recent U.S. ones (1983) for cars below 2 litres. Whereas in Japan the stock of cars is already cleaner, in the United States it will become cleaner only at the end of this decade, and in the EC only by the end of the century. Some other countries, for example, Switzerland, the Nordic countries, Austria, Canada and Australia, may have a cleaner stock of vehicles by the mid-90s.

As regards more stringent standards for noise emissions, the differences between countries are less pronounced than in the case of air pollution. In Japan and Switzerland the stock of all vehicles will be quieter by the mid-90s, since new standards were imposed between 1983 and 1986 (and not only for cars, as for air pollution). In the EC and in other countries which are gradually tightening emission standards, the whole stock of vehicles will be quieter by the end of the 90s. But since no OECD country has yet announced its intention to adopt emission standards corresponding to the goals set by the OECD Conference in 1980, it will probably not be until the end of this century that the stock of vehicles in all OECD countries will be substantially quieter.

To speed the rate at which OECD vehicles become cleaner and quieter, measures to supplement emission standards are indispensable. Some of these measures relate to the use of vehicles and infrastructures (e.g. traffic management, urban planning and transport policy). They are examined in Chapter III. Others, however, concern vehicles individually.

It could be useful to complement existing and future emission standards by other incentive measures calculated to promote the production and use of cleaner and quieter vehicles. These might include economic instruments, education and formation, labelling of vehicles in terms of their acoustic and air pollution characteristics, preferential treatment for cleaner and quieter vehicles and in-use controls of vehicles. Many such measures could be undertaken at low cost and quite quickly.

Economic instruments – such as modifications of motor vehicle prices linked to noise and air pollution characteristics; "environment" tax on fuel (as imposed in the Netherlands to combat noise and air pollution); lower tax on unleaded fuel and higher tax on leaded fuel (as in Germany and Switzerland); tax incentives for clean vehicles (as in Germany) – can play an important role in speeding the introduction and use of quieter and cleaner vehicles. Moreover, they can also play a major financing role, since the proceeds of charges, taxes, etc. can be used to implement air pollution and noise abatement policies.

Other incentives include the promotion and preferential treatment of low-pollution and low-noise vehicles, much quieter and cleaner than stipulated by the standards, whose use in sensitive areas such as residential or leisure zones could be encouraged. If enough municipalities and countries were to adopt such measures, this would be an incentive to manufacturers to produce quieter and cleaner vehicles.

Lastly, because air pollution and noise emission depend to a great extent on vehicle maintenance and drivers' behaviour, incentives to encourage regular testing of vehicles could be devised and information campaigns organised to emphasise that low noise, low pollution, low fuel consumption and safe driving go hand in hand.

Chapter III

IMPROVING THE ENVIRONMENT: ACTION RELATED TO VEHICLE USE

1. THE URBAN CONTEXT

Air and noise pollution problems persist and may worsen in many urban areas because of the suburbanisation of cities, population growth, rising rate of car ownership, increasing journey rates and failure of technology controls to perform up to design specifications.

While source controls are the highest priority for any abatement strategy, transport policies to manage vehicle use are necessary too to bring faster environmental improvement – particularly in high-growth areas and "black spots".

The case studies[2] demonstrate that transport and traffic management policies can not only make a significant contribution to pollution abatement but also produce many other transport and social benefits.

2. IMPROVING ROAD INFRASTRUCTURES, TRAFFIC MANAGEMENT AND LAND USE

In just about every case study, it is clear that budgetary constraints limit highway and transit investments. This underlines the importance of reducing emissions at source or through better management of highway and transit networks.

The case studies present many practical applications of low-cost solutions of transport and environmental problems. These include measures related to environment (e.g. purchase by local authorities of quiet or low-pollution vehicles, local inspection and maintenance programmes, enforcement of noise standards, creation of buffer zones, proper land use and building design, noise screens on existing infrastructures); pricing measures (e.g. pricing the use of cars through parking fees, supplementary licences, electronic road pricing, differential fuel and vehicle taxation, as well as simplified fare systems and public transport travel cards); financing measures (e.g. mobilisation of private funding through lease financing, transit bonds, joint property developments, tax concessions, payroll levies); physical transport management measures (e.g. traffic cells, lorry bans, preferential treatment of high-occupancy vehicles, ramp metering, area traffic bans based on alternate licence plates, rationalised goods deliveries) and institutional measures.

The improvement of public transport can also contribute to reducing noise and exhaust emissions. If public transport is allowed to deteriorate in dense, public transport-dependent areas, environmental quality can decrease significantly.

The case studies revealed extensive use of private finance and private sector finance mechanisms, with the potential for even wider applications. Much greater scope exists for the use of economic instruments to:

i) promote the use and development of quieter vehicles, and
ii) manage road use through congestion pricing.

3. IMPLEMENTATION

The most innovative and comprehensive policies stem from:

i) considering transport and environment problems together — i.e. taking environment-related questions into account early in the decision-making process; and

ii) establishing imaginative, ongoing public/private partnerships.

Central and local government each has its own role to play in developing and implementing transport policies that are sensitive to environmental considerations. For example, central government should set air quality standards and impose emission limits for new and in-use vehicles, while central and local government can co-operate in traffic management, setting fares, control of land use and innovative experiments.

Chapter IV

LOOKING AHEAD

1. GENERAL TRENDS IN ROAD TRANSPORT

For the rest of this decade and well into the next, the probable developments in the road transport sector can be summed up as follows:

- Stocks of passenger cars in use are likely to continue to grow, though at a slower rate than in the 70s. This slower rate reflects demographic factors such as ageing populations, as well as the increasing maturity of car markets in most OECD countries. The rate may, however, be influenced by future rises in income levels;
- Passenger car traffic volumes are likely to increase further, but again at a slower rate than in the 70s. On average, individual vehicles will be used less intensively as multiple vehicle ownership and the proportion of time taken up by daily travel increase, and this despite a possible stabilisation in motoring costs;
- The number and use of goods vehicles are likely to grow at sustained rates corresponding to the growth in general economic activity, with even faster rates for heavy vehicles. The continuing decline of heavy industry in several Member countries is more likely to affect the transport of freight by rail and inland waterways than the transport of goods by road;
- Road networks are likely to continue to grow, but at a slower pace than in the 70s. Maintenance problems and risks of structural failure, especially on major road systems, may well proliferate due to the normal ageing process, wear and tear by heavy traffic and, in some Member countries, the use of unsuitable construction materials and a legacy of inadequate maintenance. Thus much more emphasis is likely to be placed on protecting, improving and, where necessary, reconstructing existing networks.

2. ENVIRONMENTAL IMPLICATIONS: PRESENT AND FUTURE CONCERNS

As a consequence of these trends, a number of environmental concerns have come to the fore and yet others are emerging. All of them will be relevant for the remainder of the 80s and well into the following decade.

- Pressures on the environment from road transport, such as air pollution and noise, will persist. They may increase less rapidly than in the past, first because of slower growth in the road transport sector and secondly because of the effect of environmental policies as emission standards are enforced and made more stringent and new vehicles embodying technological progress are gradually incorporated into the stock of vehicles in use;
- Containment of these pressures will depend on the strength of policies to control the real level of emissions of new and in-use vehicles (through better vehicle maintenance, for example), as well as on policies for the management of traffic between cities (setting and enforcing speed limits, etc.) and in cities (traffic cells, lorry routing, area-wide traffic control, pricing and taxation of motor vehicle use, promotion of public transport and non-motorised modes);

- The slowdown in the extension of road networks has reduced the rate at which land is being converted to transport use and the consequent related environmental pressures. Nevertheless, environment impact assessment procedures and the integration of environmental concerns into road transport policies should be pursued, and should help reduce the potentially harmful effects of new infrastructure construction projects.

Attention should also be directed to new concerns. A first key question is how far controls on new gasoline-powered cars will contribute to reducing emissions from vehicle stocks overall, which comprise in-use vehicles whose actual performance, operation, and maintenance differ from those of new cars. The following will have to be closely monitored:

- Schemes to check that new cars comply with standards;
- Prevention of misfueling;
- Enforcement of inspection/maintenance programmes;
- Application of economic instruments; and
- Improvement of the durability of emission control devices.

A second key question is the extent to which emissions from other transport sources, in particular gasoline-powered lorries and buses, light and heavy-duty diesel vehicles and motorcycles, can be contained. Given the growth in traffic volume of *commercial and diesel-powered* vehicles, the additional development and implementation of appropriate, feasible emission standards will be a focus of attention in the years ahead, particularly as regards noise, NO_x and fine particulate matter.

A third key question relates to emissions of *other pollutants*. After a relatively early start on regulating CO and hydrocarbons and, more recently, action on NO_x and lead, it now appears that attention needs to be focussed on other "new" pollutants emitted by both gasoline and diesel-powered vehicles. Little is yet known about their effects or their magnitude, and few governments have taken preventive measures. Pollutants in this category include organic substances such as polycyclic organic matters, aromatic hydrocarbons such as benzene, heavy metals, and fibres such as asbestos. Emissions from fuel additives, from the wear and tear of tyres and brakes and from the use of regenerated lubricants should be studied, and may possibly require control.

A fourth key question relates to traffic management. The impact of transport on the environment depends on the actual performance of vehicles in a given traffic situation, which in turn depends on traffic management. Regulations and economic incentives determining both urban and non-urban traffic patterns (including buffer zones, speed limits, congestion control, etc.) can help significantly to reduce transport emissions and related adverse effects on health or on the environment.

3. STRATEGIES TO REDUCE THE ENVIRONMENTAL IMPACTS OF ROAD TRANSPORT

The OECD studies have shown that if strategies to reduce the environmental impacts of road transport are to be successful, substantial progress will have to be made in respect of: better physical and economic information; use and co-ordination of all types of measure (concerning land use, infrastructures, new vehicles, vehicles in use, traffic management); effective implementation of action decided; integration of environmental measures and concerns into policies concerned with transport, energy, industry and trade; complementary action by central and local government.

Progress in respect of the physical and economic *information* base: better understanding of the "new" pollutants; more accurate estimates of pollutant emissions by existing stocks of vehicles, and of the social costs of road transport; more data on the impacts on the international motor vehicle trade of action concerned with standards, test cycles, incentives and subsidies.

Progress in respect of *the use and coordination of all types of measures* concerning: land use and infrastructures (e.g. environmental impact assessment, installation of noise screens along existing roads); new motor vehicles (noise and pollutant emission standards); in-use vehicles (emissions, traffic management). For each type of measure, physical and economic action and regulation should be associated. Few countries have yet been able to reap the full benefits of these types of measure because they have not been co-ordinated. Strategies too often focus on a few types of measures only, and rely heavily on physical and regulatory action.

Effective *implementation* of the various types of measures should be a priority. Past policies have seldom been able to achieve the expected improvements in the quality of the ambient acoustic environment and of ambient air. This is partly due to ineffective implementation; for instance, misfuelling and rapid deterioration of control devices have been instrumental in preventing more rapid environmental improvements.

Progress in respect of the *integration of the different* environmental measures: for instance, measures to abate emission of noise or air pollutants, to reduce fuel consumption and to increase the safety of vehicles have to be coordinated, not only in order to bring down the cost to the consumer but also so that car manufacturers can plan ahead in the light of necessary technical changes and so as to reap the full benefit of technological progress. In the same way, environmental concerns must be embodied in more traditional policies concerning transport, industry, energy and trade.

Progress in respect of *the complementarity of national and local actions* is needed. Local authorities should play a greater role in supporting and adapting national policy, which is usually undifferentiated, regardless of the area concerned. Since transport movements and the impacts of transport on health and well-being are largely concentrated in urban areas, local authorities should reinforce national policies by taking proper steps to control the use of vehicles and transport infrastructures. They should aim, in particular, to eliminate pollution and noise "black spots" and enhance the quality of life in cities.

NOTES

1. The Hong Kong and Singapore case studies were conducted jointly with the World Bank.
2. OECD case studies were carried out by teams of experts in Athens (Greece), Gothenburg (Sweden), Hong Kong, London (United Kingdom), Los Angeles (United States), Munich (Germany), New York (United States), Osaka (Japan), Paris (France) and Singapore. The Hong Kong and Singapore case studies were conducted jointly by OECD and the World Bank.

Part II

THE IMPACTS OF ROAD TRANSPORT ON THE ENVIRONMENT

INTRODUCTION

In 1971, the OECD launched a major inquiry into the policy implications of the impact of motor vehicles. It singled out the problems of automotive air pollution and noise as subjects requiring priority attention, and concluded that, if trends in motorization and urban growth continued, few cities in OECD countries would be likely to escape the deleterious impact of automotive emissions.

Today, OECD countries face a common set of inter-related environmental problems concerning transport – air pollution, noise, consumption of scarce natural resources, negative impacts on the quality of life. Despite environmental regulations and policy actions implemented during the 70s, these problems and in particular the problems associated with motor vehicles (e.g. motorcycles, private cars, lorries, public transport vehicles) still remain.

In an effort to increase the benefits of motorization while minimizing the disadvantages, the OECD initiated a major new inquiry into this problem. While dealing with the very broad subject of the impact of transport on the environment, its major focus was intended to be road transport, the related air and noise pollution, and the prospects for mitigating these problems. The purpose of this study is to survey the adverse environmental impacts resulting from motor vehicles in the OECD countries. Two other related studies review policies to improve transport management (Part III of this document) and to reduce air pollution and noise emissions through motor vehicle changes (Part IV of this document).

Chapter I

TRANSPORT AND THE ENVIRONMENT

1. THE INTERFACE BETWEEN TRANSPORT AND THE ENVIRONMENT

Structural Aspects

The demand for transport is largely a "derived demand" and mainly reflects the level of economic activity; the market for passenger transport depends on the travel demands of households, particularly to go to work; the market for freight transport depends on other productive activities (Figure 1).

Transport systems play a major positive role in the economic life of industrialised countries and in the daily lives of their citizens. The production and maintenance of transport infrastructures and mobile equipment on the one hand and their use on the other hand represent a considerable weight in the economies of OECD countries: 4 to 8 per cent of GDP and 2 to 4 per cent of jobs. The balances of payments in Member countries are also strongly influenced by the international trade in transport equipment and invisible transport services. The purchase of transport services and personal transport equipment makes up a significant percentage of outlays by businesses and of household consumption expenditure (around 10 per cent, more in North America, less in Japan). A substantial share of tax revenues also goes towards public expenditures on transport, particularly for capital investment and service subsidy.

The negative effects of transport activities mainly concern the operation of transport equipment rather than the construction of infrastructure: they include accidents, congestion, air pollution and noise due to road transport, oil pollution by maritime transport, noise from aircraft, energy consumption and consumption of land and of other natural resources for the production of vehicles and infrastructures. For instance, the non-internalised social costs of road transport amount to about 5 per cent of GDP for OECD countries.

Environmental Impacts of Transport Activities

The kinds of impacts that transport acti… have on the environment and their importance de… on:

- The production of transport infrastructure and mobile equipment and their regular servicing and maintenance;
- The operation of transport modes (that is, the intensity of use of infrastructure and mobile equipment);
- The type of transport mode (for example, air, sea, inland waterway, rail, road, pipeline);
- The technologies used.

Major environmental consequences of transport activities can be summarised and structured along the following lines (see Table 1):

- Pollution problems are mainly concerned with air pollutants (CO, NO_x, HC, particulates, lead and so on) and their associated health risks and ecological impacts (See Chapter III on Air). Unpleasant odours and soiling are evident and widespread sources of annoyance. The pollution of the marine environment by the routine or accidental discharge of oil products is also a cause for concern;
- Noise disturbance, particularly due to road traffic, is an increasingly common nuisance, especially in densely built-up residential areas and at night (See Chapter II on Noise);
- Land consumption by transport infrastructures (airports, harbours, roads and railways, pipelines and associated facilities) may be in conflict with other land uses and also influence access and property values. Obsolete transport facilities (such as canals, railway lines, stations and tunnels and port facilities) give rise to difficult problems concerning the reconversion of derelict land to appropriate alternative uses.
- Solid waste problems mainly involve the disposal of earth and rubble during the building of new transport infrastructures, the …overy and recycling of metals from …ed vehicles and the disposal of certain …overable materials;
- …t risks mainly concern the daily oper… of road transport modes. Although di…rous accidents in the air, sea and rail

Figure 1: **TRANSPORT: POLICIES, STRUCTURE, PRACTICES AND ENVIRONMENTAL IMPACTS**

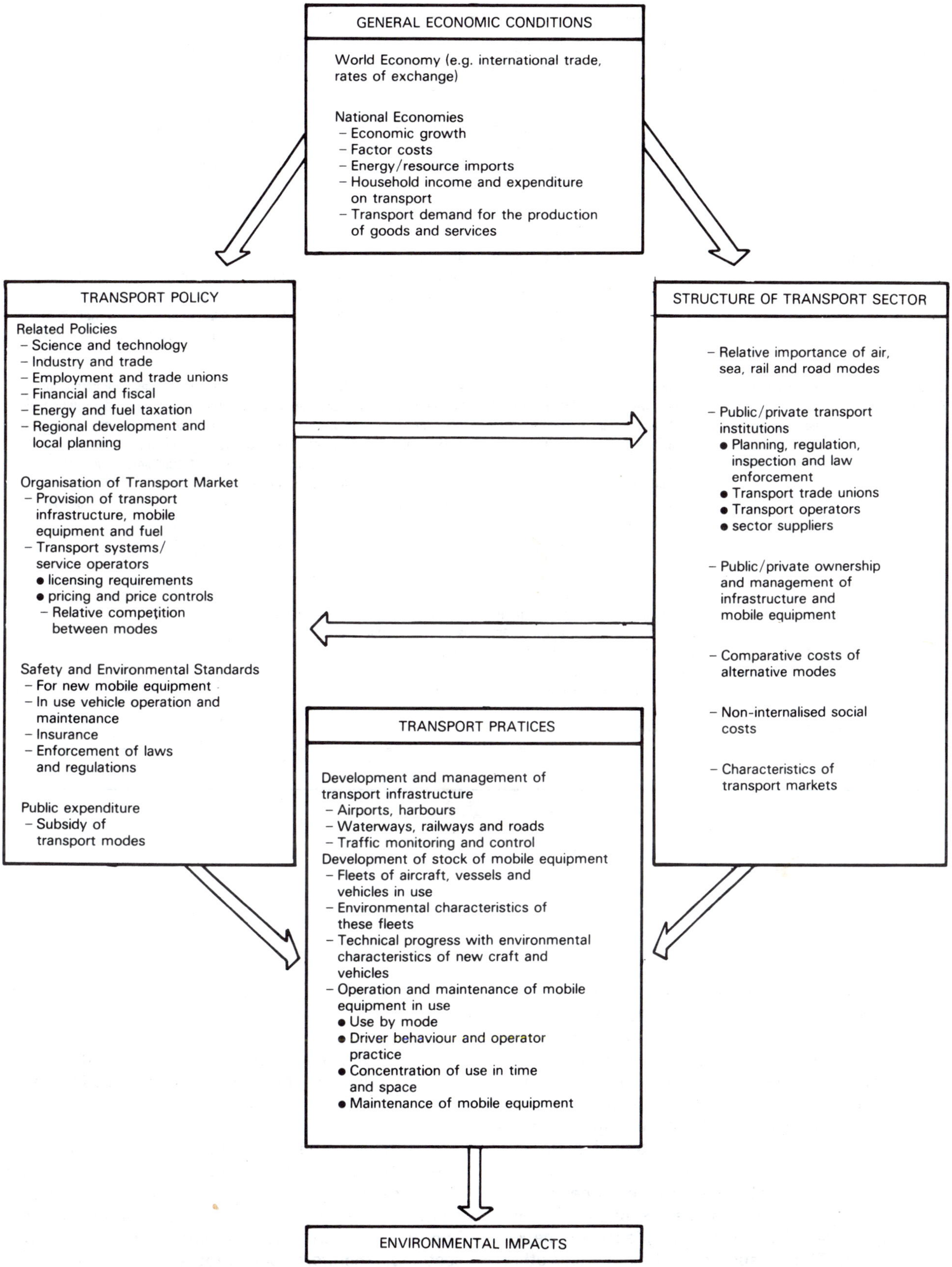

Source: OECD

SELECTED ENVIRONMENTAL EFFECTS OF PRINCIPAL TRANSPORT MODES

PRINCIPAL TRANSPORT MODES	AIR	WATER RESOURCES	LAND RESOURCES	SOLID WASTE	NOISE	RISKS OF ACCIDENTS	OTHER IMPACTS
MARINE AND INLAND WATER TRANSPORT		Modification of water systems during port construction and canal cutting and dredging	Land taken for infrastructures; dereliction of obsolete port facilities and canals	Vessels and craft withdrawn from service		Bulk transport of fuels and hazardous substances	
RAIL TRANSPORT			Land taken for rights of way and terminals; dereliction of obsolete facilities	Abandoned lines, equipment and rolling stock	Noise and vibration around terminals and along railway lines	Derailment or collision of freight carrying hazardous substances	Partition or destruction of neighbourhoods, farmland and wild life habitats
ROAD TRANSPORT	Air pollution (CO, HC, NO_x particulates and fuel additives such as lead)	Pollution of surface water and groundwater by surface run-off; modification of water systems by road building	Land taken for infrastructures; extraction of road building materials	Abandoned spoil tips and rubble from road works; road vehicles withdrawn from service; waste oil	Noise and vibration from cars, motorcycles and lorries in cities, and along main roads	Deaths, injuries and property damaged from road accidents; risk of transport of hazardous substances; risks of structural failure in old or worn road facilities	Partition or destruction of neighbourhoods, farmland and wild life habitats; congestion
AIR TRANSPORT	Air pollution	Modification of water tables, river courses and field drainage in airport construction	Land taken for infrastructures; dereliction of obsolete facilities	Aircraft withdrawn from service	Noise around airports		

Source: OECD

modes occasionally result in heavy tolls, taken together these generally represent only a small fraction of the deaths, injuries and property damage attributable to road transport activities. The risks caused by the transport of hazardous substances (chemical, nuclear) represent an increasing cause of concern because of the potential scale and intensity of the damage;

– The consumption of energy resources by the transport sector is also a major concern because of its high dependence on petroleum. The consumption of metals and other non-fuel minerals for the construction of transport infrastructures and mobile equipment raises longer-term issues of resource utilisation and recycling;
– Congestion results in loss of time that might otherwise be spent in more pleasurable or productive activities.

Although other modes have important impacts in one or two fields, road transport is responsible for much of the transport sector's impact on the environment in almost every aspect except water pollution. The analysis that follows of trends in the transport sector will therefore concentrate on the road transport sector.

2. OBSERVED TRENDS IN THE ROAD TRANSPORT SECTOR OF SIGNIFICANCE FOR THE ENVIRONMENT

Major Trends in the Road Transport Sector

Transport activity has been dominated over the period 1979-1984 by the after-effects of the 1979 energy shock and reduced economic growth. Public debates on transport policies and related environmental issues have also played an important role in many countries.

Changes in the nature and magnitude of the impact of road transport on the environment depend on trends in certain key factors:

- The total stock of vehicles in use;
- The volume of traffic;
- The network of roads.

The Stock of Vehicles in Use

The stock of passenger cars in use continued to increase over the period 1979-1984, although at a slower rate than over previous periods in North America, OECD Europe and Japan; there is some evidence, however, of stagnation (Sweden) or even decline (Denmark). The average level of motorisation is now about 75 cars per 1 000 inhabitants worldwide but reaches 540 in the USA, over 400 in Canada, Australia and New Zealand, 220 in Japan and ranges from 200 to 400 in Europe. Car markets have now reached a "mature" stage in North America and are approaching this stage in other OECD countries, with the exception of southern European countries. At this stage replacement demand typically accounts for some 85 per cent or more of total demand; the growth in the stock of passenger cars thus depends on the remaining demand from non-motorised households wishing to acquire a vehicle and from motorised households wishing to acquire a second or third vehicle (Figure 2, Tables 2).

The stock of commercial vehicles in use also grew during this period, but again usually at a slower rate than previously and even with temporary falls due to fluctuations in general economic activity. The road freight transport industry has shown its ability to recover faster than competing transport modes, however (Figure 2, Tables 2).

The growth in the stock of motor vehicles in use was accompanied by various structural changes of significance for the environment:

- The progressive introduction of less polluting vehicles, with the replacement of old vehicles by new vehicles satisfying emission standards on CO, NO_x, HC and noise emissions; these emission standards, however, differ significantly in Japan, North America, the European Communities countries and others;
- A lengthening of the average life-spans of private cars and commercial vehicles, the replacement or scrapping of certain vehicles being postponed for technical and economic reasons;
- The proportion of diesel vehicles increased. Diesel-powered commercial vehicles now account for between 70 and 80 per cent of the total in Japan and Europe but for only about 30 per cent in the United States. Changing to diesel vehicles is progressing rapidly in the United States, particularly for light and medium-weight commercial vehicles. Today diesel passenger cars account for between 2 and 12 per cent of total passenger car stocks in OECD countries, with the highest proportions and rates of increase occurring in Europe;

Figure 2 : **STOCK OF MOTOR VEHICLES IN USE, passenger cars (PC) and goods vehicles (GV)**

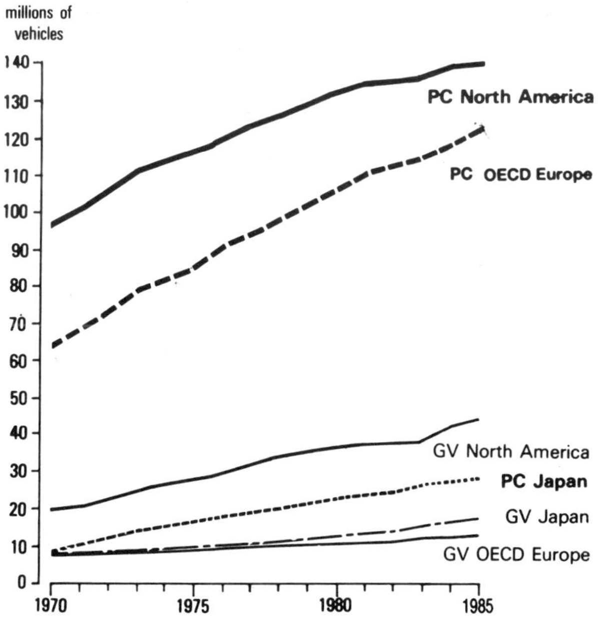

Reference: Tables 2.

Table 2A. ROAD VEHICLE STOCKS: PASSENGER CARS IN USE
OECD Countries, 1970-1985

1000

		1970	1975	1980	1981	1982	1983	1984	1985 a)
Canada		6602	8870	10256	10199	10530	10732	10781	10830
USA		89244	106719	121724	123462	123698	126728	127887	129060
Japan		8779	17236	23660	24612	25539	26386	27144	27790
Australia		3835	5016	5801	6021	6308	6470	6636	6810
N. Zealand		868	1138	1307	1332	1367	1401	1471	1500
Austria		1197	1721	2247	2313	2361	2415	2469	2531
Belgium		2060	2614	3159	3207	3231	3263	3300	3343
Denmark		1077	1295	1390	1367	1358	1390	1440	1490
Finland		712	996	1226	1279	1352	1411	1474	1546
France		12280	15555	19250	19750	20300	20600	20800	20940
Germany	b)	13941	17898	23192	23730	24105	24580	25218	25845
Greece		227	439	878	912	999	1043	1151	1264
Iceland		41	64	86	90	95	97	100	103
Ireland		394	516	734	775	709	719	711	710
Italy		10191	15060	17686	18603	19616	20389	20888	22398
Luxembourg	c)	95	115	129	133	138	141	146	152
Netherlands		2465	3399	4515	4594	4630	4728	4772	4820
Norway		694	954	1234	1279	1338	1383	1430	1514
Portugal		551	937	1269	1346	1429	1518	1601	1690
Spain		2378	4806	7557	7943	8354	8714	8874	9274
Sweden		2288	2760	2883	2893	2936	3007	3081	3151
Switzerland		1380	1794	2247	2395	2473	2521	2552	2617
Turkey		138	383	680	715	786	791	920	920
UK		11802	14061	15438	15633	16075	16612	17313	18040
Yugoslavia		721	1532	2434	2568	2703	2771	2874	2980
North America		95846	115589	131979	133661	134228	137459	138668	139890
Australia - N.Zeal.		4703	6154	7108	7353	7675	7870	8107	8310
OECD Europe	a)	63908	85366	105798	108956	112285	115319	118240	122350
EEC		57459	76694	95196	97993	100944	103695	106215	109960
OECD Total	a)	173236	224345	268544	274582	279727	287034	292159	298340
WORLD Total	a)	193516	260208	320513	331162	340262	352316	364800	377700

NOTES:
a) Includes provisional data and Secretariat estimates.
b) At 1st of July.
c) Method of calculation changed in 1975 and again in 1978.

Source: OECD

Table 2B. ROAD VEHICLE STOCKS: GOODS VEHICLES IN USE
OECD Countries, 1970-1985

1000

		1970	1975	1980	1981	1982	1983	1984	1985 a)
Canada		1440	2112	2903	3138	3239	3308	3407	3510
USA		18797	25781	33637	34451	35253	36548	38047	39610
Japan	b)	8282	10044	13178	13956	14717	15437	16241	17285
Australia		949	1198	1463	1545	1666	1718	2197	2200
N. Zealand		172	207	248	270	276	284	281	297
Austria		135	162	202	208	212	217	223	226
Belgium		251	272	299	285	285	289	294	302
Denmark	c)	248	228	253	243	235	236	244	250
Finland		108	135	158	164	172	178	185	192
France	c)	2065	2325	2457	2521	2695	3037	3111	3225
Germany	c,d)	1119	1244	1448	1487	1480	1474	1486	1502
Greece		107	198	402	454	481	556	572	602
Iceland		6	7	9	10	11	11	12	12
Ireland		50	54	66	68	69	71	85	94
Italy	b,c)	904	1170	1338	1485	1538	1654	1683	1788
Luxembourg	e)	10	12	11	12	12	12	13	13
Netherlands		303	332	363	375	377	378	370	370
Norway		134	139	153	159	167	179	198	233
Portugal	c)	112	204	367	399	448	473	492	510
Spain		717	1014	1362	1423	1490	1560	1482	1569
Sweden	c)	145	157	182	186	194	202	210	218
Switzerland	c)	107	139	169	168	178	190	193	201
Turkey		123	202	327	342	354	373	396	420
UK		1664	1820	1808	1777	1743	1582	1476	1500
Yugoslavia		107	143	191	202	212	217	223	230
North America		20237	27893	36540	37589	38492	39856	41454	43120
Australia - N.Zeal.		1121	1405	1710	1815	1942	2002	2478	2500
OECD Europe	a)	8307	9812	11373	11766	12140	12672	12724	13230
EEC		6721	7655	8445	8707	8916	9288	9333	9650
OECD Total	a)	37946	49154	62801	65125	67291	69966	72896	76130
WORLD Total	a,f)	52852	67693	90563	96216	98658	103716	109000	114600

NOTES:
- a) Includes provisional data and Secretariat estimates.
- b) Includes three-wheeled vehicles.
- c) Does not include road tractors.
- d) At 1st of July.
- e) Method of calculation changed in 1975 and 1978.
- f) Includes buses and coaches.

Source: OECD

- An increase in the proportion of commercial vehicles in the heaviest weight classes in most countries.

Total Volume of Traffic

Over the period 1979-1984, the total distance travelled each year by passenger cars in a given country grew at a slower rate than previously, and even stabilised or declined in North America and in certain European countries. This duplicates and even accentuates a pattern experienced after 1973. This is explained by the fact that the decrease in the use of an average vehicle (in terms of kilometres travelled per year) is offsetting or even in some cases compensating for the growth in the vehicle stock. The decrease in the average use of a vehicle shows the extension of multiple vehicle ownership (since second or third cars are used less than the first), a stabilisation in the time spent on urban travel and adaptation to higher motoring costs (Figure 3, Tables 3).

For goods vehicles, however, shifts among freight transport modes have led to increases in the vehicle-kilometres travelled by lorries and delivery vehicles of both commercial transport operators and company-owned fleets. This has compensated for the stagnation in general economic activity (Figure 3, Tables 3).

Figure 3 : **TOTAL VOLUME OF TRAFFIC, passenger cars (PC) goods vehicles (GV)**

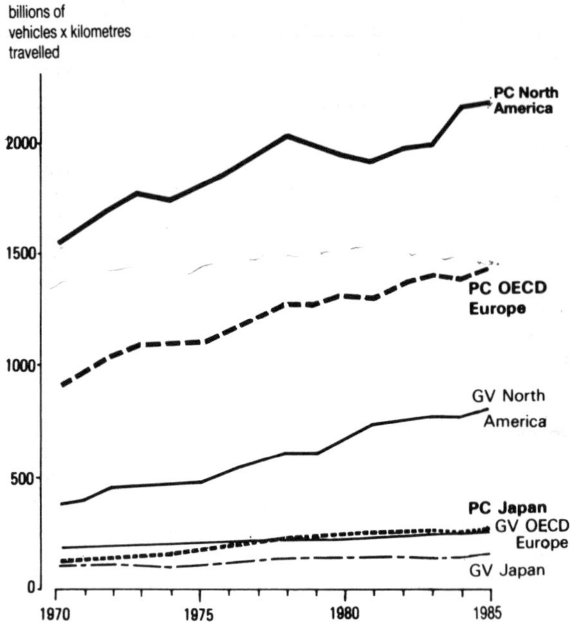

Reference: Tables 3.

Road Infrastructure

With the exception of Japan and certain Member countries in southern Europe, road development programmes have been scaled-down and/or implemented much slower in recent years. Several factors have contributed to this (Figure 4, Tables 4).

- Governments at all levels are now less prepared to spend money on roads, especially new construction. General cuts in public expenditure have coincided, in some countries, with a fall-off in revenues from taxes earmarked for road investment. This has encouraged some highway authorities to explore alternative sources of funding, including greater involvement of the private sector;
- Road building has become more expensive as land and labour costs have increased and other factor costs have been pushed up by increasing energy costs and inflation. In densely built-up areas, the costs of acquiring rights of way and of compensating or relocating households and firms displaced by projects represent an increasing proportion of the total costs. Building and improving roads in urban areas also often requires more complicated civil engineering designs (such as elevation or bridging, tunnelling, landscaping and noise protection) and the long-distance transport of building aggregates or the removal of earth and rubble;
- Political concern about adverse social and environmental impacts has resulted in the introduction of wider public consultation and elaborate impact assessment procedures. Some road building and improvement schemes have had to be abandoned or significantly modified owing to opposition from local residents and businessmen.

The Significance of These Trends for the Environment

Traffic Volumes and Road Construction

The global trends identified over the period 1979 to 1984 concerning the stocks of vehicles, traffic volumes and road networks show a slower growth compared to the previous rate. Therefore the already high pressure on the environment has increased at a lower rate. These trends have affected the emission of air pollutants and of noise disturbance, and the rates of conversion of land for building road infrastructures that were mentioned earlier.

Table 3A. ROAD TRAFFIC VOLUMES: PASSENGER CARS

OECD Countries, 1970-1985

billion/milliards veh.-km

		1970	1975	1980	1981	1982	1983	1984 a)	1985 a)
Canada	b)	101.0	134.8	152.0	146.0	147.8	147.6	145.3	143.0
USA		1433.7	1654.2	1789.4	1793.0	1824.4	1966.0	2018.1	2036.6
Japan	c)	120.6	176.0	241.5	247.2	256.0	259.7	265.1	275.6
Australia	b)	63.2	78.0	87.0	90.3	94.6	97.0	99.5	102.2
N. Zealand	b)	10.3	12.1	12.7	12.7	13.5	14.5	13.9	14.2
Austria		15.6	22.4	25.8	26.0	26.0	26.2	27.2	27.5
Belgium		28.9	33.5	40.9	41.6	41.6	41.6	41.7	42.3
Denmark		19.8	21.4	21.8	21.5	21.2	22.0	23.1	24.2
Finland		13.9	19.9	22.2	22.6	23.4	24.2	24.9	26.0
France		164.5	210.8	240.0	246.0	253.0	255.0	256.0	262.0
Germany	d)	201.1	245.1	297.4	282.7	294.4	304.4	314.0	313.4
Greece	e)	4.4	7.0	10.5	11.1	12.2	13.4	14.8	16.3
Iceland		0.6	0.8	1.0	1.0	1.1	1.1	1.2	1.2
Ireland	b)	7.9	9.3	14.7	15.1	13.6	13.7	13.5	13.5
Italy		122.5	158.7	190.6	197.5	208.5	199.3	205.3	213.5
Luxembourg	b)	1.3	1.5	2.0	2.1	2.1	2.2	2.2	2.3
Netherlands		37.5	49.5	61.4	61.0	62.9	65.6	67.9	68.5
Norway		8.8	12.2	14.4	14.5	15.1	15.4	15.8	16.7
Portugal	b)	7.1	12.0	17.1	18.0	19.1	20.3	21.4	22.6
Spain	f)	24.6	40.3	50.8	53.9	55.6	55.8	56.6	56.3
Sweden	g)	32.2	38.8	41.5	41.5	41.9	42.7	44.1	45.1
Switzerland		21.4	26.1	31.8	33.3	34.2	34.9	35.3	36.2
Turkey	f)	2.5	6.9	7.8	8.0	8.4	8.8	10.2	10.2
UK	h)	140.9	165.4	197.3	201.4	208.8	213.2	223.0	229.4
Yugoslavia	b)	6.6	14.8	21.9	23.1	24.3	24.9	25.9	26.8
North America	b)	1534.7	1789.0	1941.5	1939.0	1972.2	2113.6	2163.4	2180.0
Australia - N.Zeal.	b)	73.5	90.1	99.7	103.1	108.1	111.6	113.5	116.0
OECD Europe	b)	855.5	1081.5	1288.7	1298.9	1343.1	1359.8	1398.2	1427.0
EEC	b)	760.5	954.5	1144.4	1151.9	1193.0	1206.4	1239.6	1264.0
OECD Total	b)	2584.3	3136.7	3571.3	3588.1	3679.3	3844.6	3940.1	4000.0

NOTES:

a) Includes provisional data and Secretariat estimates.
b) Secretariat estimates based on partial data.
c) Does not include traffic by light vehicles (360 cc or less until 1975, 550 cc or less from 1976 onwards).
d) Does not include traffic by caravans and large trailers hauled by passenger-carrying vehicles.
e) Inter-city traffic only.
f) Traffic on motorways and national roads only.
g) Includes traffic by Swedish passenger cars abroad.
h) Great Britain only.

Source: OECD

Table 3B. ROAD TRAFFIC VOLUMES: GOODS VEHICLES
OECD Countries, 1970-1985

billion/milliards veh.-km

		1970	1975	1980	1981	1982	1983	1984 a)	1985 a)
Canada	b)	24.3	36.0	52.6	54.9	55.5	55.6	56.1	56.6
USA		345.5	441.6	618.9	622.1	703.1	657.3	714.0	743.4
Japan	c)	100.0	104.9	141.5	141.4	141.1	143.0	144.1	146.5
Australia	b)	15.4	19.6	27.1	27.8	29.9	30.9	39.5	39.6
N. Zealand	b)	2.8	3.4	3.5	3.5	3.7	4.0	3.9	4.0
Austria		6.1	7.3	9.2	9.5	9.7	9.8	10.2	10.3
Belgium		4.0	4.4	4.5	4.4	4.4	4.5	4.5	4.6
Denmark		3.0	3.6	4.2	4.8	4.7	4.7	4.7	5.0
Finland		3.3	3.9	3.9	4.0	4.1	4.2	4.3	4.5
France	d)	41.5	47.7	55.0	60.0	60.0	60.0	62.0	63.0
Germany	e)	26.7	26.7	32.4	32.3	31.0	30.7	31.0	31.8
Greece	b,f)	3.9	5.2	8.5	9.1	9.6	10.1	10.4	11.0
Iceland	b)	0.1	0.1	0.2	0.2	0.2	0.2	0.2	0.2
Ireland	b)	2.7	2.7	3.5	3.6	3.7	3.8	4.5	5.0
Italy	g)	22.6	24.2	33.0	35.1	36.9	36.8	39.0	40.5
Luxembourg	b)	0.2	0.2	0.2	0.2	0.2	0.2	0.2	0.2
Netherlands		5.7	6.2	8.4	8.3	8.6	8.7	8.7	5.0
Norway		1.9	1.9	2.0	1.8	1.9	1.9	2.1	2.5
Portugal	b)	2.1	3.3	4.1	4.7	5.3	5.7	5.9	6.1
Spain	h)	10.4	14.2	16.5	16.8	16.5	17.0	18.0	17.6
Sweden	i)	2.4	2.4	2.2	2.2	2.2	2.1	2.2	2.3
Switzerland		3.4	4.2	4.9	5.0	5.2	5.4	5.4	5.7
Turkey	h)	2.8	4.8	6.0	6.2	6.5	6.8	7.2	7.6
UK	j)	34.8	37.7	41.3	40.8	40.6	41.6	43.4	44.7
Yugoslavia	b)	3.3	4.9	5.9	6.3	6.6	6.7	6.9	7.1
North America	b)	369.8	477.6	671.5	677.0	758.6	712.9	770.1	800.0
Australia - N.Zeal.	b)	18.2	23.0	30.6	31.3	33.6	35.0	43.4	43.6
OECD Europe	b)	177.6	200.5	239.9	249.0	251.1	254.1	263.8	267.7
EEC	b)	157.6	176.0	211.6	220.1	221.4	223.7	232.3	234.6
OECD Total	b)	665.6	805.9	1083.5	1098.8	1184.4	1144.9	1221.5	1258.0

NOTES:

a) Includes provisional data and Secretariat estimates.
b) Secretariat estimates based on partial data.
c) Does not include traffic by light goods vehicles (360cc or less until 1975: 550cc or less from 1976 onwards).
d) Does not include traffic by goods vehicles more than 15 years old and with a load capacity of 3 tons and over.
e) Includes traffic by special vehicles.
f) Inter-city traffic only.
g) Includes traffic by three-wheeled vehicles.
h) Traffic on motorways and national roads only.
i) Does not include traffic by goods vehicles with a load capacity of less than 2 tons.
j) Great Britain only.

Source: OECD

Figure 4 : **ROAD NETWORK LENGTH AND AREA**

4a : **ALL ROAD NETWORK LENGTH**

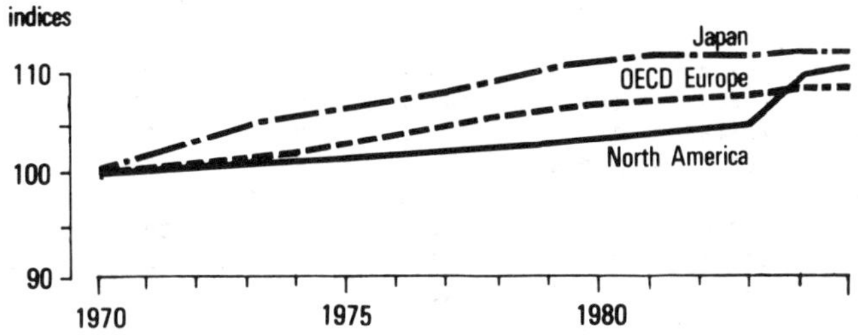

	1985 million km
Japan	1,128
OECD Europe	3,119
North America	7,530

4b : **MOTORWAY NETWORK LENGTH**

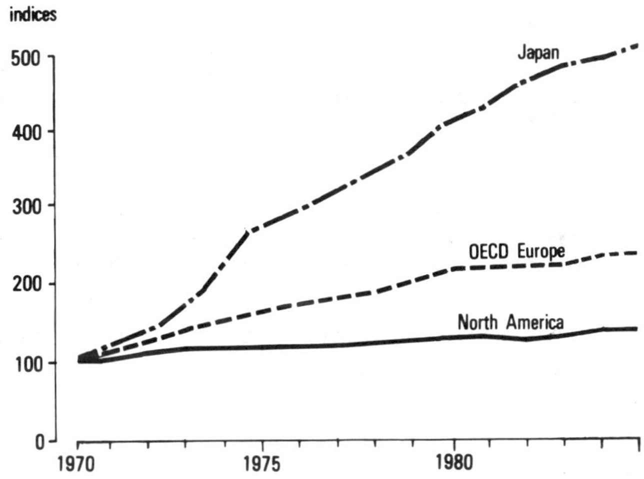

	1985 thousand km
Japan	3,5
OECD Europe	33,6
North America	77,8

4c : **ESTIMATED AREA OCCUPIED BY ALL ROADS, early 1980s**

km²

CANADA	26.000	FRANCE	8.740
USA	87.000	GERMANY	5.800
JAPAN	9.900	NETHERLANDS	1.110
NEW ZEALAND	1.930	SPAIN	1.600
		SWEDEN	1.740

Reference: Tables 4.

Table 4A. ROAD NETWORK LENGTH: ALL ROADS
OECD Countries, 1970-1985

1000 km

		1970	1975	1980	1981	1982	1983	1984	1985 n)
Canada	a)	830.3	871.6	913.7	928.3	930.0	930.0	930.0	930.0
USA	a)	6003.0	6175.6	6365.6	6400.0	6450.0	6500.0	6550.0	6600.0
Japan		1004.6	1067.6	1113.4	1118.0	1120.0	1123.3	1125.2	1127.5
Australia	b)	884.8	845.0	810.9	791.8	818.2	820.0	820.0	853.0
N. Zealand		93.8	92.5	93.4	92.9	93.1	92.9	92.6	93.0
Austria		94.2	102.8	106.3	106.9	107.1	107.2	107.4	107.4
Belgium		94.7	123.4	126.8	126.8	127.0	127.8	127.7	127.9
Denmark		62.9	66.1	68.9	69.4	69.7	69.8	70.2	70.1
Finland	c)	72.4	73.6	75.0	75.2	75.4	75.7	75.8	76.1
France	d)	792.8	802.2	803.0	804.0	804.2	804.4	804.5	804.7
Germany	e)	440.5	466.1	482.4	484.5	487.0	488.6	490.0	491.2
Greece	f)	35.1	36.6	37.1	37.5	40.2	34.5	34.5	34.5
Iceland	g)	11.4	11.8	11.7	11.7	11.6	11.6	11.6	11.6
Ireland		86.5	89.0	92.3	92.3	92.3	92.3	92.3	92.3
Italy		284.2	290.9	294.5	297.2	297.0	299.8	301.3	303.0
Luxembourg		4.9	5.0	5.1	5.1	5.1	5.2	5.2	5.2
Netherlands	h)	75.8	86.4	92.5	92.5	96.3	96.3	96.3	96.3
Norway		72.3	77.1	81.7	82.5	82.4	84.0	84.6	85.9
Portugal	i)	41.9	46.2	52.0	51.9	51.9	51.9	51.9	51.9
Spain	j)	139.4	144.5	150.7	152.5	153.8	153.6	150.4	151.8
Sweden		125.4	124.8	129.0	129.5	129.5	129.7	130.4	130.7
Switzerland		59.2	61.6	64.0	65.1	66.7	68.8	70.8	70.6
Turkey	k)	59.5	59.3	60.5	60.8	61.1	59.4	59.4	59.4
UK	l)	322.5	330.0	339.6	341.9	343.6	345.4	347.2	348.3
Yugoslavia	m)	92.0	101.1	115.8	116.1	115.8	117.0	116.6	116.0
North America	a)	6833.3	7047.2	7279.3	7328.3	7380.0	7430.0	7480.0	7530.0
Australia - N.Zeal.	n)	978.6	937.5	904.3	884.6	911.3	912.9	912.6	946.0
OECD Europe	n)	2875.6	2997.3	3073.0	3087.3	3101.8	3106.0	3111.5	3118.7
EEC	n)	2381.3	2486.3	2544.8	2555.7	2568.0	2569.6	2571.4	2577.1
OECD Total	n)	11692.1	12049.6	12370.0	12418.1	12513.1	12600.0	12700.0	12800.0

NOTES:

a) Secretariat estimates for 1981 to 1985.
b) Coverage of types of road changed in 1985.
c) Does not include urban streets (10446km in 1985).
d) Does not include certain rural roads: 700 000km in 1985.
e) Estimates.
f) Does not include local roads: 68 800km in 1985.
g) Does not include urban roads prior to 1974.
h) Surfaced roads only.
i) Includes forest roads.
j) Motorways, national roads and secondary roads only. Other roads (167200 km in 1985) include rural paths and unsurfaced forest trails.
k) National and provincial roads only. Does not include village roads (243000 km in 1985).
l) Great Britain only.
m) Does not include urban streets.
n) Includes Secretariat estimates.

Source: OECD

Table 4B. ROAD NETWORK LENGTH: MOTORWAYS
OECD Countries, 1970-1985

km

		1970	1975	1980	1981	1982	1983	1984	1985 g)
Canada	a)	2759	3633	4718	4939	5848	5848	6268	6268
USA	b)	53701	64653	69202	69500	70000	70500	71000	71500
Japan		698	1888	2579	2860	2993	3232	3435	3551
Australia	a)	1027	1056	1086	1092	1100	1100	1100	1100
N. Zealand		100	108	120	120	125	130	134	134
Austria		478	722	938	956	1047	1109	1137	1261
Belgium		501	1052	1193	1246	1317	1375	1375	1456
Denmark		198	345	504	525	526	528	549	603
Finland		108	180	204	204	204	204	204	204
France		1553	3401	5080	5520	5700	5845	6005	6150
Germany		4461	6213	7538	7784	7919	8080	8198	8350
Greece		65	76	91	91	91	92	92	92
Iceland		..	..	..	..	..	..	..	..
Ireland		..	..	..	..	..	8	8	8
Italy		3913	5329	5900	5900	5901	5901	5941	5955
Luxembourg		7	27	44	58	58	58	58	58
Netherlands		975	1525	1798	1838	1841	1884	1971	1975
Norway	c)	79	165	266	267	270	283	294	294
Portugal		66	66	127	127	154	181	183	183
Spain	c)	268	800	1842	1877	1882	1927	1977	1977
Sweden		403	692	850	854	868	881	892	897
Switzerland		377	662	876	957	986	1006	1030	1054
Turkey		24	189	205	205	205	205	205	205
UK	d)	1057	1975	2556	2628	2666	2720	2802	2838
Yugoslavia	e)	9	84	547	547	613	630	714	714
North America	a)	56460	68286	73920	74439	75848	76348	77268	77768
Australia - N.Zeal.	a)	1127	1164	1206	1212	1225	1230	1234	1234
OECD Europe	f)	14533	23419	30012	31037	31635	32287	32921	33560
EEC	f)	13064	20809	26673	27594	28055	28591	29151	29637
OECD Total	a)	72818	94757	107717	109548	111701	113097	114858	116113

NOTES:

a) Secretariat estimates based on partial data.
b) Secretariat estimates for 1981 to 1985.
c) Includes dual-carriageways.
d) Great Britain only. Does not include slip roads.
e) Secretariat estimates for 1970 and 1975.
f) Includes Secretariat estimates.

Source: OECD

Environmental, Energy and Transport Policies

Some progress has been made over the period 1979 to 1984 with environmental, energy and transport policies relating to new vehicle standards, with environmental impact assessment procedures for new infrastructures, and in fuel savings, fuel quality and traffic management.

Concerning emission standards for new motor vehicles, most OECD countries have implemented such standards for air pollution (CO, NO_x, HC) and noise and have progressively tightened them. Progress with regard to vehicle emissions has been greater in Japan and the United States, which have both adopted stronger standards and implemented them earlier (see Chapter III on Air). Not all implemented standards have however been effective in improving the environment (e.g. NO_x in Europe). Concerning noise, progress on emission standards has been slow, although some progress has recently been made in agreeing lower levels in the European Communities. This progress has not compensated for the increase in noise due to the growth in traffic volumes (See Chapter II on Noise). However, this progress should be consolidated and extended because of the delay between the adoption of a regulation and the date it is actually effective for the full stock of vehicles in use, and because of the deterioration of emission control devices with the age of vehicles. In particular, the increase in the average life span of vehicles means further deterioration of emission control devices and slower replacement by cleaner vehicles.

With regard to environmental impact assessment, it is now fairly common practice to consider environmental impacts in the design of new infrastructure projects, and this has helped prevent environmental disruption. For instance, noise barriers and noise insulation of buildings help to protect the most exposed populations. However, these advances must be extended in OECD countries (particularly where countries have not adopted specific efficient and public procedures), as well as in relation to bilateral and multi-lateral aid for transport infrastructure projects in developing countries.

Concerning fuel consumption, actual average energy consumption per vehicle has been markedly reduced, particularly in North America, where it was very high, but also in Japan and Europe, owing to major technological improvements in the energy efficiencies of vehicles. The full effect of this on the vehicle stock has yet to be realised, however, owing to the slow rate of replacement of the vehicle stock.

With regard to fuel quality, 97 per cent of the fleet in Japan now uses unleaded petrol. In the United States the figure should have reached 50 per cent of vehicles, but the actual level is much lower owing to misfuelling practices. In European Communities countries, the lead content of petrol has been reduced to levels between 0.15 and 0.40 grams per litre, and some countries have already introduced unleaded petrol. This has contributed to reducing lead emissions and thus reducing the exposure of the population to lead.

With regard to traffic management, some progress has been made, particularly in dealing with "black spots" in polluted and noisy areas of a number of cities and with the introduction of speed limits in a number of countries.

Structural Changes in the Stock of Vehicles and in Traffic Volumes

The major structural changes identified earlier for the period 1979 to 1984 are: the rapid advancement of diesel vehicles in general, and the spread of heavy lorries. These have immediate environmental implications.

Diesel vehicles contribute to air pollution not only by way of pollutants such as NO_2 and sulphur compounds but also with fine particulate emissions, some of which have potential mutagenic and carcinogenic effects. Diesel vehicles are also exacerbating environmental pollution through noise and odours.

Heavy lorries not only aggravate the general problems of diesel vehicles but have additional environmental effects relating to noise, both airborne and ground-borne vibrations and the deterioration of road surfaces and bridges. It is well known that the external environmental costs of heavy freight vehicles are particularly high in comparison with other commercial and private vehicles. Moreover, the effects are increasingly perceived by the public and give rise to complaints and conflicts.

3. PROSPECTS AND CONCLUSIONS

The major changes that have occurred in the road transport sector over the past 10 years have had important and sometimes contrasting impacts on the environment. The impacts of and concern with air pollution and noise due to road transportation remained or became important in OECD countries.

- The slower growth in vehicle use, particularly of passenger cars, has made the overall pressure on the environment increase at a reduced rate;
- The progressive incorporation of environmental emission standards for new vehicles into the technical specifications of the stock of vehicles in use has also contributed to a stabilisation or even reduction in certain air pollutions and noise in some countries;
- Traffic management policies have been fairly successful in eliminating "black spots", where road users and local populations are most exposed to accident risks, pollution or noise disturbance. They have also prevented congestion from imposing unacceptable delays on business traffic and personal travel, especially in urban areas;
- The slackening in the rate of development of road networks has reduced the rate at which land is being converted to transport use and related environmental pressures;
- Environment impact assessment procedures and the integration of environmental concerns into road transport policies have reduced the potentially harmful effects of new infrastructural construction projects as well as reducing existing problems for local populations, for instance by means of anti noise barriers, or traffic diversion.

Throughout the remainder of the 80s and well into the following decade, the major developments in the road transport sector can be summarised as follows:

- Stocks of passenger cars in use are likely to continue to grow, though at a slower rate than in the 70s. This slower rate reflects demographic factors such as ageing populations, as well as the increasing maturity of car markets in most OECD countries. However, the rate may be influenced by the future growth of income levels;
- Passenger car traffic volumes are likely to grow again, but also slower than in the 70s. Individual vehicles will be used less intensively on average owing to the increase in multiple vehicle ownership and the high proportion of time taken up by daily travel, despite a possible stabilisation in the cost of motoring;
- The number and use of goods vehicles are likely to grow at sustained rates corresponding to the growth in general economic activity, with even higher rates for heavy vehicles. The continuing decline of heavy industry in several Member countries is more likely to affect the transport of freight by rail and inland water than the transport of goods by road;
- Road networks are likely to continue to grow but at a slower pace than in the 70s. Maintenance problems and risks of structural failure, especially on major road systems, may well multiply owing to the natural ageing process, wear and tear by heavy traffic and, in some Member countries, the use of unsuitable construction materials and a legacy of inadequate maintenance. Thus, much more emphasis is likely to be placed on protecting, improving and, where necessary, reconstructing existing networks.

As a consequence, a number of environmental problems are pending and new problems are emerging for the remainder of the 80s and well into the following decade:

- Pressures on the environment from road transport, such as air pollution, noise and land consumption, will remain. They may be moderated by a double effect: the effect of the slower rate of growth in the road transport sector and the effect of environmental policies, with the progressive implementation and tightening of emission standards and technological progress in new vehicles, and their gradual incorporation into the stock of vehicles in use;
- The actual containment of these pressures will depend on the strength of policies to control the real level of emissions of vehicles in use, however (by vehicle maintenance, for example) and of policies to manage traffic between cities (for example, the setting and enforcement of speed limits) and in cities (such as by traffic cells, lorry routing, area-wide traffic control, through the pricing and taxation of motor vehicle use or by the promotion of public transport and non-motorised modes);
- Increased pressures from heavy lorries and diesel vehicles in general are likely;
- The use of new fuels and of new additives and their potential environmental impacts should be reviewed in order to prevent related problems.

Chapter II

ROAD TRAFFIC NOISE

Surveys and opinion polls in many OECD countries have found that the disturbance most frequently cited by respondents is noise in the home. This finding also emerges from an analysis of complaints relating to the environment, the majority of which concern noise. The prime offending source of noise in terms of the number of people disturbed is road traffic, followed by neighbourhood and aircraft noise. Road traffic noise thus seems to be the principal cause of disturbance in the home.

Noise may be defined as any acoustical phenomenon producing a sensation perceived as disagreeable or disturbing by an individual or a group. This definition encompasses the three fields of analysis of sonic phenomena: their physical (acoustic) effects, their physiological effects (those that are directly measurable) and their psycho-sociological effects (annoyance and other reactions to noise).

Noise is measured in decibels[1]. In daily life one is generally exposed to noise levels fluctuating between 30 to 40 decibels and 80 to 90 decibels or even more (Figure 5). Various indices have been developed for assessing the impact of noise and for regulating exposure to it. Some countries use statistical indices such as L10, L50, L1 (i.e. noise levels exceeded for 10 per cent, 50 per cent or 1 per cent of the time). Many countries tend to favour the Leq ("equivalent sound level" in decibels, A-weighted), a scale that can be used for assessing the impact of noise from most sources. For this reason, data concerning noise exposure in this Chapter will generally be expressed in Leq dB(A)[2].

The effects of noise on people are various (annoyance, behavioural changes, stress effects, hearing damages and physiological reactions) and often interrelated. For instance, interference with speech can result in tiredness and annoyance but tiredness may exacerbate annoyance and exacerbated annoyance may aggravate the feeling of tiredness. There are also interrelationships between the individual's general state of health and the effects of noise: noise-induced stresses trigger off various reactions in the body and demand a constant effort of "adaptation" to noise.

1. THE EFFECTS OF NOISE

Effects on Health

Physiological Effects

It was thought for a long time that the body could adjust relatively well to noise but recent observations have shown the opposite. Laboratory tests have demonstrated that such habituation does not take place in the case of certain motorcycle noises, for instance (the heart rate speeds up and muscles tense); this type of noise thus seems to be particularly pernicious.

There has been a growing awareness that hearing damage is only one of the harmful effects of noise and that continuous noise can induce non-auditory physiological effects. Noise is thus seen to be pathogenic; it comes into the vast category of contributory stress factors in disorders of the cardiovascular and digestive systems.

Sleep Disturbance

Sleep serves to repair damage caused by physical and mental fatigue; it helps maintain the metabolism in good working order and helps keep people fit. A chronic pattern of poor sleep can impair health in a number of ways.

Research and surveys have shown that exposure to noise during sleep both changes the duration of

Figure 5: **EXAMPLES OF NOISE LEVELS**

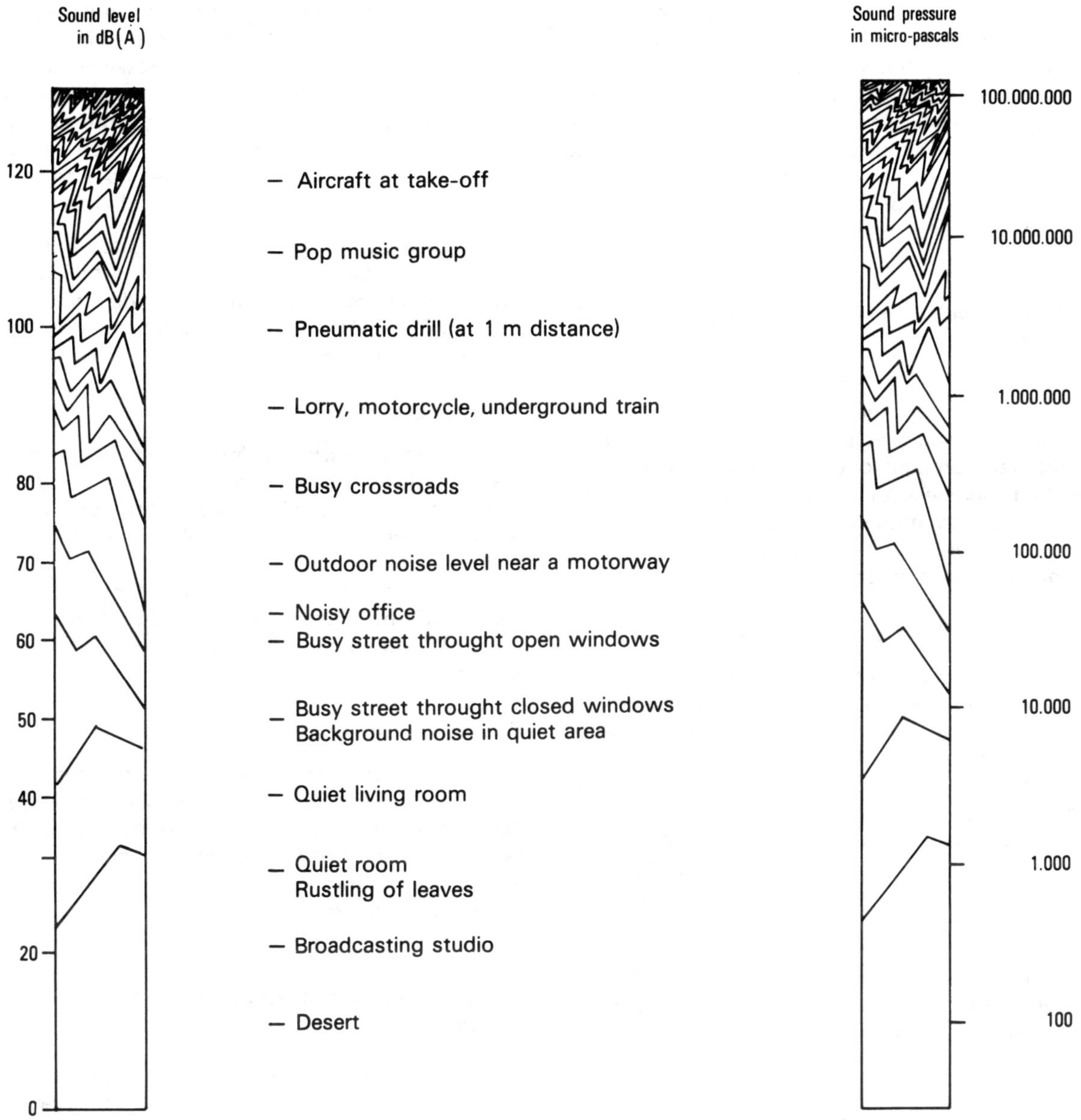

sleep and diminishes its quality by inducing qualitative changes (from deep to light sleep) which are not perceived by the sleeper. Noise is particularly harmful to those who do not sleep well and thus to the frail and elderly. Research in Europe has shown that even after several years' exposure to noise, cardiac reaction is still high, demonstrating that people do not "get used" to noise.

The Pathological Effects of Noise

Effects on hearing

Among the pathological effects of noise, deafness is the only one that can be pinpointed with any certainty. The auditory fatigue caused by noise exceeding 75-80 dB(A) is reflected in a transitory decrease in auditory acuity (a raising of the hearing threshold).

Long-term exposure to such levels of noise can result in permanent hearing loss in the form, for instance, of occupational deafness resulting from working in a very noisy environment (forges, bottling factories, textile mills and so on). Other groups of workers (e.g. roadworkers, postal workers, traffic police, car or delivery van drivers) who are exposed for considerable lengths of time to high sound levels are also liable to suffer a permanent loss of auditory acuity.

Overall effects: noise and consumption of medicaments

The consumption of medicaments and the number of medical consultations made by the population groups exposed to noise can be a useful yardstick. This has been brought out in several studies which show that numbers of medical prescriptions and psychiatric or psychotherapy sessions and the consumption of tranquillisers or sleeping pills all tended to be higher in noisy districts than in quiet ones.

The non-auditory consequences of noise

Without reviewing research in this area in depth, it can nonetheless be said that physiological disorders, once they become chronic, carry a risk of such long-term pathological effects as high blood pressure and greater proneness to heart and circulatory diseases. This implies that in assessing response reactions to noise, particularly of the autonomous nervous system, priority attention should be accorded to certain factors, such as differences in individual reactions to noise and poor habituation, probably because of fluctuations in levels. This latter point is of special importance inasmuch as lack of habituation may well be a major causal factor in chronic disorders and diseases of this kind.

The Effects of Noise on Communication

Intelligibility and Ease of Conversation

If conversation, radio, music, television and sound signals of various kinds are unintelligible, an essential part of life is missing; intelligibility is a prerequisite for acoustic comfort in every place of habitation, in public places and for safety in industry and transport.

Interference with speech occurs at noise levels frequently encountered in the street, in gardens or on balconies. Residents generally find themselves obliged to close their windows in order to enjoy reasonable acoustic comfort indoors: an ill-tolerated constraint on behaviour, especially in summer.

Consequences for Communication by the Hard-of-Hearing

Most studies defining ranges for intelligibility and ease of conversation take persons with excellent hearing as their point of reference. However, a sizeable proportion of the population (8-10 per cent in France) have a hearing loss of 20 dB(A) or more due to the natural effects of age (presbyacusis); such people are especially disadvantaged when they have to follow a conversation against a background of noise.

A Swedish study has shown that while in the case of a control group loss of intelligibility in conversation occurred when outside traffic noise reached 60 dB(A), for individuals with auditory impairment loss of intelligibility began at 45 dB(A).

The Effects of Noise at School

Interference with the intelligibility of communication is particularly serious for the education and mental development of schoolchildren and the younger generation generally. Environmental noise due to surface traffic or aircraft impedes language development and the acquisition of reading skills in infants (one to four years old) and primary schoolchildren (five to seven years old) during crucial periods for intellectual development.

Perception of Auditory Warnings

Apart from interfering with verbal communication, the noise of road traffic, as well as building sites, can obscure auditory warnings, putting pedestrians, cyclists and roadworkers at risk. In addition, building site noise and industrial noise can obscure auditory warnings at the work place.

Psychological Annoyance and Effects on Behaviour

The psychosociological factors in noise discomfort are complex, being bound up with the perceptive and affective reactions of those subjected to the noise. Annoyance is often a generalised sensation and the interrelationship between levels of individual annoyance and noise levels are statistically significant. It is therefore possible to establish noise indices which take due account of annoyance to the immediate community and to assign "threshold values" for defining an acceptable or comfortable environment.

As well as provoking response reactions in terms of annoyance, noise also induces individuals to take steps to reduce the annoyance, and research has revealed such noise-induced behaviour in various areas of daily life in the home.

Closing the windows for certain activities (watching television, reading, sleeping) is a standard behavioural response to noise. A French study has shown that above 60-62 dB(A) (daytime Leq), the greater the noise, the more marked is the behaviour. At 65 dB(A) more than two-thirds of the sample reported that they shut their windows to watch television, while almost half did so for reading. The study also showed that in dwellings with differential noise levels, certain activities (such as reading or intellectual work in the home) were shifted to rooms less exposed to noise, particularly where noise levels exceeded 68 dB(A). It is generally at or above this level that it is decided to soundproof dwellings.

Lastly, noise not only disrupts home life, it also affects the use of outdoor amenities. It has been noted, for instance, that less use is being made of private gardens for recreation and relaxation, while public parks and gardens are also receiving fewer visitors.

It is also an interesting fact that noise can serve to fuel personal grievances (such as disputes between neighbours), sometimes triggering off violent reactions. High noise levels may result in formal complaints to authorities, culminating on occasion in community action or litigation. However, complaints are not necessarily a reliable guide to the significance of noise problems, mainly because social and political factors may influence the "representativeness" of the complaint.

Summary of the Effects of Noise

Noise disrupts activity, disturbs sleep and hinders people carrying out their work. Many examples have been given: it has been seen that noise impedes the learning process (particularly in school), psychological development, social activity and verbal communication and impairs job performance and safety in the workplace and in transport.

Noise also generates stress. Quite apart from the permanent damage it causes to hearing, it also has a very considerable impact on how the individual functions physiologically, psychologically and socially, both because of the effort required to acclimatise to noise and because of the frustration resulting from the deterioration in the quality of life and sleep.

The findings of the many studies undertaken in OECD countries on the effects of noise and its wider repercussions point to the fact that in order to comply with desirable limits for well-being indoors, the outdoor level should not exceed 65 dB(A) (Leq by day). In the case of new residential areas, the outdoor level should not exceed 55 dB(A) (Leq by day).

2. THE PRESENT STATE OF THE ENVIRONMENT WITH REGARD TO NOISE

The last twenty years have seen a rise in noise levels. This may be ascribed to three phenomena: a 50 per cent growth in the urban population of the Western countries, increased mobility (the number of motor vehicles has tripled and air traffic has increased tenfold) and the spread of mechanisation to virtually every activity.

It has been estimated that in the early 70s in the OECD countries some 100 million town dwellers were exposed in their daily environment to noise levels of more than 65 dB(A). Today more recent data are available on the exposure of national populations to the various sources of noise in the environment.

Present Exposure of the Population to Noise

With regard to road traffic, 5 per cent to 30 per cent of the population according to country are exposed to a noise level of over 65 dB(A). Approximately 110 million people are exposed to road traffic noise levels in excess of 65 dB(A) in OECD countries. It has also been estimated that over half of this same population is exposed to noise levels exceeding 55 dB(A), though there are of course differences between countries. These figures, in comparison with those available earlier, show that in the last 10 years or so the situation, while not deteriorating, has equally not improved (Table 5).

Overall, there would therefore be about 16 per cent of the population of OECD countries – appproximately 130 million people – exposed to noise levels in excess of 65 dB(A) from various types of environmental noise. Furthermore, more than 50 per cent of the population of OECD countries are exposed to noise levels in excess of 55 dB(A), and it is recognised in many countries that the percentage of population living in these "grey" areas, that is those exposed to noise levels between 55 and 65 dB(A), is increasing and therefore has become a more significant problem than it was thought to be a few years ago.

Principal Sources of Noise and Factors Influencing Levels of Exposure

Transport is by far the major source of noise, ahead of building or industry, with road traffic the chief

Table 5. NATIONAL POPULATION EXPOSURE TO ROAD TRANSPORT NOISE
Selected Countries, Early 80s

Percent (c)

		Sound level in Leq (dBA) outdoor				
		>55	>60	>65	>70	>75
United States	b)	37.0	18.0	7.0	2.0	0.4
Japan	a,d)	80.0	58.0	31.0	10.0	1.0
Austria	a)	50.0	35.0	16.0	7.0	1.0
Belgium	a)	69.0	39.0	12.0	1.0	-
Denmark	b)	38.0	24.0	12.0	4.0	1.0
France	a)	44.0	25.0	13.0	4.0	0.4
Germany	a)	34.0	17.0	8.0	3.0	-
Greece	b)	50.0	30.0	20.0	10.0	2.0
Netherlands	a)	40.0	18.0	6.0	0.6	-
Norway	b)	18.0	10.0	5.0	1.8	-
Spain	a)	74.0	50.0	23.0	7.0	1.0
Sweden	b)	38.0	24.0	11.0	4.0	1.0
Switzerland	a)	54.0	28.0	11.0	4.0	1.0
United Kingdom	a,e)	50.0	25.0	11.0	4.0	0.6

NOTES:
a) Daytime Leq (6-22 hours).
b) Leq over 24 hours.
c) Percentages are cumulative and not additive (e.g. percentage of persons exposed to >55 dB(A) includes percentage of persons exposed to >60 dB(A), etc.)
d) OECD estimates.
e) Road traffic noise: Leq averaged (06.00-24.00), 1973 survey, England only.

Source: OECD

offender. Aircraft noise comes next in terms of population exposure. This is particularly high in the United States where the proportion of population exposed is four times higher than in Europe or Japan.

Railway noise and noise from fixed sources such as industrial establishments generally affect a more limited proportion of the population. However, in some countries these sources may rank second to road transport. This is the case in Switzerland and in Germany, for instance, where a high proportion of the population is exposed to railway noise, owing to the greater importance of railways in relation to other modes of transport, the density of the rail network and topographical factors.

Even within countries, noise exposure can vary considerably from region to region, from town to town and even from one district to another within the same town. Factors such as population density and type of conurbation can play a very significant role. Generally speaking, noise exposure levels are higher in urban areas, which are more densely populated and where traffic density is therefore higher.

Multi-Exposure to Various Sources of Noise

These data do not tell the whole story, however. Until now researchers have tended to study each type of noise exposure separately. In reality, people are subjected to noise from a multiplicity of sources, either simultaneously (road traffic and aircraft noise for example) or successively (in the home, while commuting, at work). Noise exposure at work, outdoors, during travel, at home, during recreation and so on should all be considered in order not to underestimate the real level of exposure to noise and its effects.

A preliminary study carried out in Japan has shown that individuals are subjected to environmental noise to differing degrees. A difference of more than 10 dB(A) (a doubling of the noise level) in Leq (24 hours) has been found between workers in noisy industrial establishments on the one hand and those working in quiet plants and in the home on the other. Moreover, and this is perhaps the most striking finding, 33 per cent of housewives and 36 per cent of workers were exposed to sound levels over 24 hours in excess of 70 dB(A); this would imply that the total amount of noise experienced is significantly higher than might be deduced from the incomplete figures on the external noise environment. The problem of multi-exposure is thus likely to become a matter for increasing concern and attention in coming years.

3. THE FUTURE STATE OF THE NOISE ENVIRONMENT

How the noise environment is likely to develop in the coming decades will depend both on certain aspects of socio-economic development (lifestyles and technological change) and on the noise abatement policies adopted.

Thus, apart from such target-specific measures as tightening up vehicle regulations and soundproofing the facades of buildings, other socio-economic and technical factors can augment or reduce community exposure to noise in the medium and long term. These factors may be broken down into four categories:

- Mobility trends and their consequences in terms of the vehicle stock and its use in space (urban, rural and tourist areas) and time (daytime, night-time, weekends and holidays);
- Technical developments in vehicles;
- Characteristics of the noise-impacted areas; for example, the type of urban development and the acoustic quality of the buildings;
- Characteristics of the social groups affected: age, sensitivity to environmental problems and so on.

Forecasts in some countries suggest that despite the current regulations, some of which have been strengthened in recent years, and specific noise abatement measures, the impact of noise, particularly from surface transport, will increase unless greater determination is shown on the policy front. Moreover, the future could well see the emergence of other noise sources and noisy locations.

Future Noise from Surface Transport

In France, failing the strengthening of noise abatement policies, there is likely to be a 15 per cent growth in urban populations subjected to levels of more than 65 dB(A) and a 40 per cent growth in populations subjected to levels of more than 55 dB(A), in the year 2000: The number of noise black spots would increase sharply and there would be a considerable extension in "moderately noise-impacted areas". In the United States the proportion of the population exposed to levels in excess of 55 dB(A) would be 28 per cent higher in 1990 than in 1980, while the proportion exposed to levels in excess of 75 dB(A) would be 50 per cent higher. This would result principally from increases in the volume of traffic and urban development.

However, new and stricter noise limits should help to improve the situation in the future. In France, lower emission limits for private cars (75 dB(A)) and heavy vehicles (80 dB(A)) should halve the proportion of the population subjected to levels of over 65 dB(A), though the percentage of the community living in moderately noise-impacted areas would remain unchanged. In Switzerland, a reduction of 3 dB(A) in present noise emission limits for private cars and of 6 dB(A) for heavy vehicles would cut down the numbers exposed to levels in excess of 65 dB(A) and 55 dB(A) by a third and a quarter respectively. The estimates for Denmark are very similar. The full effect of these measures would of course be felt only once the vehicle stock had been totally replaced.

Mitigating the impact of noise from surface transport, particularly in the moderately noise-impacted areas, would require the decision-makers and implementing authorities to pursue a deliberate policy of reducing permissible levels for vehicle noise together with a series of back-up measures in such areas as infrastructure, town planning, habitat and individual behaviour patterns.

Possible New Noise Sources and Sites and New Nuisances

Traffic is likely to remain the prime source of noise. But with changing lifestyles, the coming years are likely to see the emergence of other more limited sources of noise with a more localised impact and which are less easy to apprehend and control. Such noise may derive from an expansion in leisure and tourism, with a rapid growth in recreational "toys" such as trailbikes, ultra-light airplanes and snowmobiles and so on, the use of motorised vehicles and craft in country and mountain areas as yet untouched. As a result silence will become an ever scarcer commodity in terms of both time and place.

4. CONCLUSIONS

Noise is an important feature of the environment, from both the social policy and the economic point of view.

The nature of disturbance and damage caused by noise are today fairly well understood – annoyance, stress effects, disturbed sleep, and auditory and non-auditory impairment; such damage clearly has an economic cost, even if this is sometimes poorly understood. The economic implications of noise abatement policies are also important, associated not only with the cost of such policies but also with the international character of the production, distribution and consumption of the goods and services which are the main source of noise – surface transport vehicles and aircraft in particular – where national regulations have a major impact on such products, in terms of output levels, domestic sales and trade with other countries.

In addition to these economic aspects, noise influences interpersonal and social relationships. The importance of noise pollution from the policy standpoint is clearly established and noise today is seen as a high priority environmental problem by the community, as is borne out by various surveys on undesirable features of living conditions.

The last twenty years have seen a rise of noise levels. At national level, transport is by far the prime source of noise, ahead of building or industry, with road traffic being the chief offender. Aircraft noise is generally next in terms of overall population exposure in most countries, before rail transport and stationary sources.

There is evidence of the results of past and current efforts towards more stringent vehicle noise emission standards, though the full effects of such measures will only be felt some ten to twenty years hence. Moreover considerable efforts have been and are being made to retro-equip existing infrastructures and housing by installing anti-noise screens and soundproofing especially close to the noisiest infrastructures, i.e. in "black spot" areas. Greater account is being and will be taken of noise abatement objectives at the design and construction stages.

All this will not in itself greatly improve the quality of the noise environment, however. If trends are to be reversed, given the conclusions of the various studies on the future outlook, there is a clear need to strengthen these noise abatement policies in all areas in order to counter the almost certainly adverse trend in the state of the noise environment, particularly as regards the extension of areas subject to moderate noise (what may be called the "grey areas").

There are subjects of growing or new concern for the future state of the environment with regard to noise. These mainly relate to the emergence of new sources of noise (e.g. recreational vehicles, increasing use of diesel vehicles) and trends in the communities at risk (a higher proportion of old people), multi-exposure to noise from several sources and the encroachment of noise into rural, tourist and unspoilt areas that have hitherto been spared.

Chapter III

AIR POLLUTION

1. INTRODUCTION

Air pollution is caused by a wide variety of man-made and natural sources. Fuel combustion has been identified as the largest single contributor to air pollutant emissions; in this category, stationary and mobile sources (internal combustion engines) are responsible for approximately equal overall shares, however, varying significantly for individual pollutants. Mobile sources include motor vehicles, aircraft, ships, railways, etc., of which road traffic is by far the dominant source of air pollutant emissions. Road traffic, in turn, includes light and heavy duty vehicles fuelled with either gasoline, diesel, compressed natural gas (CNG) or liquified petroleum gas (LPG), and motorbikes usually fuelled with gasoline.

Motor vehicle exhaust emissions include emissions from the exhaust pipe, blow-by from the engine crankcase, fuel evaporative emissions from the fuel tank and carburettor as well as particulate emissions from the wear and tear of tyres and brakes. The air pollutants emitted from gasoline driven vehicles are carbon monoxide (CO) and hydrocarbons (HC) or more correctly volatile organic compounds resulting from incomplete combustion, nitrogen oxides (NO_x) generated under high combustion temperatures mainly from oxygen and nitrogen in the combustion air, and lead (Pb) from fuel-lead which is added to attain the desired octane rating. CNG and LPG-driven cars have lower HC and CO emissions from the exhaust pipe because of more complete combustion; nitrogen oxide emissions are comparable to those from gasoline cars. No lead is emitted from CNG- and LPG-fuelled cars. Diesel driven vehicles also have better combustion efficiencies, therefore emitting lower rates of HC and CO, and they emit fewer NO_x (on an uncontrolled basis) due to lower ignition temperatures. Diesels emit no lead. However, diesel engines emit fine particles including polycyclic organic matter (POM) – a group of genotoxics –, SO_2 due to the higher sulfur content in diesel compared to gasoline, and more aromatic HCs which cause an unpleasant odour and simultaneously have negative health effects, and of which some are carcinogenic. Aromatic HCs are not only emitted from diesel vehicles but also from gasoline cars. An example of a carcinogen emitted in this group is benzene which, to a large extent, is formed during combustion. Particulate emissions from the wear and tear of tyres and brakes include asbestos which is also carcinogenic. Further, the use of regenerated lubricants containing PCBs may lead to emissions of dioxines.

Comparing emissions from the transport sector to overall man-made emissions on a national basis, the following can be concluded (Table 6): about 90 per cent of all CO emissions originate from the transport sector, mainly automobiles. In most OECD countries, anthropogenic NO_x emissions stem to approximately equal parts from the transport sector and the energy and industrial sectors. In urban areas, 50 per cent of total HCs are often emitted from automobiles. Of all benzene emissions around 80 per cent originate from gasoline-powered motor vehicles if uncontrolled. Lead emissions are due to automobiles to at least 50 per cent with the exception of Japan; their share can, however, be much higher depending on the lead content in gasoline and the importance of the metallurgical industry in the specific country.

The relative contribution from motor vehicles to ambient air quality in cities is higher than their emission shares on a national basis. In the centre of an average built-up area, traffic usually accounts for 100 per cent of CO and lead levels, for at least 60 per cent of NO_x and hydrocarbon levels, for about 10 per cent of SO_2 and 50 per cent of particulate levels. These shares can increase further with respect to the street environment itself.

To appreciate the impact of the transport sector on the environment, and in particular on human health, one needs to elucidate the following: 1) transport emissions and the related ambient pollutant concentrations; and 2) the health and other effects on people or other sensitive species (including trees, etc.) exposed to these concentration levels. The following sections briefly review these two topics and lead to some conclusions regarding the overall impact of transportation on the environment.

Table 6. MAN-MADE EMISSIONS OF AIR POLLUTANTS,
OECD countries, 1980

EMISSIONS OF TRADITIONAL AIR POLLUTANTS, total and share of mobil sources, selected countries, 1980

		Total emissions (1000 tonnes/year)										Transport emissions (% of total)				
		SOx		Part.		NOx		CO		HC (1)		SOx	Part.	NOx	CO	HC
Canada		4650		1907		1942		9928		2100		3%	6%	66%	74%	40%
USA		23200		8400		20300		76000		22800		4%	17%	45%	70%	40%
Japan	b)	1259		133	i)	1339		..		..		9%	..	40%	..	..
Australia	c)	1479		271		915		3704		423		..	..	63%	95%	61%
N. Zealand	c)	88		21		89		566		38		..	..	..	..	..
Austria		354		50	d)	211		1126	d)	251		4%	20%	68%	66%	..
Belgium		856		267		317		839		..		1%	..	38%	..	..
Denmark		455		47	c)	241		602	f)	106		2%	..	26%	100%	..
Finland		584		97	a)	284		660	g)	112		2%	18%	34%	91%	..
France		3558		252	j)	2567		5200	c)	2185		4%	20%	56%	..	..
Germany		3200		730		3090		8960		1860		4%	9%	53%	65%	38%
Greece		700	a)	40	c)	196	c)	695	c)	82	c)	..	..	..	..	..
Ireland		217		94		71		497		62		2%	9%	30%	77%	53%
Italy		3800		196	c)	1550	o)	4036	c)	496	c)	..	..	..	..	..
Luxembourg		23		..		21	k)	..		..		7%	..	> 50%	..	..
Netherlands		445		150		500		1368		452	m)	4%	7%	53%	72%	22%
Norway		141		66	e)	125		632		158	n)	13%	5%	80%	79%	44%
Portugal		293		208		248		533		91	p)	6%	13%	84%	96%	..
Spain		3622	g)	1521	g)	778		3780		739		2%	2%	63%	99%	..
Sweden		483		170	a)	328		1250		410	m)	5%	4%	62%	98%	56%
Switzerland		126		28		196		711		311		5%	..	78%	83%	55%
Turkey	c)	714		138		380		3707		201		..	..	..	..	..
UK		4670		442		1932		5127		1954	m)	1%	17%	29%	89%	16%
Yugoslavia		815		..		..		..		..		..	..	..	..	..

NOTES:

a) 1978.
b) Fiscal year April 1st. to March 31st.
c) Secretariat estimates refering to 1978; 'industrial process' excluded.
d) 'Industr.process' and 'miscell.' excluded.
e) 'Miscellaneous' excluded.
f) 'Mobile sources' only.
g) 1979.
h) Secretariat estimates.
i) Stationary sources only.
j) 'Industrial process' excluded.
k) 1983.
l) Non-methane hydrocarbons.
m) Total hydrocarbons.
n) Including emissions from natural sources.
o) Estimate: 1,410 - 1,550 (1000 t).
p) 'Fuel combustion' excluded.

Source: OECD

2. ADVERSE EFFECTS OF AIR POLLUTANTS EMITTED FROM TRANSPORT SOURCES

Total environmental damage costs due to all sources of air pollution have been estimated to be around one to two per cent of national GDPs. Most transportation sources emit some substances that pose a potential risk to health, the general human well-being, or the natural environment. In industrialised countries, such as those of the OECD and, particularly in urban and densely populated areas, human activities are responsible for almost all air pollution generated, of which transportation sources make up about 50 per cent. In general terms, a major portion of overall health effects resulting from air pollution can therefore be attributed to the transport sector, and mainly the road transport sector.

This section summarises effects of the major air pollutants emitted from the transport sector as well as their atmospheric reaction products. These include carbon monoxide (CO), nitrogen oxides (NO_x), hydrocarbons (HC), lead (Pb) and other particulate matter (TSP), as well as photochemical oxidants, acid deposition, and carbon dioxide (CO_2). They may cause the following direct and indirect effects:

- Health effects (irritation of respiratory, eye, or other systems; acute toxic systemic effects; mutagenic or carcinogenic actions; adverse effects on defense mechanisms against infections);
- Environmental damage (material soiling; corrosion; loss of agricultural productivity; acidification of soil and water; forest die-back); or
- Nuisance (odour, decreased visibility);

Certain of these effects may be immediately apparent and relatively easily traceable to the transportation source. The odour of diesel vehicles is an illustration of these. Other effects may occur in the short term, but the precise contribution of vehicle emissions to these is not always clear. Examples of this are the toxic effects of gasoline lead on children, or the link between NO_x emissions from cars and respiratory tract irritation. Certain effects may take long periods to become apparent, and drawing a causal link to vehicle emissions becomes dramatically more difficult, complicated often by lack of complete scientific understanding of the process, as is the case with many carcinogens. Some of these pollutants have also been implicated in more complex environmental problems, such as photochemical smog and acid deposition.

Until recently, most attention to air pollution problems has focused on the impacts of individual pollutants. However, growing evidence is emerging that the whole problem may be much greater than the sum of its individual parts. For example, a careful review of the dying German forests indicates that it may be due to synergistic effects of both acid rain and photochemical reaction products, as well as direct effects of sulphur dioxide and nitrogen dioxide. Other studies have found adverse health effects from SO_2 and NO_2 in combination to be much more serious than from these pollutants individually; similar results have been found for crops. Also, the US National Academy of Sciences has noted that high levels of SO_2 and coexisting particulate pollutants have been associated repeatedly with increases in respiratory morbidity and mortality rates. Therefore, considering each of these pollutants separately may lead to erroneous conclusions regarding the relative and absolute need for and cost-effectiveness of individual control measures.

Direct Adverse Effects of Primary Pollutants Emitted from Transport Sources

This section discusses the direct adverse effects of CO, NO_x, hydrocarbons and other toxic organic compounds on man and his environment. "Direct" is to be understood as short- and long-term effects which are caused by the responsible pollutant before it undergoes chemical transformation in the atmosphere, or without such transformation.

Carbon Monoxide (CO)

Carbon monoxide can cause adverse health effects because it interferes with the absorption of oxygen by red blood cells. It combines with haemoglobin over 200 times faster than oxygen and blocks its function, thus restricting the supply of oxygen by the blood to body tissue. When 50 per cent of the haemoglobin has been transformed into carboxyhaemoglobin (CHb), this can lead to death. The reactions leading to incorporation of carbon monoxide into the blood are reversible. Thus, the inhalation of a CO-free atmosphere for a few hours removes most of the gas from a victim with mild CO poisoning. The first symptoms for healthy persons appear at carboxyhaemoglobin levels of 10 per cent, which corresponds to atmospheric concentrations of about 100 ppm of CO. For susceptible persons, symptoms appear already at CHb levels of 2-3 per cent .

Carbon monoxide in urban atmospheres has been linked to loss of worker productivity and general discomfort. It can affect the central nervous system, impairing physical coordination, vision and judgement. It can further affect the cardiovascular system, exacerbating cardiovascular disease symptoms, particularly angina. Numerous studies carried out on humans and animals have now demonstrated that those individuals with heart disease are placed under special strain by the presence of excess CO in the blood. Angina pectoris is a cardiovascular disease in which mild exercise or excitement produces symptoms of pressure and pain in the chest because of insufficient oxygen supply to the heart muscle. Clinical health studies have shown a decrease in time to onset of angina pain in those individuals suffering from angina pectoris and exposed to elevated levels of ambient CO. Individuals suffering from peripheral vascular disease may experience similar symptoms aggravated by CO exposure. A study has shown more rapid leg pain in patients suffering from occlusive arterial disease who were exposed to CO, and then exercised.

Lastly, fetuses, sickle cell anemics, and young children may be especially susceptible to exposure to low levels of CO. Several experimental animal studies have exposed pregnant females to CO and have shown resulting effects in the offspring; for example, when pregnant female rabbits were exposed to CO, this resulted in lower birth weights and increased newborn mortality. Since the fetus operates much closer to critical levels in terms of tissue oxygen supply than normal adults, exposure to CO and interference with fetal tissue oxygenation during important developmental stages may have particularly serious effects on fetal development.

Another danger of carbon monoxide is its synergistic action, in conjunction with other air pollutants, to promote morbidity, particularly in subjects with pre-existing respiratory or circulatory ailments. It is one of the most directly acting toxic substances in high concentrations of automobile exhaust emissions. All these effects together have led the World Health Organisation (WHO) to recommend a long term goal of 10 mg/m^3 of ambient CO as an eight hour average.

Nitrogen Oxides (NO_x)

Nitrogen oxides, a class of compounds, can have a variety of direct and indirect effects on human health and the environment. Nitrogen dioxide (NO_2) is of great concern with respect to human health; acute exposure to NO_2 decreases gaseous exchanges in blood and increases respiratory symptoms producing lower lung-function values. These effects can cause irritation and eventually lead to oedema, or even emphysema. Even short-term exposures to NO_2 have resulted in a wide range of respiratory problems in school children – cough, runny nose and sore throat are among the most common. Studies have shown that asthmatics are especially sensitive to even one-hour exposures. A small group of asthmatics were initially exposed to carbachol, a bronchoconstrictor, and then to NO_2; adverse effects such as increased airway resistance were experienced by some of the individuals at levels as low as 0.1 ppm for one hour.

In general, the most serious human health effects attributed to nitrogen oxides are in combination with other air pollutants, or they affect mainly persons with existing health problems. The World Health Organisation (WHO) concluded that a maximum one-hour exposure of 190-320 ug/m^3 (0.10-0.17 ppm) should be consistent with the protection of public health, and that this exposure should not be exceeded more than once per month.

Oxides of nitrogen have been shown to affect vegetation adversely. This effect is even more pronounced when nitrogen dioxide and sulphur dioxide occur simultaneously. Further, nitrogen dioxide has been found to cause detrimental effects on a wide variety of textile dyes and fabrics, plastics and rubber. Nitrogen dioxide is further responsible for a portion of the brownish coloration observed in polluted air, and in combination with particulate nitrates, contributes to pollutant haze, reducing visibility.

Hydrocarbons (HC) and Other Toxic Organic Compounds

Organic compounds, including the entire class of hydrocarbons, have long been considered traditional air pollutants because of the role they play in photochemical oxidant formation and not because they constitute a class of pollutants exhibiting intrinsic health or ecological effects. However, further study has shown that particular organic compounds such as aldehydes, polycyclic aromatic compounds, benzene or organic acids, for example, have adverse effects on human health, while others, such as ethene, exhibit adverse effects on plants. On the other hand, low-molecular-weight hydrocarbons are relatively non-toxic, although they can cause unpleasant effects, which may include eye irritation, coughing and sneezing, drowsiness and symptoms akin to drunkeness. However, these effects have only been observed at relatively high concentrations.

With respect to the more serious health risks, benzene, as a constituent of gasoline and automobile exhaust, is a known human carcinogen causing leukemia. Also, polycyclic aromatic compounds (such as benzo(a)pyrene), as by-products of incomplete combustion of diesel fuel, are known mutagens and carcinogens. It further appears that there are substantial synergistic effects of polycyclic aromatics (PAH), such that the mutagenicity of multiple types of PAH, and in combination with other substances, may be greater than of individual PAH. This is important, especially because of the wide variety of PAH found in diesel exhaust. Yet another toxic organic compound released with car exhaust gases is acetaldehyde.

In addition, lead scavengers, most notably ethylene dibromide and ethylene dichloride, added to gasoline together with lead to encourage greater volatility of leaded combustion by-products, have been found to be carcinogenic in animals and have been identified as potential human carcinogens by the US National Cancer Institute. In October 1983, the US EPA concluded that the harmful effects were so serious that it banned the use of ethylene dibromide in pesticides, which, on the other hand, is still used today in leaded gasoline.

Lead (Pb)

Lead has long been known to damage the kidney, liver, reproductive system, blood formation, basic cellular processes, and brain function at relatively high levels in humans; clinical lead poisoning and encephalopathy (brain and marrow-damage) occur at blood lead levels over 80 ug/dl. It has only been recently that its adverse impacts at very low level are starting to be fully appreciated, potentially bringing many more people into the population of concern.

Lead enters the body primarily by absorption of some ingested lead from the gastrointestinal tract and by absorption of some inhaled lead from the lower respiratory tract. It takes the human body weeks or months to come to equilibrium with intake and excretion of lead. In the body, lead is transported by the blood and stored in bone and teeth (about 95 per cent of stored lead in adults is in bone, slightly less in children) and soft tissues including the brain. Lead is excreted in urine and faeces. Measuring blood lead, which is the easiest and thus most common method, gives a fair measure of recent exposure, whereas measuring bone marrow lead reflects long-term concentrations.

The highest susceptibility is found in children, whose activities tend to expose them more to lead in dust and soils and who absorb a much greater proportion at a given level of exposure (about 50 per cent as opposed to approximately 10 per cent for adults). In 1979, it was found that children with high levels of lead accumulated in their baby teeth experienced more behavioural problems, lower IQs and decreased ability to concentrate. The latest series of health studies in the United Kingdom tends to confirm this result. Even after taking up to 15 social factors into account, a 3 IQ number deficit was consistently found. While not necessarily statistically significant in any individual study , data consistently show the above effects. It is important to note that it is not only the length and severity of exposure to lead which results in the health damage but the age at which exposure occurs. The newborn child is the most prone to injury from overexposure to lead, and the damage that may be caused will have the greatest long-term social and economic consequences. Studies in Germany offer additional evidence that neuropsychological effects can be caused already by very low blood lead levels.

Studies have been carried out to quantify the effects of gasoline lead on human health and on children's health in particular. It has been found that both average blood lead levels and cases of lead poisoning in children correlate more strongly to gasoline lead than to lead in the air alone. Because of this close relationship, reducing the lead content of gasoline has been demonstrated to significantly reduce the health risks in urban areas in the United States. For example, based on data collected in more than 60 United States cities by the Center for Disease Control, the decline in mean blood lead levels computed by six month intervals almost parallels the amount of lead used in the production of gasoline from 1976 to 1980.

In Europe, Ispra has completed a study in the Northern Italian region of Piemont, designed to determine the relationship between gasoline lead and human uptake, and came to the conclusion that the gasoline lead correlates best with the finest lead particles in the air, and that the gasoline fraction of blood lead in Turin is on the order of 24 to 27 per cent, whereas, in nearby countryside, the range is from 12 to 21 per cent and, in further countryside, from 11 to 19 per cent. These results show that the relationship between airborne lead and blood lead seems approximately the same in Europe and the United States, i.e. an increase of about 1 ug/m^3 of ambient lead will result in an increase of about 1 to 2 ug/dl of blood lead.

Lead is recently receiving further increased attention because of other health concerns, especially the high suspicion of potential carcinogenic activity, which would mean that no "safe" concentration level exists.

Particulate Matter (Aerosols) and Fibers (Asbestos)

Particulate matter or aerosols, are emitted with vehicle exhaust gases as well as from the wear and tear of tyres and brakes and from entrainment of road dust during vehicle use. Particulate matter consists of small solid or liquid particles of varied chemical composition suspended in the atmosphere. It is sometimes perceived as visible smoke, as e.g. in diesel exhaust emissions. Fine particulate matter may be toxic in itself or may carry toxic (including carcinogenic) trace substances absorbed to its surface. Fine particulate can penetrate deep into the respiratory system, irritating lung tissue and causing long-term disorders. Fine particles emitted from diesel-fuelled vehicles and asbestos fibers from the wear and tear of brake-linings are of particular concern.

In urban areas, a strong correlation has been established between suspended particulate and variations in infant mortality and total mortality rates. The US EPA has further found clear evidence from the epidemiological literature that implicates particles in aggravating disease among bronchitics, asthmatics, cardiovascular patients and people with influenza. Diesel particulate emissions are further of special concern because of their potential carcinogenicity. For example, the US National Academy of Science notes that, because of their small size, diesel particles remain suspended in the air for a week or more and can be inhaled and deposited in the narrowest passages of the lungs, and because of their small size they offer a relatively large surface on which toxic, mutagenic, and carcinogenic compounds can be absorbed. A pilot study of US railroad workers, conducted by researchers at Harvard, indicates that the risk ratio for respiratory cancer in diesel exposed subjects relative to unexposed subjects could be as great as 1.42, i.e. the possibility of developing cancer may be 42 per cent greater in individuals exposed to diesel exhaust than in individuals who are not exposed.

Asbestos, a group of naturally occurring hydrated mineral silicate fiber, has been shown to induce, at high concentrations, asbestosis, lung cancer, mesothelioma (a rare cancer of the abdomen and lung linings). No conclusive data are, however, available to show that current ambient asbestos levels are high enough to induce these diseases, and the risk of the general population to develop lung cancer or mesothelioma from ambient exposure is estimated to generally be low.

Fine particulate matter is in the size range of the wavelength of visible light, and can thus significantly reduce visibility. Since diesel particulate falls into this size range, and because it is primarily composed of elemental carbon, it strongly scatters and absorbs light. A study conducted for the State of California found that fine diesel soot particles have a light extinction efficiency of three to four times that of other fine aerosols.

Lastly, diesel particles are associated with soiling, which can result in increased cleaning and painting costs for building and other materials, and reduction in the useful life of fabrics. Since the soiling of fabrics and vertical surfaces has been ascribed to fine particles, particularly dark carbonaceous materials, it is believed that the oiliness of diesel particulates might cause a more serious soiling problem than an equal weight of particulates from other sources. Therefore diesel car exhaust is of some special concern.

Indirect, Secondary Effects of Pollution Caused by Transport Sources

This section discusses the more complex environmental problems of photochemical oxidants, acid deposition, and carbon dioxide build-up in the atmosphere. "Indirect, secondary" is to be understood as short- and long-term effects primarily on the natural environment, which are caused by generally a mix of pollutants after they have undergone atmospheric transformation. These effects are of concern, not only in areas close to emission sources, but also at distant sites with no pollution sources. Carbon dioxide is discussed here because it is not a pollutant in itself, but may cause long-term environmental effects via its build-up.

Photochemical Oxidants

Photochemical oxidants are defined as compounds with a strong oxydising potential formed by chain reactions between unsaturated hydrocarbons and other reactive organic compounds, nitrogen oxides and oxygen in the presence of sunlight. Ozone (O_3) is the most prevalent photochemical oxidant, being formed in the largest quantities; other oxidants include hydrogen peroxide, aldehydes, peroxyacetyl nitrate (PAN), peroxybenzoyl nitrate (PBzN), and other peroxyacyl nitrates. Approximately 50 per cent of both precursor emissions (HC and NO_x) stem from the transport sector. The effects of photochemical air pollution first became manifest in the 40s in the Los Angeles basin through eye irritation, plant damage and visible smog. The primary toxicological effects of oxidants are increased susceptibility to infections, pulmonary disease, pulmonary and systemic biochemical changes, impairment of pulmonary functions, and eye, nose and throat irritation. To avoid these symptoms, the World Health Organisation (WHO) has recommended a maximum one-hour ozone concentration in ambient air of 100 to 200 ug/m^3 (0.05-0.10 ppm); as a best single value estimate of exposure limit, WHO recommends a total oxidant concentration of 120 ug/m^3 (0.06 ppm).

Oxidants can further cause significant damage to vegetation, including agricultural crops and forestry. The Congressional Research Service estimates short-term crop yield losses in the United States alone at between US $1.9 and 4.3 billion per year due to ambient ozone concentrations; in the long term, ozone damage may have resulted in the disappearance of high yielding crops from certain localities and even from the genetic base. Other negative impacts include seed yield reductions of 10 to 22 per cent in field corn, up to 33 per cent reductions in wheat yields and from 24 to 50 per cent reductions in soybean yields. A recent Swedish study concludes that timber volume may also be significantly reduced. Ozone and other oxides attack the cell walls of plants; the susceptibility to this attack varies appreciably from one species of plant to another and, although thin-leaved vegetables are particularly vulnerable, forest trees may also suffer.

Photochemical oxidants and, in particular, ozone accelerate the deterioration processes of materials, especially rubber. They contribute significantly to visibility degradation owing to a number of photochemical reactions that lead to the formation of aerosols in the light scattering range.

Acid Deposition

Sulphur and nitrogen oxides emitted by natural and man-made sources can undergo chemical transformation in the atmosphere, forming acids and acid salts (sulfates and nitrates) and returning to the earth as acid deposition. The single most important source category of NO_x emissions is the transport sector. These NO_x emissions are converted to nitric acid and contribute approximately one-third of the acidity in rainfall; under certain conditions such as spring thaw when snowfall accumulated over the winter melts, this NO_x impact can be much higher. Further, photochemical oxidants are suspected of playing a key role in the conversion of sulfur and nitrogen oxides into acids; by contributing to the formation of photochemical oxidants, motor vehicle hydrocarbon and nitrogen oxide emissions can, therefore, indirectly contribute to the acid deposition problem in addition to the direct contribution of nitrogen oxides.

It is now generally accepted that acid deposition does impair sensitive aquatic ecosystems and corrodes materials. Decreases in the pH values of fresh water bodies, indicating higher acidity, have occurred throughout Europe and North America. As a result, there has been a decline in or an elimination of the fish population in acidified lakes and, in more general terms, a reduction in the number and variety of species, or changes in and replacement of certain aquatic organisms and nutrients. Some evidence suggests that essential nutrients can be removed from sensitive soils releasing metals that are toxic to plants. Based on a growing body of research, it has been suggested that this mechanism may be responsible for very substantial damage to the West German forests. Some recent evidence also suggests that some adverse effects on human health may be attributable to acid deposition.

Carbon Dioxide (CO_2)

Even though CO_2 is not an air pollutant by definition since it is a natural component of the earth's atmosphere, its constant increase from fossil fuel combustion, to which, in turn, the transport sector contributes an important share, may significantly add to the "greenhouse" effect (i.e. a global warming of the atmosphere). The possible climatic and biological changes and resulting social, economic, and political impacts are currently the object of debate among experts.

3. TRENDS IN EMISSIONS FROM THE TRANSPORT SECTOR AND RESULTING AIR QUALITY

This section sequentially reviews facts concerning:

1. Overall trends in emissions from vehicular traffic, in North America, OECD-Europe and the OECD Pacific region;
2. Emissions per vehicle-km ;
3. Trends of resulting ambient air quality and the current state; and
4. Prospects concerning the environmental impacts from transportation in light of new legislation and traffic volume growth. Focus is on road traffic, and particularly on gasoline driven cars; statements concerning OECD-Europe do not necessarily apply to Southern European countries in view of the lack of available data for these countries.

Overall Trends in Emissions from the Transport Sector

Chapter I has shown that the number of motor vehicles in use in OECD countries has increased since 1970 by 70 per cent and that the amount of miles travelled in OECD countries has increased by about 50 per cent. Most OECD countries introduced legislation at some point in the 70s regulating the maximum allowable emissions (CO, HC and NO_x) per vehicle; such legislation, however, has usually been limited to new gasoline driven passenger cars (see tables in this section and Part IV for a detailed review of emission standards). The resulting emissions to ambient air are reviewed here.

Considering individual pollutants, *CO and HC emissions* from transportation sources have significantly declined in the United States and Japan; they have increased and then stabilised in Europe. The decrease in the United States and Japan was a consequence of the introduction of stringent automotive emission standards, starting in 1975 with the mandatory use of oxidation catalysts, and their subsequent further tightening[3]. Total emission reductions achieved today from US transportation sources have been 23 per cent for CO and 30 per cent for HC since 1975, with the most noticable decrease taking place after 1978. In Europe, CO and HC emissions from transport sources have, in the 70s, generally increased in proportion to the increase in vehicle-miles travelled. A stabilisation in CO and, to a lesser degree, also in HC emissions has been observed in some European countries since about 1980, partly due to a slower rate of increase in total vehicle-miles travelled, partly because of implementation of emission regulations whose impact is delayed by the necessarily progressive replacement of the old vehicle fleet. The difference in European and North American trends can be attributed to the fact that European emission regulations have been much more lenient than in the United States and Japan including regulation ECE 15.03 currently enforced by all EC member states and regulation ECE 15.04 currently applied by some EC members (Tables 7 and 8, Appendix 1).

Regarding *NO_x emissions* from the transport sector, an increase was observed in all OECD countries in the 70s, with the exception of Japan, related to the

Table 7. CO EMISSIONS FROM THE TRANSPORT SECTOR
Selected Countries, 1970-1983

		Transport emissions (1000 tonnes)				Changes 1970-1983 (Index 100 = 1975)			
		1970	1975	1980	1983	1970	1975	1980	1983
Canada	a)	13022	9803	7245	..	133	100	74	..
USA		71800	62000	52700	47700	116	100	85	77
Japan		..	..	..	..	..	..	..	..
France		6000	7000	..	..	86	100	..	..
Germany	b,c,d)	5800	6200	5665	5330	94	100	91	86
Italy	e)	4620	..	..	..	..	..	..	..
Netherlands	f)	1400	1400	1050	875	100	100	75	63
Norway	d)	360	520	483	487	69	100	93	94
Portugal		270	440	511	..	61	100	116	..
Spain		..	3010	3748	..	..	100	125	..
Sweden		1480	1370	1230	..	108	100	90	..
Switzerland	d)	434	440	448	440	99	100	102	100
UK		5920	6709	7941	8327	88	100	118	124

NOTES:
a) 1980 refers to 1978.
b) 1980 data are arithmetic averages based on 1978 and 1982 data.
c) 1975 refers to 1974.
d) 1983 refers to 1982.
e) 1970 refers to 1971.
f) 1983 data are estimates.

Source: OECD

Table 8. HC EMISSIONS FROM THE TRANSPORT SECTOR
Selected Countries, 1970-1983

		Transport emissions (1000 tonnes)				Changes 1970-1983 (Index 100 = 1975)			
		1970	1975	1980	1983	1970	1975	1980	1983
Canada	a)	2139	1197	851	..	179	100	71	..
USA		12300	10300	8200	7200	119	100	80	70
Japan		..	..	..	..	..	..	..	..
France		460	430	..	..	107	100	..	..
Germany	b,c,d)	530	580	642	624	91	100	111	108
Italy	e)	509	..	..	..	..	..	..	..
Netherlands		240	225	105	170	107	100	47	76
Norway		69	82	69	..	84	100	84	..
Portugal		49	82	82	..	60	100	100	..
Spain		..	522	693	..	..	100	133	..
Sweden		310	250	230	..	124	100	92	..
Switzerland	d)	89	94	99	104	95	100	105	111
UK		397	457	535	548	87	100	117	120

NOTES:
a) 1980 refers to 1978.
b) 1980 data are arithmetic averages based on 1978 and 1982 data.
c) 1975 refers to 1974.
d) 1983 refers to 1982.
e) 1970 refers to 1971.

Source: OECD

steady increase in road traffic volume and the relatively late implementation of stringent emission regulations. In Japan, NO_x emission standards for automobiles were already considerably tightened in 1975, reducing allowable levels from 3.0 g/km to 1.6 g/km. In 1977, Japan further regulated maximum allowable emissions from trucks, buses, and diesel-powered vehicles.

In general, transport emissions in early 80s decreased in the United States and stabilised in Europe. In the United States, NO_x emission standards for new gasoline driven cars were progressively tightened since the early 70s but were only significantly lowered in 1977 and 1981 from 1.9 g/km to 1.2 g/km and 0.6 g/km, respectively, now implying the use of the three-way catalyst; this considerable reduction of allowable NO_x emissions for automobiles has off-set the increasing trend in emissions of the 70s and resulted in a zero increase in 1983 compared to 1975 in spite of continued traffic volume growth. In Europe, NO_x emissions exceed 1975 levels by 15, 23, and 42 per cent for the United Kingdom, France, and Germany, respectively, and by 3 per cent in Sweden (Table 9).

Lead emissions have closely corresponded to the amount of leaded fuel consumed and its lead content. With the introduction of catalyst equipped cars in Japan and the United States in 1975, lead-free fuel had to be available. In the United States, 1983 unleaded gasoline sales made up 54 per cent of the total US gasoline marketed; lead content in other gasoline has also been limited to 0.29 g/l since 1983; as a result, lead emissions from the transport sector have dropped substantially by 68 per cent since 1975, the sharpest decrease being observed after 1979 (Table 10). In Japan, in 1983, over 95 per cent of all gasoline sold was already unleaded (less than 0.004 g/l). In Europe, as well, lead emissions from transportation sources have been decreasing due to legislation on the maximum lead content in gasoline and its stepwise reduction. The EC passed a regulation in 1978 setting 0.4 g/l as a maximum and 0.15 g/l as a minimum allowable lead content. In 1980/81 this regulation was enforced by most European countries, and many countries have already, or are in the process of, lowering their lead content further to the lower limit of 0.15 g/l. Further decisions have been taken to introduce unleaded gasoline between now and 1988 by the latest, and some European countries have already introduced it (Appendix 1).

Few data are available on *particulate emissions* from transport sources. However, increases in especially fine and toxic particle emissions are expected in countries where the use of diesel cars has increased and is further increasing, for example North America, Japan, and some European countries like France, Germany, Italy and Spain.

Emissions per Vehicle-Kilometre

The evaluation of vehicle emissions based on the distance travelled would reveal the effectiveness of the national emission standards more clearly than the global quantities described above. Unfortunately not enough reliable data are yet available.

Preliminary studies have shown that there may be a large difference between the prescribed emission standards on new vehicles and the real emissions of the fleet of vehicles actually in use. This large difference can be explained by:

- The fact that the full benefits of current emission standards are not yet achieved because it takes ten to twelve years to replace a fleet of cars in Europe and North America;
- The fact that actual tail pipe emissions of motor vehicles deteriorate with time and use, and that they deteriorate faster and more in the absence of proper maintenance of the vehicles. Misfuelling, in particular may lead to high increases in emissions; for a given vehicle, up to several hundred per cent;
- The possible difference between actual traffic conditions and hypothetical traffic conditions expressed by the driving cycles used for the definition of emission standards;
- The fact that emission standards are actually much less stringent with respect to commercial and/or diesel vehicles than for gasoline driven automobiles.

Due to the importance of these aspects, it is hoped that additional research efforts will be made to obtain reliable data of this kind separately for each vehicle category.

Trends in Air Quality Changes

Changes in emissions always result in changes in air quality that are, however, not always directly proportional. With respect to pollutants directly emitted from mobile sources (e.g. CO, NO_x, certain HCs, Pb, TSP), air quality changes are generally observed in the direct vicinity of emission changes, for example, along highways, in streets, tunnels and in urban areas. Emissions from transport sources, however, also contribute to the formation of secondary pollutants in the atmosphere as conversion products of precursor emissions. HC and NO_x emissions together cause photochemical oxidation, thus being responsible for ozone (O_3) and smog formation; nitrogen oxide emissions are being seen as increasingly important in the formation of atmospheric acidity, thus, contributing significantly (at least 30 per cent) to the acid rain (and dry deposition) problem. In

Table 9. NO_x EMISSIONS FROM THE TRANSPORT SECTOR
Selected Countries, 1970-1983

		Transport emissions (1000 tonnes)				Changes 1970-1983 (Index 100 = 1975)			
		1970	1975	1980	1983	1970	1975	1980	1983
Canada	a)	760	1206	1114	..	63	100	92	..
USA		7600	8900	9200	8800	85	100	103	99
Japan	a)	..	804	567	..	..	100	71	..
France		537	879	1042	1085	61	100	119	123
Germany	a,b,e)	1008	1188	1637	1692	85	100	138	142
Italy	c)	331	..	..	..	..	..	..	..
Netherlands		210	250	280	270	84	100	112	108
Norway	d)	..	95	100	105	..	100	105	111
Portugal		55	78	208	..	71	100	267	..
Spain		..	357	501	..	..	100	140	..
Sweden		162	195	199	202	83	100	102	104
Switzerland	e)	79	105	131	145	75	100	125	138
UK	f)	440	473	533	546	93	100	113	115

NOTES:
- a) 1975 refers to 1974.
- b) 1980 data are arithmetic averages based on 1978 and 1982 data.
- c) 1970 refers to 1971.
- d) 1975 refers to 1976.
- e) 1983 refers to 1982.
- f) For UK, 'mobile source' data neither include aviation fuel nor marine fuel.

Source: OECD

Table 10. PB EMISSIONS FROM THE TRANSPORT SECTOR
Selected Countries, 1970-1983

		Transport emissions (1000 tonnes)				Changes 1970-1983 (Index 100 = 1975)			
		1970	1975	1980	1983	1970	1975	1980	1983
Canada		..	11.8	8.1	6.5	..	100	69	55
USA		..	123.0	60.0	40.0	..	100	49	33
Japan		..	..	..	..	..	..	..	..
France		..	..	..	..	..	..	..	..
Germany		..	..	..	..	..	..	..	..
Ireland	a)	0.7	0.7	0.9	0.5	100	100	129	71
Italy		..	..	..	..	..	..	..	..
Netherlands	b)	1.8	2.4	1.4	1.3	75	100	58	54
Norway	c)	..	0.7	..	..	..	100	..	..
Sweden	c)	2.0	1.6	1.1	0.7	125	100	69	44
Switzerland		1.3	1.1	1.1	0.5	114	100	100	45
UK		6.5	7.4	7.5	6.8	88	100	101	92

NOTES:
- a) 1970 refers to 1972.
- b) 1983 refers to 1982.
- c) 1975 refers to 1977.

Source: OECD

these cases, precursors and products can be transported over long distances (several hundred to thousand kilometres), and their effects are felt not only in the source vicinity but also in relatively remote areas.

This section presents air quality trends in the various OECD countries, discusses them in light of the emission changes from the transport sector, and describes the current state of the ambient air in relation to recommended air quality values.

Regarding *carbon monoxide*, the sharp decrease in CO emissions in North America and Japan during the 70s is directly reflected in ambient concentration levels. In Japan in 1982, all except for one effective roadside monitoring stations met the Japanese ambient air quality standard (8-hour standard: 20 ppm); the annual averages of CO concentrations in Tokyo and Osaka decreased by about 45 per cent between 1973 and 1982 from 1.7 ppm and 1.9 ppm to 0.9 ppm and 1.1 ppm, respectively. In the United States, in 1983, the ambient air quality standard (8-hour standard: 9 ppm) was met by 70 per cent of all monitoring sites, which compares to 35 per cent in 1975; the composite average of 8-hour concentrations from all stations decreased by 33 per cent between 1975 and 1983 from 12 ppm to 8 ppm. Ambient CO data concerning European cities present a decline or stabilisation of CO concentrations. For instance, the annual mean value of hourly CO concentrations decreased in Paris from about 17 ppm in the early 70s to 10 ppm in the late 70s and early 80s. The recorded levels are within the limit values recommended by WHO both for periods less than one hour (25 ppm) and for exposures between 8 and 24 hours (10 ppm).

Regarding *lead*, emission reductions achieved through reduced amounts of lead in gasoline or the use of unleaded gasoline usually are directly reflected in reduced ambient concentrations. In the United States, an emission drop of 68 per cent from transportation sources corresponded to a drop in ambient lead levels of 67 per cent (1975-1983); average quarterly maximum lead concentration from 1975 to 1977 were about 1.0 ug/m^3, steadily falling thereafter to an average of 0.3 ug/m^3, all well below the national ambient air quality standard (NAAQS) of 1.5 ug/m^3. In Europe, a decrease in ambient concentrations is reported in countries which have reduced the lead content of their gasoline such as France, Germany, the Netherlands, Sweden, and the United Kingdom. However, maximum ambient lead concentrations in major European cities such as Paris still reach up to almost 4.0 ug/m^3. A further reduction in ambient lead levels is to be expected from measures under way to decrease the gasoline lead content and introduce unleaded gasoline in Europe (Appendix 1).

The impact of reduced lead emissions can be seen beyond changes in air quality in actual lead levels in the blood of people, this being a more direct measure of health implications from air pollution caused by transportation sources. In the United States, for instance, mean blood lead levels in children declined by almost 37 per cent from 1976 to 1980.

Regarding *nitrogen oxide* concentrations available data in selected cities show that NO_2 levels remained relatively stable between 1975 and 1983, with a few exceptions where NO_2 levels either increased (e.g. Lausanne) or decreased (e.g. London) substantially. National data from the United States and Japan confirm the relative stability of NO_2 concentrations observed in urban areas elsewhere in OECD countries in the period 1975-1980, but show some improvements after 1980. The United States noted a 10 per cent improvement in the composite average of NO_2 levels at all monitoring sites between 1980 and 1983, while Japan registered a 20 per cent improvement measured at road side monitoring stations during the same period. The 1983 annual averages of daily atmospheric NO_2 concentrations in cities in OECD countries were generally below 80 ug/m^3, with some exceptions in Southern European cities. NO_2 concentrations were therefore generally lower than the US National Ambient Air Quality Standard of 100 ug/m^3 as an annual average. In Japan, about 2 per cent of all NO_2 monitoring stations recorded values exceeding the upper limit of a range given as the national air quality standard for NO_2 in 1982. Background NO_2 levels in OECD countries have been stable, the annual average usually being in the range of several ug/m^3, rarely exceeding 10 ug/m^3.

As already pointed out in the beginning of this section, NO_x emissions are significant contributors to *photochemical pollution and atmospheric acidity*. Therefore, trends of secondary pollutants are shortly discussed here. Regarding photochemical smog pollution, no clear trends can be discerned in Europe other than the more frequent occurrence of high ozone levels in rural and relatively remote areas in more recent years. In the United States, a 18 per cent decrease in the composite average of the second highest daily O_3 concentration was observed between 1978 and 1982 whereas this trend was reversed by a comparable increase in 1983. Over the entire period the composite average exceeded the US national ambient air quality standard (NAAQS) of 0.12 ppm, even though the number of days with concentrations higher than the NAAQS decreased from around 13 in 1975 to about 6 in 1982, followed by an increase to 8 in 1983. Improved air quality with respect to urban photochemical oxidant levels in the United States is attributed to reduced HC emissions, not to reduced NO_x emissions.

A decreasing trend in photochemical oxidants has also been observed in Japan where the average number of days exceeding 0.12 ppm O_3 at roadside monitoring stations decreased from 2.8 in 1975 to 0.3 in 1982. The number of people reporting health damage from photochemical air pollution to authorities had reached a peak of more than 46 000 in 1975, followed by a downward trend to a low of 450 in 1982, which then again increased to over 1 700 in 1983. Most smog alerts are issued in the Tokyo and Osaka Bay areas where traffic emissions and population density are highest. In Japan as well, urban O_3 trends are more closely related to HC emissions and ambient concentration trends, which decreased by 25 per cent between 1977 and 1982, than to NO_x emissions and concentrations.

Nitrogen oxide emissions also play a major role in atmospheric acidification; however, no quantitative conclusions can yet be drawn regarding the contribution to the acid rain phenomenon from the transport sector. Acid deposition has been significantly increasing in North America and Europe over the last decades whereas the phenomenon has not yet been observed in the OECD Pacific region. Over a relatively short period, however, it has not been possible to delineate clear trends in increasing acid deposition in Europe or North America.

Although concern is increasing with respect to ambient pollution of other trace substances from motor vehicles, including small particles, polycyclic organic matters, etc., no actual air quality data are available to review the situation.

Prospects Concerning Future Environmental Impacts from Transportation

The development and implementation of policies aimed at reducing the environmental impact of the transport sector should take into consideration an analysis of possible future emissions, their likely effect on air quality and the resulting potential impacts on health and the environment estimated in physical and economic terms to the degree possible.

To predict future (5 to 10 years) emissions from transportation sources, the following need to be considered: trends in traffic volume (including the future composition of the vehicle fleet), and emissions of the vehicle fleet (including planned legislation for new vehicles and deterioration of emissions over vehicle life).

Stocks of passenger cars are likely to continue to grow, though at slower rates than in the 70s, and the corresponding road-traffic volume is also likely to further increase but, as well, at decreased rates (Chapter I). The trends in air pollutant emissions from gasoline driven passenger cars will depend on how fast the fleet becomes cleaner through:

- The full translation into the fleet of already implemented standards for new vehicles and fuels;
- The development and implementation of additional tighter standards for new vehicles and fuels; and
- The improved performance of in-use vehicles.

Prospects concerning CO suggest a general decrease in emissions, with the exception of Southern European countries. Future lead emissions and concentrations are also projected to decrease for those countries that have reduced or have scheduled to reduce the lead content in their gasoline. Prospects concerning NO_x are less favourable. Standards already introduced in Japan and the United States, as well as recent decisions in Europe for passenger gasoline cars may lead, if properly implemented and translated into the actual vehicle fleet, to decreases in NO_x emissions from the transport sector which could, however, be offset by increasing emissions from trucks, etc.

Considering goods vehicles, their number and use is expected to grow at sustained rates (Chapter I). Such increases, together with the growing share of diesel vehicles in a number of countries, will lead to increasing environmental pressures from commercial and diesel vehicles. This development implies that emissions of and concerns with non-traditional pollutants (e.g. fine particles, polycyclic organic matter, and emissions from fuel additives) will become significantly more important in the future.

4. CONCLUSIONS

Air is an environmental resource; it is a fundamental necessity for almost all forms of terrestrial life. It is also an economic resource; unhealthy air reduces man's production potential and it may reduce plant productivity, resulting in potential crop and timber losses. Environmental damage costs due to air pollution from all sources have been estimated to one to two per cent of national GDPs. Further, socially there is a demand for clean air. Lastly, the general perception of air pollution has been changing. While in the 60s, air pollution was perceived as a local problem mostly concerned with direct health effects on man in heavily industrialized and densely populated urban areas, it is now increasingly being recognized that pollution can also have an impact on areas far removed from emission sources, can be transported across national frontiers, and may exert effects on water bodies, forests and agricultural crops.

In industrialized countries, and particularly in urban and densely populated areas, human activities are responsible for almost all air pollution generated. Transportation sources make up about half of these emissions, of which road traffic is by far the dominant source. The overall contribution from the transport sector appears therefore significant and crucial, even though its precise contribution cannot always be quantified. The understanding, monitoring and assessment of the impacts of pollution from various source categories needs , therefore to be improved. Human and environmental exposure to pollution has been studied and treated in a sectoral approach. Growing evidence is becoming available that simultaneous and sequential exposure to several pollutants not only outside and at work but also in garages, parking areas, inside vehicles as well as in homes and commercial premises may produce more serious health problems than traditionally expected. Ecological damages such as damages to lakes, forests and crops are today well documented and of concern to the public as well as to governments. While the qualitative linkages between the pollutants and the adverse effects are generally well established, quantification is still difficult and controversial (e.g. the contribution of nitrogen oxides to photochemical smog and acid rain, as well as their direct contribution to effects from transport sources only). Beyond the physical estimates of these health and ecological damages, the economic estimates should be further assessed.

The most prevalent air pollutants emitted from transport sources include carbon monoxide (CO), lead (Pb), volatile organic compounds (VOCs), nitrogen oxides (NO_x), and other particulate matter (TSP). They may cause the following direct and indirect effects:

- Health effects (irritation of respiratory, eye, or other systems; acute toxic systemic effects; mutagenic or carcinogenic action; adverse effects on defense mechanism against infections);
- Environmental damage (material soiling; loss of agricultural productivity; acidification of soil and water; forest damage); or
- Nuisance (odour, decreased visibility).

Carbon monoxide transport emissions and resulting air quality levels are already improving, especially in Japan and the United States. These gains should be sufficient to achieve and retain, in Japan and the United States, air quality levels considered healthy. Similar progress is starting to occur in Europe, but will need to be monitored and probably strengthened, particularly in Southern Europe.

The health effects of *lead* exposure, especially in children, have been of growing concern in most areas of the world. The use of lead in gasoline is declining in many countries, and translates clearly into reduced ambient lead concentrations. However, further progress is necessary in all OECD countries, except Japan where decisions were taken early and have been effectively implemented. Evidence is building that no safe concentration level may exist for lead.

Progress has also occurred in reducing *hydrocarbon* emissions and resulting urban photochemical pollution in Japan and the United States, and should continue in the foreseeable future. In Europe, no clear trends can be discerned. It is, however, expected that photochemical smog remains a major problem in large urban areas in Europe as well as North America where precursor pollutants are still not decreasing; this may particularly be true in Southern European countries. Also, recent observations of increasingly frequent, high oxidant concentrations in rural and remote areas tend to indicate that photochemical smog formation is a major long-range transport phenomenon which may contribute significantly to currently observed forest damages.

The lack of progress in reducing *NO_x* emissions from transport sources is a cause of concern, especially in Europe, because of associated secondary pollution problems such as acid rain and photochemical oxidants. Acid deposition is a major concern in North America and Europe. Widespread deterioration of forests and lakes has taken place in many parts of Europe and North America and has been attributed to these problems.

Lastly, increasing concentrations of CO_2 in the atmosphere resulting from fossil fuel combustion, and thus traffic sources, and their possible climatic, economic and social impacts are also of some concern.

Generally, the effectiveness of policies aiming to abate air pollution from the transport sector can be evaluated in two ways:

- Comparison of trends with and without implementing a specific policy; and
- Comparison with air quality objectives.

With respect to the first, countries that have implemented emission standards have seen the effectiveness of these regulations. Many European countries have been able to prevent emission increases of traditional pollutants from vehicles from keeping pace with the road traffic growth; Japan has even achieved an absolute reduction in emissions despite a very rapidly growing vehicle fleet. With regard to attainment of ambient air quality objectives, success has been much more limited. Only Japan and the United States have been capable of showing better attainment of ambient air quality standards in the 80s compared to the 70s even though exceedances are still observed. In Europe, emission reduction policies for the transport sector have not been strong enough to achieve absolute environmental improvements, even though this might well be expected as a consequence of the introduction of the new standards in the EC as from 1988. In conclusion, only those countries that have already, for a considerable number of years, been enforcing most stringent emission requirements per individual vehicle, have until now been able to reverse significantly trends of rising pollution from the transport sector.

Attention should also be directed to new issues of concern. A key question is: How well will controls on new gasoline driven cars improve emissions from the actual fleet? This fleet is indeed made up of in-use vehicles which differ in their actual performance, operation, and maintenance from new cars. To guarantee an efficient and effective implementation of control programmes, the following needs to be closely monitored and assured:

- Prevention of misfueling;
- Enforcement of inspection/maintenance programmes;
- Application of economic instruments; and
- Improvement of the durability of emission control devices.

A second key question is: How well will emissions from other transport sources, in particular from gasoline trucks and buses, light and heavy duty diesel vehicles and motorcycles be contained? Given the growth in traffic volume of commercial and diesel powered vehicles, the development and implementation of appropriate, emission standards will be a focus of attention in the years ahead. Of special concern is fine particulate matter.

A third key question relates to emissions of "non-conventional" pollutants. After having started relatively early with the regulation of CO and hydrocarbons, and more recently with action on NO_x and lead, it appears now that other "new" pollutants emitted by both gasoline and diesel driven vehicles deserve attention. Knowledge about the effects and magnitude of such pollutants is still limited, and preventive measures have hardly been taken by any governments. Pollutants in this category include organic substances such as polycyclic organic matters, aromatic hydrocarbons such as benzene, heavy metals, and fibres such as asbestos. Emissions from fuel additives, from the wear and tear of tires and brakes and from the use of regenerated lubricants should be studied, and may possibly require control.

A fourth key question relates to measures regarding traffic management. Indeed, the impact of transport on the environment depends on the actual performance of vehicles in a given traffic situation, which, in turn, depends on traffic management. Regulations and economic incentives that determine both urban and non-urban traffic patterns (including buffer zones, speed limits, congestion control, etc.) can help significantly to reduce transport emissions and related health or other environmental effects.

NOTES

1. A decibel (dB) is a unit of sound pressure level related to a standard reference level of 0.00002 Newtons per square metre. The decibel scale is logarithmic so that a very wide range of audible sound can be described in terms of a manageably small range of numerical expressions. A sound level of 0 dB at 1000 Hertz is just audible to a person with good hearing. A sound level of 120 dB would cause pain in the ear. The acoustical pressure of the second is one million times greater than that of the first.
   A decibel A-weighted (dB(A)) is a unit of measurement of sound in which greater emphasis is given to medium and high frequencies to which the human ear is most sensitive. The dB(A) measure, which is the most usual in noise abatement and control activities, gives a good correlation with the subjective impression of loudness.
   A 10 decibel increase in the sound doubles its subjective intensity (that is, its loudness or noisiness), whereas a doubling of the acoustic energy results in an increase of 3 decibels only.
2. The Leq gives the average sound level over a given period, e.g. a full day.
3. Emission limits were sequentially reduced for CO from 17 g/km to 2.1 g/km in the United States, and from 26 g/km to 2.7 g/km in Japan; regulations for VOC's were tightened from 1.9 g/km to 0.25 g/km in the United States and from 3.8 g/km to 0.39 g/km in Japan.

Part III

ASSESSMENT OF INNOVATIONS IN URBAN TRANSPORT MANAGEMENT

Chapter I

SUMMARY

1. SOURCES

This part is about the use of traffic management to pursue environmental and economic goals in urban areas. It draws on Part II, which is about the impact of road transport on the environment. It is complemented by the results of Part IV which is about the reduction of vehicle emissions at source.

The main sources of this report are ten city case-studies carried out in 1984 and 1985: Athens (Greece), Gothenburg (Sweden), Hong Kong, London (UK), Los Angeles (USA), New York (USA), Munich (Germany), Osaka (Japan), Paris (France), Singapore; and a variety of documents supplied by delegates to the Ad Hoc Group on Transport and the Environment.

Case-studies prepared for the seminar 'Urban Transport and the Environment' (1979) have also been taken into account.

2. PROBLEMS

Not all the cities studied are at a similar stage of development. Some are distinguished by fast and concentrated development. Others exhibit growth of a slower and more dispersed kind. Notwithstanding this important distinction, certain environmental, economic and transport problems were found in all of them. The following are amongst the most significant:

Changes to the Structure of Urban Areas

- Continuing and in some cases rapid population growth;
- Changes in urban form in the direction of lower inner city densities coupled with a decentralisation of employment and a shift from manufacturing to services.

Changes in Travel Patterns

- Continuing growth in car-ownership and in the distances travelled by car fleets;
- Growth in travel by car;
- Inability of rail transit to accommodate the growing demand for travel emerging in the less densely developed suburbs.

Economic Stringency and Uncertainties About Energy Costs

- A shortage of public funds to modernise rail transit;
- A shortage of public funds for the construction of major roads and, even where resources are available, opposition to such roads from affected residents;
- Uncertainties about future energy costs.

Noise and Air Pollution

- Persistent public dislike of traffic noise;
- Continuing high levels of air pollution; increases in the contribution of motor vehicles to total emissions; public concern about the health effects of vehicle pollutants.

Traffic Congestion

- Worsening traffic congestion leading to falling speeds and increased emissions in growing cities.

Fragmentation in Policy-making

- An absence of close-coupling between policies for land-use development, transport and environmental management due to divisions of responsibility between different levels of government.

3. SOLUTIONS

A Combined Approach

In searching for solution to these and other problems governments in all OECD countries are being obliged to pay increasing attention to managing existing highway and transit systems, developing new technologies and managing existing vehicle fleets. The days of massive investment in new roads and railways are, for the time being and in most countries, past.

The evidence of this report is that the better management of both highways and vehicle fleets can, nevertheless, produce more travel at reduced financial and environmental cost. It also makes clear that in reducing emissions of noise and air pollution, by far the most effective and long lasting policies are those which limit environmental nuisances at source but that drastic reductions can only be obtained through the implementation of complementary policies, including better management of existing vehicles.

This report, in addition to providing a list of solutions, underlines the importance of developing new policy instruments. In particular, it shows that, amongst existing and new instruments, a range of economic tools exists that can be used to influence vehicle technologies, purchasing decisions and the use and management of transport systems.

Economic Policy Instruments for Traffic and Transport Management

These economic tools, many of which are designed to influence markets, are of various kinds. They include:

- Differential taxation for leaded and lead-free fuel designed to promote the use of the latter and to limit the risk of mis-fuelling vehicles equipped with exhaust catalysts;
- Purchase tax reductions for low polluting cars designed to offset the cost of emission control devices and promote the sale of cars fitted with them;
- Government purchasing of low or non-polluting vehicles to expand the market for them, reduce unit manufacturing costs and assist further sales;
- Road user charges designed to promote the staggering of travel times and increase the occupancy of private cars thereby raising the efficiency of highway systems while stabilizing vehicle emissions;
- Taxing employers to help pay the transit costs of their employees in order to offset such inducements to commute by car as free parking, company vehicles and fuel allowances;
- Transit "travelcards" covering periods from a day to a year giving easy and "free" access to networks of buses, metros and trains;
- Special, short-term, reduced-rate, "environment tariffs" sold exclusively to car-drivers to persuade them to experiment with transit travel;
- The trading of "air rights" and land-use zoning advantages above or near railway and metro stations in return for the building or rebuilding of interchanges;
- The leasing of rapid transit cars to reduce the need for capital borrowing and to obtain the tax advantages on capital investment open to private companies;
- The financing of transit modernisation by the sale of bonds secured by future fare revenues, a linkage that obliges transit operators to pursue efficiency and good service.

It may be argued that none of these policies or measures is an innovation in the strictest sense of the word. They would, however, be new to the many cities that have not tried them. More important the actions described, if refined and combined in new ways, promise to increase the efficiency of urban transport and be effective in reducing air pollution and noise from vehicles. In the face of persistent transport-induced environmental problems, this prospect is noteworthy.

Chapter II

ENVIRONMENTAL, ECONOMIC AND TRANSPORT PROBLEMS

1. THE CASE STUDY CITIES: BASIC FACTS

The ten urban areas vary in their population, density, area, urban form, economic activities, travel characteristics, topography, transport infrastructure and car-ownership levels. Selected statistics from the cities are therefore presented to assist readers in drawing comparisons with urban areas in their own countries and in assessing the transferability of the results (Table 1).

2. GENERAL ISSUES

A number of general trends were identified in the cities studied. These included increases or shifts in population and increases in vehicle ownership and use not matched by increases in road or transit capacity. For example:

a) By the year 2000 Los Angeles will experience substantial increases in car-ownership and use while its population is forecast to grow from 11.5 to 14.15 million people. No comparable growth is projected in the capacity of the bus service. In the case of the highway system, where innovative traffic management has already been used to squeeze out additional capacity, no major new roads are in prospect. In the light of current levels of highway congestion, officials and the public recognise that continued reliance on travelling by car at low occupancy rates can only lead to continued environmental problems;

b) Athens experienced a 205 per cent increase in car-ownership in the period 1968 to 1978, the highest in Europe. The Athens region also contains 58 per cent of all cars in Greece but less than 3 per cent of the land. Yet the city's dense structure ill-suits it to accommodate the growing volumes of road traffic resulting from urban expansion and the growth of car-ownership;

c) Singapore, which saw the number of cars in use grow by 8.5 per cent per year in the period 1962 to 1973 suffers, like Athens, from incompatibilities between its dense structure and high levels of car-ownership. Hong Kong likewise, with a metropolitan area population of 5.3 million living at an average density of 28 000 people per square kilometer, is ill-suited to high levels of car-ownership and use;

d) In London and Munich population shifts rather than population growth have caused a dispersion of activities and a change in the pattern of commuter journeys that does not fit existing radical rail transit routes and is ill-suited to public transport in general;

e) Osaka's employment base of 2 470 000 nearly equals its population of 2 650 000 and results in a large daily influx of commuters from neighbouring areas. The city's daytime population is accordingly 1.38 times its evening one (an addition of over one million people) while its four central wards attract 69 per cent of the inflow (860 000 workers) giving them a daytime population 6.1 times greater than their evening one. This daily influx, concentrated in specific areas at similar times, creates transport and environmental problems.

Some of the above trends, sometimes happening at the same time, may be observed in the other cities which have been studied.

Table 1. SELECTED STATISTICS, early 80s

City	Population (millions)	Population density (persons/km^2)	Employment (millions)[b]	Auto population/ownership[b]
Athens	3.0 [a] 0.4 [d]	7 026[a] 17 391[d]	1.1	734 000 cars[a] 1 car/4.1 persons
Gothenburg	0.7 [a] 0.43 [c]	953[c] 1 667[d]	0.240[c] 0.025[d]	1 car/3.1 persons[c]
Hong Kong	5.3	28 000[a, e]	NA	211 000 cars 1 car/24 persons
London	6.7 [a] 2.0 [c] 0.5 [d]	4 938[a]	3.65 [a] 0.85 [c] 1.25 [d]	NA
Los Angeles	11.5 [a]	793[a] 1 815[d]	NA	NA
Munich	2.3 [a] 1.3 [c]	460[a] 4 194[c]	0.771[c]	1 050 000 cars[a] 1 car/2.2 persons[a] 472 000 cars[c] 1 car/2.8 persons
New York	13.2 [a] 7.0 [c]	6 775[a] 25 000[d]	3.7	1 514 391[c] 1 car/4.7 persons[c] 161 494 cars[d] 1 car/9 persons[d]
Osaka	14.513[a] 2.626[c]	3 458[a] 12 383[c]	6.862[a] 2.473[c]	750 772 cars[c] 1 car/3.5 persons
Paris	10.0 [a]	840[a]	4.58	3 610 000 cars 1 car/2.8 persons
Singapore	2.5 [a] 2.25 [c] 0.15 [d]	4 251[a] (12 800max)	0.270	184 150 cars[a] 1 car/14 persons[a]

a) Greater urban area.
b) NA = Not available.
c) City.
d) Central Business District (CBD).
e) Data refer to the metropolitan zone near the harbour: average density is 5 000 persons/km^2.

3. TRANSPORT AND THE ENVIRONMENT

Roads, vehicles and transit services are major conditioners of cities. They occupy land, contribute to the structure of urban development, and are a source of air pollutants, noise, vibration and accidents. With the growth of road transport, the spreading out of cities and in certain cases the diminution of emissions from stationary sources, road traffic's share of total emissions has tended to increase.

In cities where maintenance and renewal of transit systems and highways have been deferred, citizens find themselves travelling in dingy and even dangerous trains or riding along streets damaged by potholes.

Noise

The case studies identified noise as the most serious and frequent environmental complaint. Several examples may be quoted. In *Munich*, for instance, the public's sensitivity to and resentment of noise disturbance has increased over the past decade. Heavy lorries, cars and motorcycles are the predominant source of disturbance. Along the city's main roads representing 23 per cent of the network, high noise levels disturb thousands of people.

A 1975/76 noise survey of 2 000 *Athenians* reported that 44 per cent identified noise as the chief environmental nuisance while 31 per cent mentioned air pollution. Few abatement actions have however been undertaken and the enforcement of existing regulations is still at an early stage.

Traffic noise, particularly from heavy lorries, is perceived by *Londoners* as the city's greatest environmental nuisance and densely populated areas are most affected by it.

In the *Paris* region over a quarter of the population is exposed to noise with a Leq of 65 dB(A), an unacceptable level, between 8 a.m. and 8 p.m. In the city of Paris conditions are even worse and nearly half the 2.3 million inhabitants are subjected to such levels until late into the evening. In a high proportion of streets noise levels attain 80 dB(A) for at least five hours per day. Certain routes, such as the Peripherique (the inner ring motorway), bear intense vehicle flows both day and night, with lorry traffic accounting for 50 per cent of the night time total and causing widespread sleep disturbance. Approximately 400 000 inhabitants live adjacent to the Peripherique and other urban expressways, half of them where the daily Leq between 8 a.m. and 8 p.m. is at or above 70 dB(A) and sometimes as high as 80 dB(A).

Over the past decade public dissatisfaction with noise in the Paris region has grown from isolated complaints to general manifestations of discontent. Complaints about noise outweigh all others and amounted to 70 per cent of total complaints about environmental nuisances in 1971 and over 90 per cent in 1981.

In *Osaka* traffic noise along trunk roads is generally high and has remained fairly constant since 1971. It ranges from 60 to 75 dB(A) with an average of 69 dB(A).

Air Pollution

Air pollution problems are nowhere more extensive than in *Los Angeles* where car travel amounts on average to 221 million vehicle miles and 39 million person trips per day. Throughout the region emissions from cars account for one half of reactive hydrocarbons, two thirds of nitrogen dioxide and 80 per cent of carbon monoxide. The highly mobile residents of Los Angeles use 5.6 billion US gallons of fuel annually, one of the highest per capita rates in the United States. The combustion of all this fuel contributes significantly to smog alerts and forecasts indicate that even by the year 2000 Federal clean air standards will continue to be violated and suggest that the Federal ozone standard may never be met.

Atmosphere pollution is *London*'s most pervasive environmental nuisance. Motor vehicles, which account annually for 1.05 out of a total of 1.3 million tons of pollutants, are the dominant source of carbon monoxide, nitrogen oxide, hydrocarbons, smoke and lead. London's busiest roads frequently exceed the EEC limit for atmospheric lead (2 ug/m^3). Ozone concentrations exceeding government guidelines were recorded repeatedly in July 1983.

In *Athens* the high average age of the car fleet, poor vehicle maintenance, traffic congestion and low quality fuel all help to contribute to extremes of air pollution. In 1982 the Greek government concluded that these conditions had assumed the dimensions of an 'environmental crisis', but that the crisis was surmountable and would be faced 'without any compromise'. However car-ownership in Greece is forecast to double by the year 2000 and emissions from vehicles in Athens are likely to grow by 60 per cent over the next decade.

In *Osaka* although emissions of all major pollutants, including nitrogen oxide, have shown a downward trend over the past ten years, the Japanese nitrogen oxide standard was exceeded at nearly half the general environmental monitoring stations and at all eleven motor vehicle exhaust gas monitoring stations (1982). While 60 per cent of all emissions are accounted for by vehicles, the spatial distribution and diffusion of mobile sources gives them a greater impact than this figure implies. Furthermore the rate of fall in nitrogen oxide levels has begun to slow down because the rate of scrapping of older, higher emitting vehicles is declining.

4. THE ECONOMIC CONTEXT

Transport and environmental problems regularly have economic effects and vice versa. Thus in the US a reduction in Federal and State purchasing power has been caused by a fall in gas tax revenues due to energy efficient cars and reduced travel; political decisions to reduce public spending and inflation-driven escalation of the cost of building, operating and maintaining transit systems.

In *New York*, for instance, the Federal government share of operating subsidies for transit in *New York* City had by 1982 shrunk to 6 per cent with 28 per cent coming from State and city sources. The Federal share of capital financing shrank likewise and between 1982 and 1984 fell from 58 to 25 per cent.

In *Los Angeles* highway and transit improvements will cost $61 billion up to the year 2000. Despite private sector contributions, a $14 billion shortfall is projected. Environmental constraints will also severely limit the building of new roads.

In *Athens* although revenue from fares increased by 43 per cent in the three years up to 1980, operating costs rose 55 per cent leaving a deficit of US $150 billion with fares covering only about 32 per cent of operating costs.

In *London* a complex set of interactions involving industrial changes, population decline and traffic congestion have been associated, particularly in the inner Boroughs where road access is poor, with the outward migration or closure of factories and the development of a service economy.

In *Paris* the economic recession has diminished the resources available for financing public transport. Politically set limits on increases to fares, a decline in income from employers' contributions to employee travel, and the growing weight of debt incurred in modernising and extending the Metro and Metro Express all affect the availability of resources. High annual increases in operating costs coupled with diminishing revenues and uncertainty about the financing of shortfalls add to difficulties.

In *Hong Kong*, where car-ownership levels are low and where public transport is run on commercial principles, high levels of efficiency are achieved. The number of employees per bus is three compared with 4 in Brazil and 19 in India.

5. TRANSPORT

Increased travel demand, rising car usage, traffic congestion, accidents, pollution and public transport delays were all noted in the case study cities. Most of them also reported that few new roads or public transport links would be built in the foreseeable future due to environmental objections and financial constraints.

Traffic Delay

In *Los Angeles* the severity of future traffic congestion will depend on success or otherwise in reducing single-occupant car travel and on the introduction of demand management techniques such as staggered work hours and goods delivery, the rerouting of traffic away from bottlenecks and special bus services. Unless the growth of single-occupant car commuter trips is limited it is unlikely that current freeway service levels can be maintained. Driver response to the control measures which have already been tried has been good, but the response to stricter measures is unknown.

In *Gothenburg* worsening traffic congestion throughout the 1970s caused increases in vehicular and pedestrian casualties and interfered with tram and bus services. Transit travel was unpunctual and involved trip times double those of cars.

In *Athens* traffic speeds in the city centre average 7 to 8 km/hr during peak periods. This compares with 18 km/hr in *Paris* and 20 km/hr in *London* though not necessarily measured over comparable networks. In Greater London traffic increased by 70 per cent over the past 20 years but with only a 10 per cent increase in road area.

In *Munich* volumes of car and truck traffic have increased rapidly in recent decades while road space has increased only marginally. During peak periods traffic jams occur regularly on *Munich*'s partially completed ring roads, the main radials and river bridges. In the inner city a lack of off-street parking is thought to cause congestion because it extends the time visitors take to find parking spaces.

In *New York* City congestion is common but road traffic to and from Manhattan, which accounts for 16 per cent of all people entering the CBD, reached a new peak in 1982. In that year crossings increased by 8 per cent despite a 25 per cent increase in tolls.

In *Paris* traffic congestion is spreading, the average speed of vehicles on city streets is 18 km/hr and major bottlenecks are emerging on the urban motorway system. Bus priority measures have been introduced in both Paris and its suburbs but in a slow and piecemeal fashion. The occupancy of cars (1.25 passengers for every 4.5 seats) is low and their journeys are concentrated on motorways which, while representing less than one hundredth of the highway network, carry one third of all vehicle trips. Within Paris illegal parking has reached crisis proportions with 60 000 violations occurring every day by noon.

In *Osaka* while transportation policy aims to decrease dependence on cars, growth in the use of them, particularly in peripheral areas, is outstripping travel by railway. A five to six fold increase in the frequency and duration of traffic jams took place in the decade up to 1980. Environmental damage from severe congestion is particularly serious on the narrow roads in the city centre.

Public Transport

In *New York* City years of deferred maintenance and lack of investment have brought the subway and the commuter railways to the verge of collapse. The system has lost over 800 000 daily passengers since 1950.

In *Athens* growth of car-ownership and an absence of traffic management measures contributed to a fall in per capita transit travel of one half over the 20 years up to 1978. A 10 per cent annual increase in per capita car-ownership coincided with an annual decline in transit riders of 8.7 per cent. Transit travel peaked in 1965 at one billion passengers and then fell to the current level of 450 million, notwithstanding rapid population growth. Despite service improvements and very low fares, bus passengers still declined by 7 per cent in the years 1978 to 1980.

In *Los Angeles*, which has the second largest bus fleet in the United States, less than 3 per cent of all vehicular trips are made by bus and services outside the denser inner parts of the city are poor. Even if financial constraints did not limit expansion of the fleet and prevent service improvements, the buses would continue to carry a small percentage of all trips. The spread of activities in Los Angeles that has been caused by the availability of cars creates a pattern of travel demand ill-suited to bus transit. Two rapid transit lines, scheduled to be in operation by the year 2 000 will accommodate only 400 000 to 500 000 trips per day, or about one per cent of the forecast regional total.

In *Paris* public transport runs on average at 18 per cent of its capacity despite being filled or overfilled during peak periods. Substantial latent capacity accordingly exists for off-peak travel and the staggering of work hours.

In *Osaka*, while trains are very overcrowded during rush hours, the city has, over the past ten years, reduced the bus fleet by 40 per cent, cut operating mileage by 50 per cent and witnessed a decline in passengers of 60 per cent. As deficits mounted and riders were lost the management, caught in a vicious cycle, raised fares and lost even more riders.

In *Hong Kong* all forms of public transport saw increased patronage in the decade up to 1984 with the exception of ferries, trains and minibuses. Total daily travel by all modes increased from 5 to 8.4 m trips.

6. INSTITUTIONS

Government in large cities is inevitably complex and it follows that the institutional arrangements for environmental and transport policy-making are complex too. In many cases, however, this complexity appears to hinder the concerted action needed to deal with transport and environmental issues.

In *Los Angeles* responsibility is spread among agencies at several levels and no central authority exists to try and resolve conflicts between mobility and environment. While cooperation and coordination take place, an increasingly complicated institutional structure causes decision-making to be uncertain in its outcome and drawn out in its processes.

In *Osaka* the railways are run by national and municipal government and by private companies, while the buses are run by the city and by private companies. This complex and sometimes uncoordinated arrangement makes transfer between line haul and local area services difficult and also complicates the fare structure.

In *Paris* transport decision making involves national, regional and local government authorities often with overlapping responsibilities and often providing uncoordinated services. Despite nearly a decade of decentralisation, the national government continues to play an important role in metropolitan transport. The Paris Region authority is, in theory, responsible for transport and traffic but it lacks commensurate resources. It is involved solely in co-financing with central government, an arrangement that makes procedures complex and causes delay between decisions and implementation. The Region neither takes part in traffic or transport management, a key to short term improvements, nor is it responsible for the operating cost implications of its decisions.

In *Hong Kong*, which is a city state, decision-making has traditionally been centralized. However with the prospect of the UK lease on the territory running out in 1997, constitutional changes have been made. District Boards have been set up to give the citizens an increased voice in government and one of their first actions was to oppose a new traffic management scheme involving road pricing.

Chapter III

MAIN MEASURES AND RESULTS

1. CONTROL OF EMISSIONS

The case-studies make clear that the control of air pollutants and noise depends on complementary national and local actions. In all except the largest countries, such as the United States, national Governments take responsibility for setting emission standards for new vehicles and introducing regimes of inspection and maintenance. Traffic management, which requires detailed local knowledge, is typically a complementary local action.

Nevertheless several cities had taken initiatives that not only produced local environmental benefits but sometimes contributed to action at the national level. Thus in *Munich* the municipal fleet of 4 000 vehicles was converted to run on lead-free petrol or liquified petroleum gas in advance of a Federal Government decision on removing lead from fuel. Furthermore all lorries and buses bought by Munich were required to be low polluting models.

Other local initiatives include the promotion of electric goods vehicles in *London* and, in the State of California, the introduction of new car emission standards, new vehicle testing and certification procedures, anti-tampering tests, in-use vehicle surveillance, and gasoline vapour recovery.

Air Pollution

Far-reaching measures for controlling vehicle emissions are in use in the State of California where emission standards for new cars coupled with periodic inspection and maintenance have been identified as the most effective controls. The effectiveness of this approach is unquestioned. Studies in *Los Angeles* show that 90 to 95 per cent of the reduction in vehicle emissions so far achieved results from the replacement of old, high-emitting cars by newer, cleaner and better maintained ones.

The presence of vapour recovery systems at fuelling stations is indicative of the scope of emission control in California. It reduces emissions by an amount equivalent to 15 per cent of state-wide hydrocarbon emissions in 1980.

Biannual inspection and maintenance of in-use vehicles implemented in Los Angeles in 1984 after prolonged controversy, covers cars and light trucks. Inspection costs $10, with repair bills of failed vehicles limited to $50.

In *New York* City inspection and maintenance is forecast to cut hydrocarbon emissions by 38 per cent and carbon monoxide by 34 per cent by 1987. When these gains are added to those from vehicle turnover, the reduction in emissions of those two pollutants should be 66 and 45 per cent respectively. Between 1980 and 1987 the contribution of vehicles to total hydrocarbon emissions is expected to fall from 47 to 26 per cent.

However notwithstanding the efforts made to control emissions in Los Angeles during the past decade ozone levels remain high; the ozone standard will not be met by the 1987 Federal deadline, by the year 2000, or perhaps ever while emissions of nitrogen oxides are an emerging problem. The growth of smaller stationary sources, new *co-generation* facilities and delays in implementing controls account for these pessimistic forecasts. Some trends in travel are unfavourable too. Although transit travel is increasing, car-pooling is declining due to the falling price of fuel.

Noise

Opinion surveys of environmental problems often indicate that people consider noise to be a more serious nuisance than air pollution yet the amount of noise abatement action reported in the case-studies is substantially less than action against air pollutants. Amongst measures implemented are the following:

- Trials of electric trucks with one to two ton pay loads were carried out over a three year period in *London*. The objective was to build up experience of battery-powered vehicles amongst transport managers and also feed it back to manufacturers. Both national and metropolitan government were involved;
- In *New York* City action against noise was concentrated in the subways. A rail transit noise code was enacted by New York State in 1982. This was followed by a programme covering revised noise specifications for new subway cars. The improvements included air conditioning coupled with new doors and windows designed to reduce noise by 8 dB; thickened car floors; machining to reduce wheel noise by 10 to 14 decibels; and track grinding;
- In *Munich* action was taken to reduce noise at source and to deflect it. Measures adopted include controls over the design and location of new buildings; the doubling of windows on façades exposed to noise; changing layouts of apartments; and sinking new sections of the middle ring road into tunnels;
- Noise conditions in the *Paris* region are widely acknowledged to be severe. Authorities at all government levels are therefore working jointly on two programmes. The first involves improvements to new roads. This programme, which adds on average 10 per cent to construction costs per kilometer, involves earth mounds and screens or covering highways in part or whole. In the case of the new A86 motorway around Paris, noise abatement measures are adding 40 per cent to costs.
  However with the slowdown in the construction of new roads in France, abatement action is being concentrated on another programme for remedying nuisances from existing roads. The aim is to reduce daily external noise levels to between 65 and 70 dB(A) for the 90 000 people living along motorways in the Paris region. Because of the high cost of covering roads, noise barriers and the insulation of building façades are the most widely used techniques. The full cost of the remedial programme is Frs. 1 170 million (US$167 million) of which Frs. 300 million (US$43 million) is being devoted over the period 1980 to 1988 to the Paris "peripherique".
- *Osaka*'s abatement efforts take three forms. Reliance on national vehicle regulations aims to reduce noise at source. These regulations, introduced in 1971 and subsequently tightened, are now in a second phase although large trucks and compact cars are still excluded from them. A second measure is a 1980 zoning law which requires 'appropriate and efficient use of land' adjacent to trunk roads. A third initiative involves the abatement of expressway noise by means of plastic panels, the planting of barriers of trees and shrubs, and subsidies for insulation and air conditioning at road-side houses afflicted by noise.

2. ECONOMIC MEASURES

Economic instruments appear in many forms in the case studies. Examples may be found of instruments aimed at influencing the purchase, use and technology of vehicles, at harnessing property development to the improvement of transit, at compensating individuals for environmental nuisances, at improving the image of transit by tariff policy, and at widening the scope for private investment in transit modernisation. Three studies in particular focus on charging for the use of roads, attracting private investment to transit modernisation and partnerships between public and private agencies.

Influencing the Purchase and Use of Cars: Singapore

Two pre-1974 transport studies of *Singapore* both concluded that limits on car-ownership and use would be necessary before 1992. The studies pointed to a need for changes in government policies and public attitudes and a reorientation of both from cars towards public transport.

The Government was quick to act and 1975 saw the deployment of a three pronged economic policy designed to limit the use of cars for commuting to the city centre. This involved road user charges, parking management and vehicle taxes.

Supplementary Licenses

Motorists wishing to drive into the central area in the morning rush hours were obliged to obtain and display a special supplementary license. Both cars and taxis were required to buy the licenses while carpools of four or more riders are granted free passage. The system is still in existence.

The licenses were initially set at S$3 per day or S$60 per month for private cars and created a four to one ratio between the cost of commuting by car and going by park-and-ride bus service. These fees were subsequently increased to S$5 and S$100 respectively. Company owned cars pay double. (One Singapore dollar equals approximately US$2.2).

This economic regime was originally imposed between 7.30 am and 9.30 am from Monday to Saturday. It worked well on this basis but congestion began to occur after 9.30 am. The Government therefore extended the restricted period to 10.15 am to remove the new peak. Extensions of the scheme to cover the full working day were considered but rejected due to concerns about possible damage to business. A notable aspect of the scheme was that the morning restrictions failed to bring about, as had been expected, a reduction in the evening peak.

Parking Controls

Fees at off-street car-parks were raised by S$50 to S$80 per space per month depending on location at the same time as the supplementary licenses were introduced. Hourly on-street parking fees were raised too in order to discourage longer term stays and surcharges were imposed on privately-owned off-street car parks so as to induce increases in their charges and prevent profiteering on the difference between the cost of private and public parking places.

Vehicle Taxation

Singapore has four main types of vehicle taxes: import duties; registration fees; additional registration fees aimed at encouraging the scrapping of old cars in favour of new ones with more economical engines; and annual road taxes based on engine capacity. For a new 2 000 cc car not replacing an old one and with an open market price of S$10 000, the duties and taxes amount to S$21 700 bringing the total cost of registering and licensing a car for private use to S$31 700.

Results

The effects of Singapore's nine-year old package of economic traffic management measures are difficult to isolate. Not only do factors such as oil price changes, the economic recession and Singapore's rapid urban development cloud any analysis, but the impacts of closely related individual measures are hard to single out.

All that can be identified is the overall effect of supplementary licensing and the other measures accompanying it. The main effects were: reduced car use; reduced car ownership growth; reduced congestion in the city centre during the morning peak; a shift in morning peak travel from car to carpool and bus; a fall in traffic accidents; and a hypothetical saving of S$1.5 billion which it would otherwise have been necessary to spend on roads to maintain levels of service.

Without the economic measures, cars would have accounted for 50 to 60 per cent of city-centre peak period trips rather than the current 23 per cent. Morning peak traffic volumes would have been 114 000 rather than 57 000 vehicles. The result would have been worse congestion than the high levels currently experienced in the evening peak.

The business community in Singapore perceives the scheme as beneficial and necessary to keep congestion in check. Reduced traffic and improved flows enhance business activity. Travel conditions for central area employees have suffered few detrimental effects.

Singapore's relatively low level of car-ownership helped to make the traffic management scheme politically feasible. Coming as it did at the beginning of a period of expansion in office employment in the central business district, the scheme was also extremely timely. Had car-ownership rates been greater, the provision of alternative transport would have been more difficult. Obtaining public and business support for the scheme would have been correspondingly more difficult.

Assuming such problems can be solved supplementary licensing provides a low-cost means to increase the efficiency of urban roads and defer capital investment. Congestion pricing thus provides a valuable instrument for cities with serious traffic congestion, increasing travel demand and lack of resources.

Amongst the many effects of the Singapore economic package the following are notable:

- *Changes in Traffic Volumes*: In 1975 a total of 74 000 vehicles entered the restricted zone in the morning peak. Immediately after licensing was introduced, the total fell to 43 000. By 1983 the number had risen to 57 000 although up to 114 000 vehicles might have been expected given the prevailing levels of income and car-ownership;
- *Modal Shift:* Prior to the scheme buses accounted for 33 per cent and cars (including carpools) for 56 per cent of all city-centre bound work trips. After licensing was introduced bus trips increased to 46 per cent while those by car fell to 46 per cent. By 1983 the share carried by the buses had grown to 69 per cent while the car share had dropped to 23 per cent;
- *Traffic Speeds:* Inbound traffic on arterials moves smoothly at 40 to 50 km/hr during

the morning peak. On other routes within the restricted zone speeds of 30 km/hr are recorded while during the unregulated evening peak they fall to 18 km/hr;

- *Costs:* The capital cost of the licensing scheme amounted to S$66 million of which 92 per cent was for park and ride car parks which, when they failed to attract travellers, were sold or devoted to other purposes;
- *Car-Ownership:* The vehicle taxation that accompanied road pricing limited car-ownership to 71 cars per 1 000 persons. It is estimated that without the effect of the Government's economic measures, ownership levels would have risen to 107 cars per 1 000 persons;
- *Road Safety:* All types of traffic accidents within the Central Area have declined since 1975. The total fall was nearly 25 per cent;
- *Park and Ride:* Park and Ride was unpopular from the outset. Car commuters switched to regular buses rather than to the special shuttle services based on the park and ride car parks. The shuttles were therefore re-routed to serve residential areas;
- *Air Quality:* Six air quality monitoring stations in Singapore's central area all indicate increases in CO due to gradual increases in total daily traffic since 1976. CO levels are, however, low compared with other Asian cities. Furthermore falls in total acidity, smoke and NO_x have been recorded although they cannot be attributed solely to supplementary licensing. Much of the improvement results from better monitoring and control of industrial pollutants, better vehicle inspection and repair requirements and the replacement of old by new cars;
- *Effects on Business and Land Use:* The Singapore case study notes that the effects of area licensing are difficult to single out from changes caused by the recession and other economic shifts. The results of an analysis of rent changes and interviews with businessmen, which revealed no identifiable effects of area licensing on rents, retail sales and hotel occupancy rates, should therefore be treated with caution. However labour availability appears to have been improved as a result of upgraded bus services and the expansion of carpooling while the availability of taxis seems to have declined.

Electronic Road Pricing: Hong Kong

Transport in *Hong Kong* is run on commercial principles. The use of charges for road use in order to maintain traffic flows and reduce noxious emissions is therefore consistent with the economic philosophy of the H.K. Government.

Road congestion arises in Hong Kong because of the very high density of development and the intensity of economic activity. Most road junctions in the Metropolitan area are therefore running at or near capacity. The Government commissioned a study of road pricing, and then of electronic road pricing, because of its promise to reduce traffic flows over a wide area.

The benefits of reducing flow by about ten per cent are considerable. If, at a junction where the flow is 900 vehicles an hour and the delay 1.2 minutes per vehicle, the flow can be reduced to 800 vehicles, the delay per vehicle falls to 36 seconds. The effect on emissions is comparable.

An experiment with electronic road pricing has demonstrated that the technology, including enforcement with the aid of remote controlled cameras, is practical.

There are also grounds for believing that if the charges are to be effective it is necessary to make them apparent to drivers. The Hong Kong technology accordingly encompasses road-side displays that would indicate the charge in force.

In three charging plans examined by consultants the reductions in congestion would be 14, 16 and 17 per cent giving daily time savings of 98 000, 113 000 and 124 000 hours.

In June 1985 when the Hong Kong Government considered whether to expand the pilot scheme into a city-wide one, the effects of the economic recession on activity and car-ownership, plus opposition by the District Boards, led to the introduction of road pricing being deferred. However economic analysis led to a clear definition of the benefits it would bring and its superiority over limits on car-ownership.

Following the decision of June 1985 consideration was turned to finding ways of introducing road pricing bit by bit.

Financial Innovations in New York City

In 1981 the *New York* State legislature provided the New York City Transit Authority with $7.2 billion over the five year period from 1982 to 1986. The resulting $1.4 billion per year was seven times greater than the Authority's income up to 1979 and substantially greater than the $600 million a year provided between 1979 and 1981. Out of the $7.2 billion nearly $5 billion was allocated to go into the subways, $1.4 billion into commuter railways and the remainder to the buses. The operating subsidy part of the finance was provided by tax revenues. Capital funds came from bond sales.

Lease Financing

One financing technique used by New York City transit is 'safe harbour' leasing. This practice, a provision of the Federal Recovery Act 1981, allows the transit authority, which has no Federal tax liabilities, to sell and lease back buses or subway cars to corporations which are entitled to offset depreciation against their Federal tax liability.

Transit Bonds

Another technique involves the sale of transit authority bonds covered by 'earnings' from fares, road tolls and subsidies. Investors are given an incentive to buy these transit bonds because interest from them is exempted from income tax. This securing of transit bonds on revenue from future fares without any government guarantee is an innovation in the United States.

Joint Property Development

Funds are obtained for improving transit stations at locations where the public authorities are involved in promoting comprehensive redevelopment, by requiring developers, who benefit from transit improvements, to contribute to the cost of the stations.

Financial Innovations in Los Angeles

Transit Benefit Assessment District

In *Los Angeles* 'benefit assessment districts' have been created around the stations of the first subway line to be built in the city. Within such districts, land-owners whose properties appreciate due to proximity to future stations, become liable to special taxes. Benefit districts in Los Angeles will produce at least $170 million by the year 2 000.

Private Finance for Highways

Private sources have contributed $941 million to highway improvements ($97 million in 1981 alone) since 1972. In Los Angeles private investment in the State highway system has been approximately $50 million a year over the past five years. Private funds have paid for new streets, widened existing ones, and financed freeway access ramps and interchanges. One $30 million freeway addition has been built entirely by private sector funds. The State of California set up an Office of Transportation Economic Development in 1981 with the express purpose of soliciting this kind of private financial support for highway works.

Tax Concessions to Promote Car-Pooling

In a State such as California where the role of transit is negligible, the major opportunities for increasing transport capacity lie in building new highways or improving the management of existing ones. The State legislature has accordingly devised several tax laws designed to take advantage of the second option. These laws: allow employees to deduct the cost of transit or car-pool costs before paying their State income taxes; exclude income received for giving rides from taxable income; and grant tax credits to corporations which spend money on programmes for reducing single-occupant car commuting. Developers of down-town sites in Los Angeles who are obliged to provide parking spaces (the cost of which currently averages $25,000 per space) can avoid up to 75 per cent of this investment by providing car parks elsewhere and linking the two by shuttle buses.

Taxes on Employers to Pay for Transit

In France a transport levy on employers was introduced in 1971 in the *Paris* region. The object was to pass some of the heavy cost of providing peak hour Metro and bus services from employees to employers. Revenues from the levy are dedicated to public transport and paid to the Syndicat des Transports Parisiens, the body responsible for organising public transport in the region. The levy is paid by employers with 10 or more employees and affects some 55 000 firms with 3.7 million employees. It is 2 per cent of wages in Paris and its three neighbouring Departments and 1.2 per cent elsewhere in the metropolitan region. It covers the cost of depreciation and revenue lost through the granting of concessionary fares.

- In 1982 the levy raised more than FF 4 000 million (US$571 million), about 20 per cent of the overall cost of transit in the Paris region. The levy is easy to administer and has made employers pay part of the cost of commuter travel just as they already pay part of the cost of health insurance and pensions.
- The levy is supported by both unions and employers because it was brought in gradually, is set at an acceptable level and involves exemptions for small firms and new towns.
- The levy spreads transit costs over users, taxpayers, and employers although the reduction in the contribution of national taxpayers is less than appears because the levy reduces company profits and tax revenues.
- In recent years the product of the levy has diminished because the economic recession has reduced the value of the wages on which it is calculated. Furthermore an increasingly high percentage of its proceeds is required to cover the subsidy of fares and is not therefore available to pay for improvements to equipment or services.

- The scope for increasing revenues by raising the level of contribution or broadening its assessment is limited by the climate of economic stringency.

This levy on employers has now been extended to all French cities with more than 50 000 inhabitants but it has been set up at a lower level than in Paris, generally around 1 per cent of the salaries.

3. PUBLIC TRANSPORT

Improvements to public transport in the case-study cities varied but were nowhere seen by themselves as solutions to the environmental effects of road traffic. They were seen instead as part of wide-ranging urban transport policies designed to sustain economic activity and limit the environmental ill-effects of increased car travel.

Rail Service Improvements

In *New York* City, *Munich* and *Hong Kong* improvements of a highly capital-intensive kind were made to existing rail systems. In Munich the city authorities built a new underground and transformed two separate sets of suburban lines into a single system. New York concentrated on renewing its old subways. In *Osaka* the already extensive network of railways was seen as a tool for limiting the growth of car traffic and in *Hong Kong* three new metro lines have been built.

- In 1981 New York State declared a 'transportation emergency', passed the Transportation Systems Assistance and Finance Act, and acknowledged that restoring public transport to a state of 'good repair' would cost $14.5 billion over ten years. Former policies for deferred maintenance and the construction of new lines were abandoned.
  In a new approach priority was given to safe and reliable operation to be achieved by the rehabilitation of existing equipment and the upgrading of inspection and maintenance procedures. Great importance was attached to performance targets and monitoring.
- Munich's 1965 General Transport Plan aimed to reverse the decline of travel by transit to the city centre and raise it from its 1965 level of 50 per cent of all vehicular trips to 65 per cent in 1990. The authorities decided to concentrate on improving reliability and on cutting the time taken by transit commuters by up to 50 per cent.
  The city's 413 km long S-Bahn, or suburban railway, now carries 600 000 passengers a day on weekdays. The new underground began operation in 1971 and also carries 600 000 passengers on weekdays. It is a 41 km network designed to serve travellers within 4 to 5 kilometers of the city centre. It also collects and distributes travellers on the S-Bahn who come in from places as far as 45 km from the centre.
  The main objective of the 1965 plan was to create an efficient, co-ordinated regional transit system. This aim was pursued by creating a small, central public transport policy-making body; eliminating duplicate tram and bus services; improving feeder services to stations; making transfers between modes quicker and more convenient; and providing for park and ride in the suburbs.
  Since 1973 total public transport travel has increased by 30 per cent with travel on the two railways and the city buses growing by 41 and 44 per cent respectively. Modal split between transit and cars has shifted from 37/63 in 1970 to 46/54 in 1980.
- Osaka has a 209 km rail network which was largely complete by 1935 but a further 390 km of lines has been proposed. Recent improvements to the quality of service include the doubling of single track lines, new cars and stations, automated ticket gates, the elimination of at-grade road crossings and the provision of passenger amenities.
- In Hong Kong a new mass transit system is under construction. It was started in 1975 and by 1984 was carrying 13 per cent of all transit passengers. Apart from a subsidy for interest payments on one third of the capital cost of the system all construction and operating costs are paid from fares and land development revenues. All debt is due to be repaid by 2004.

Bus Service Improvements

Improvements to bus services were made in many OECD cities in the ten years up to 1985. New vehicles were brought into service nearly everywhere, and in cities such as Los Angeles where efforts were made to improve the quality and availability of services, bus fleets were expanded.

In *Los Angeles* the per capita increase in buses actually exceeded that for cars in the decade up to 1980. In *Singapore* the fleet was increased by over 46 per cent between 1974 and 1982 – from 2 188 to 3 203 buses.

Bus operators in many cities also increased their investment in telecommunications systems designed to improve the management of services running on congested streets, assist crews to report emergencies and assaults, and give information to intending passengers about waiting times.

In *Osaka* a location system was introduced on two routes that informs waiting passengers of the approach and destination of oncoming buses. Surveys found that 65 per cent of passengers watched the indicator and that the displays generated an 11 per cent increase in travel.

Simplified Fare Systems

Many cities simplified their fares in the 1960s and 1970s in order to reduce the inconvenience of buying tickets and to speed up access to buses without conductors. *London* retained graduated fares long after most cities but in May 1983 the cost of bus and metro fares was cut by 25 per cent and a period ticket good on all services was introduced. These "Travelcards" carry photographs of their holders and are available for periods from one day to one year. Their cost is related to a series of annular zones that cover the 625 square miles of Greater London.

In 1985 "Travelcards" were augmented by "Capitalcards" covering the suburban services of British Rail as well as the red buses and the metro. At the same time a change in political control over London Transport led to increases in fares.

Experience of period tickets of the travel card type suggests that at least three years of strong growth can be expected to follow their introduction. Travelcards may be subsidised in the conventional way. They may also be financed by employers voluntarily or compulsorily.

Preliminary results of the fares simplification in London were a 16 per cent increase in public transport travel or about twice the amount attributable to the reduction in the cost of travel. The new cards were bought by about 600 000 people or about one in ten Londoners. A fall of 10 to 15 per cent in cars entering central London in the morning peak was counted. Air quality benefits are estimated to be on the same scale. The full benefits of the change were estimated at £171 million compared to costs of £75 million.

A non-transferable monthly or yearly ticket giving unlimited travel by bus and Metro (the "Orange Card") was introduced in *Paris* in July 1975. The new fare structure underpinning the Orange Card results in the same price being charged for equivalent journeys regardless of the form of transport used. It reduces travel costs for the longest commuting trips. It encourages inter-suburban travel, and it simplifies travel for people changing modes.

In 1982 the French Government obliged employers to reimburse employees half of the cost of their Orange Cards in order to promote travel by public transport and to make employers aware of the external costs of their choice of location. This measure replaced an obligation on employers to pay their employees a fixed sum regardless of their mode of travel.

When Orange Cards were first put on sale their take up exceeded forecasts by 50 per cent after six months and continued to increase thereafter. By 1984 Orange Card sales were between 1.4 and 1.7 million per month depending on the season. User surveys found that the new tariff enhanced the image of public transport and led the number of bus passengers to increase from 750 000 to one million per day. The tariff also led to the shift of 70 000 journeys per day from car to bus or Metro. This shift represented a 2.8 per cent drop in car use over the entire day or 4 per cent during the evening peak. It is attributed as much to the added convenience and improved image of public transport as to considerations of cost or time.

Improving the Image of Public Transport

In an attempt to stop a fall in travel and attract new customers, the *Paris* Transport authority (RATP) has taken a series of steps to influence the way in which the public sees its services. Action followed a 1973 opinion survey which showed that the RATP lacked a corporate image, that the Metro, while viewed as efficient and reliable, was felt to be an oppressive place disconnected from life in the streets, and that the buses, while much more friendly, were considered to be inefficient, unreliable and incomprehensible. Apart from introducing the Orange Card action was taken on three other fronts.

Information and Animation

Public information skills were used to create a positive corporate identity and to depict the RATP as a dynamic enterprise actively engaged in expanding and improving its services. Information on services and on improvements to speed and reliability were broadcast via the media and by postal brochures. In the Metro itself station lighting and design were brightened up and shops installed. Where space within the Metro permitted it, concerts and exhibitions were arranged so as to capture some of the spirit of the streets and reduce passenger anxiety.

Advertising

One finding of the RATP opinion surveys was that users of public transport were generally perceived to be inferior. Advertising was accordingly used to portray the Metro as a place where one might find happy, interesting and pleasant people.

Security

Parisians believe the risk of aggression in the Metro to be greater than it is. This reputation is the result of the Metro's image as a menacing underground place coupled with unbalanced media coverage of incidents of violence. The RATP has therefore concentrated on highly visible security actions to try and persuade Parisians that the risk of aggression is being reduced.

Surveys suggest that the actions taken by the RATP have improved the image of transit in Paris and that transit travel (including intentions to travel by transit) has been increased slightly beyond what could be explained by other actions. Expenditure by the RATP on public communication is nevertheless low by the standard of French companies. Expenditure by the RATP on communications is 0.2 per cent of its operating budget. The average for French companies is 0.85 per cent.

4. TRANSPORT MANAGEMENT AND ROAD IMPROVEMENTS

In cities such as *Gothenburg* and *Singapore* increases in road capacity have contributed to transport and environmental improvements. In both cities ring roads were built or upgraded in order to divert through traffic from places of greater to lesser environmental sensitivity. A number of cities also used parking controls to manage city centre bound cars.

Traffic Cells

In 1969 *Gothenburg* established a policy under which traffic cells were to be used incrementally to reduce traffic throughout the city. It was also agreed that the building of new roads would be limited and priority given to ones allowing the creation of traffic cells.

The city centre had already been divided into five parts and all through traffic that had previously passed across it was re-routed onto a ring road. The resulting cells led to a reduction in accidents and improved environmental conditions. They also brought about better time-keeping by trams and buses and, as a side-effect, produced some reduction in traffic. Similar benefits flowed from the second generation of cells created in some of the city's inner residential and commercial district. As the introduction of the cells was linked to various other traffic management measures the effect of different components of the city's traffic policy are impossible to isolate. The favourable nature of the results overall is, however, indisputable.

CBD Traffic Cells

The first generation of cells reduced traffic flows across the borders of the central area by 45 per cent between 1970 and 1982. Casualties were cut by 45 per cent within the cells and by 40 per cent on boundary streets. Since the successful introduction of the central cells the City has turned to parking policy as its main instrument for reducing the use of cars in the centre.

Inner Area Cells

All through traffic amounting to 2 400 cars per day was diverted on to peripheral streets. Accidents were reduced by 27 per cent within the cells and by 9 per cent on roads surrounding them. Information of travel time changes is incomplete but preliminary evidence suggests that car drivers going in and around the cells had their travel distances increased by 7 per cent. (In the CBD longer trip lengths seem to have been cancelled out by shorter trip times.) The cells reduced noise by 8 dB(A) for one third of affected residents, increased it by 4 dB(A) for another third and caused no difference to the other third. In the case of dwellings where a noise increase was unavoidable a change of use to offices will be permitted.

The effects of the traffic cells on trade are uncertain and this matter merits further study. Gothenburg's long experience of traffic cells would be of greater benefit to other cities if such a study was carried out. The adverse effect on trade caused by traffic cells at *Groningen* in the Netherlands makes clear that this type of traffic management may not be satisfactory in all conditions.

The implementation of the five original cells was helped by the presence of ring road with spare capacity and a simple traffic pattern. Implementation of the outer ring of cells was more difficult and time consuming because of complicated land use and traffic patterns, increased emphasis on consultation and a need for major works. However the consultation evoked little response and with the benefit of hindsight it appears that the scheme should have been executed without it and modified as necessary.

Selective reductions in traffic provide the only low cost way to create the spare road capacity needed to implement traffic cells in congested city centres. Gothenburg's central area parking policy represents the first practical experiment with this approach to urban traffic management. However as half of the parking stock in the city centre is privately owned, the City Council may need to introduce additional traffic management techniques to achieve its traffic restraint objective.

Heavy Lorry Bans

In the early 1980s the Greater *London* Council (GLC) focussed its traffic management resources on protecting the environment and assisting public transport, pedestrians and cyclists. Amongst proposals that flowed from this policy was a licensing scheme for heavy lorries designed to reduce through movements and shift access movements away from the night-time and weekends. The goods vehicles identified for control were those over 16.5 tons and the assumptions made by the GLC were that the 400 to 500 firms affected would switch to smaller vehicles, switch to weekday operation, use exempted roads or make use of hushed lorries. The ban, although opposed by the Secretary of State for Transport, was introduced by the GLC early in 1986 but its effectiveness was undermined by lack of enforcement and by the impending abolition of the GLC.

Management of Traffic on Urban Freeways

Congestion is a major problem on the freeways of *Los Angeles* and only traffic management enables them to operate as well as they do. The network, largely completed in the 1960s, accounts for one per cent of all highways and streets in Los Angeles but carries 55 per cent of all vehicle miles of travel. A variety of management techniques have been used to keep traffic on the freeways flowing.

High-Occupancy Vehicle Lanes

On the El Monte freeway two lanes have been dedicated to high-occupancy vehicles in order to raise the capacity of the highway as a mover of people. During peak hours, the El Monte Busway is filled to capacity with car pools, van pools and express buses. It carries 42 000 persons daily.

Ramp Metering

Traffic signals that limit the entry of vehicles to freeways at access ramps enable demand to be balanced with capacity and so reduce stoppages. Some 600 ramps are already metered and 400 additions are expected in the next five years.

Sharing Rides

Commuter Computer is a carpool promoting organisation that has worked with 1 800 companies assisting 93 000 people to share rides to work. The agency provides employers with lists of potential sharers and promotes transit use as well as pooling. In 1985 the agency had 300 000 people on its books including 45 000 active ride-sharers.

Transport Management for the 1984 Olympics

The 1984 Olympic Games caused Los Angeles to experience the travel demand of the future. The transport and environmental problems created by the resulting surge in demand were met in various ways. A total of 550 additional buses, 40 000 special bus operations, 1 000 new public transport workers and an unparalleled public information programme were set in motion. A total of 1 175 000 extra passengers were carried using park-and-ride and express buses.

Company Buses

Companies in Southern California have long provided car parks for their employees. In recent years groups of employers have begun to form associations charged with improving transit and providing economical alternatives to it. The best known of these bodies is the El Segundo Employers Association. It represents 50 000 employees and, in addition to negotiating with public transport companies to provide services, it organises subscription and charter buses, van and carpooling, preferential parking for car pools, cycle facilities and other variants to single-occupant car commuting.

Transport Management

During the Olympic Games assistance to employers to arrange ride-sharing was intensified. Bus lanes were created and effort devoted to the staggering and re-routing of car travel and trucking.

Selected freeway on-ramps were closed, mini-freeways were created on some arterial roads, enforcement was increased and the monitoring and management of bottle necks intensified. Demand management techniques of the kind used during the Olympic Games, all of which involve modification of travel behaviour, are expected to become essential in Southern California in the future if freeway service levels are to be maintained at present standards.

Area Traffic Bans Based on Alternate License Plates

An emergency traffic management scheme aimed at alleviating air pollution and traffic congestion in *Athens* was introduced in 1981. The main feature of the scheme is a ban on the use of private cars on and within the inner ring road. The ban is in operation from Monday to Friday during business hours and on any given day only cars with license plates ending in an odd or even number are allowed to circulate. Taxis, doctors, and tourists receive limited exemptions. Violations suffer fines ranging from US$50 to 1 000. The ban locks within the ring road about 40 000 cars belonging to residents. Limited monitoring of the exercise suggests that total traffic within the ring road is reduced by 20 per cent.

Management of Signals, Goods Deliveries and Bicycles

In *Osaka* the authorities aim to reduce dependence on car travel, to limit traffic to 22 million vehicle kilometers per day and to channel as much as possible of this flow onto expressways and trunk roads which are associated with measures to improve the environment. While the extent of the road network has grown by only 7 per cent in ten years, elevated toll roads have been increased by 150 per cent. The resulting increase in expressway travel has allowed sidewalks to be widened, bicycle lanes to be introduced and trees to be planted on some main roads.

Residential Areas

'Living zone' traffic regulations, designed to reduce vehicle impacts on people in their houses have been introduced in many districts. A before and after survey in 65 such zones found that traffic accidents were down by 9 per cent, deaths by 11 per cent, injuries by 10 per cent and property damage by 5 per cent.

Signal Control

An extensive control system embracing 2 299 traffic signals, 4 460 vehicle sensors, 108 bus sensors, 155 traffic signs and 62 cameras covers nearly all of the city's 325 km of trunk roads and the entire 137 km^2 central area. The system, designed to prevent or alleviate traffic congestion, monitors and analyses vehicle volumes and automatically controls signals and signs. Between 1972 and 1982 vehicle speeds were increased by 20.7 per cent, the frequency of stops was cut by 30 per cent, stopping time cut by 33 per cent and travelling time shortened by 16 per cent.

Goods Deliveries

Reductions in the amount of goods vehicle traffic in the centre of the city are being sought by means of grouped delivery services based on data processing.

Bicycles

Bicycle ownership and use have expanded as the quality of Osaka's bus service has declined. Use of bicycles for feeder journeys to railway stations is particularly marked and in 1982, 127 000 bicycles were counted at 144 stations. Bicycle parking is being provided at stations. A total of 450 km of bicycle lanes and 80 km of exclusive bicycle ways have been created. Bicycle ownership is at the level of 1.4 machines per household.

5. INNOVATIONS IN INSTITUTIONS

Where new ideas are being tried or new policies introduced it is often necessary to create new institutions or use existing ones in new ways. Local conditions nevertheless play a powerful role in deciding what changes are practical. Innovations in institutions are thus, of all aspects of transport and environmental policy, the most difficult to transfer from one country to another.

Some lessons may however be drawn from the case studies. In *Singapore*, the prospect of the growth of a major financial centre without the possibility, in the short term, of building underground railways to sustain it, led to the setting up of a high level, inter-ministerial committee to design and implement a traffic management scheme that would prevent the otherwise inevitable congestion. In a further act of centralisation an Urban Redevelopment Agency was set up to marshall the sites necessary for the buildings in which the new financial services could locate themselves.

Day to day management of the bus services and even enforcement of the selected area licensing scheme were however left as far as possible in the hands of competing private operators. A clear distinction was thus drawn between the high level of organisation needed for policy-making and the grass-roots level needed for the successful operation of services.

In both *Munich* and *Athens* a comparable distinction may be observed in the management of public transport. In both cities, despite their different stages of development, policy issues including the setting of fares, are decided by small-scale, high-level, 'holding companies' while the running of services is in the hands of competing and even private operators.

Further steps towards reducing the scale of public transport operations and towards a more passenger-centered style of work may be observed in other cities. In *Stockholm* groups of bus drivers are being given responsibility for managing many aspects of the services in which they work. In *London* a growing number of suburban services, formerly run by London Transport using the familiar red buses, has been put out to tender and in a number of cases contracts have been won by small, private companies using quite different vehicles. The next step, and one that is being discussed in some cities, is the franchising of groups of city bus routes. Such franchises might be bought by groups of drivers or small companies. In *Hong Kong* the franchising of bus routes is already established.

Chapter IV

CONCLUSIONS

1. GENERAL ISSUES

The Problem

Vehicle air pollution and noise persist and may worsen in many urban areas. The suburbanization of cities, population growth, rising car-ownership, and increasing trip rates are all tending to increase the use of vehicles, congestion, and emissions.

Constraints

In the presence of resource constraints scope for the expansion and improvement of urban highway and transit networks and the subsidisation of transit services is limited. This underlines the over-riding importance of adopting an approach, that works through low-cost techniques and private financing, which promises to reduce vehicular environmental impacts at source and which is based on the enhanced management of existing transport systems.

Priority Solutions

Control of emissions at source needs to be given the highest priority in any abatement programme. However, due to increases in trip-making and the failure of source controls to perform to specification, such measures will not by themselves eliminate all pollution problems. The case studies indicate that transport and traffic management policies do also contribute to the abatement of air pollution and noise.

Government Roles

Distinct roles exist for central and local governments in implementing urban transport policies that take account of the environment:

- The principal roles of central government are the setting and enforcing of emission standards for new and in-use vehicles, laying down national air quality and noise standards, and establishing economic incentives designed to reduce noise and exhaust emissions;
- The principal roles of local governments are the management of highways, the setting of transit tariffs, selective vehicle purchasing policy, public education, controls of land use and various local actions against pollution and noise.

Policy Innovations

The most notable innovations identified by the case-studies addressed the institutional problems of fragmented and overlapping authority and acted to consolidate decision-making; established partnerships between public and private agencies; created new pricing and financing techniques; and adopted a comprehensive approach towards abating vehicle air pollution and noise.

2. SPECIFIC POLICY FINDINGS

a) Urban form has a significant effect on the transport and environment policy options open to governments;

b) Scope appears to exist for a wider use than at present of economic instruments. Road use and traffic congestion can be brought within an economic framework by means of road-user charges. These provide a low-cost means to maximize the use of available road space and defer heavy investment in highway and transport systems. Economic incentives may also be used to promote the development and the use of quieter and cleaner vehicles;

c) Road pricing based on supplementary licenses has been demonstrated to work in Singapore. Electronic road pricing has been shown to be technically practical in Hong Kong. The obstacles to the wider use of such techniques are ethical and political. If concerns about unfairness can be satisfactorily resolved, the use of road pricing is likely to depend on finding ways to introduce it gradually. One possibility is to use it to collect bridge or tunnel tolls. Another is to persuade car-owners to choose to pay their motoring taxes through road pricing instead of by more traditional methods;

d) There is a marked tendency for the high-performance transport facilities – be they express Metro lines or urban freeways – to be overcrowded and congested. Management resources should therefore be concentrated on smoothing flows on such facilities. Capital resources should be devoted to expanding them or providing alternatives to them;

e) Major changes are taking place in the management of urban bus services. Large, centrally planned companies are giving way to smaller private and franchised operators. The smaller operators are closer to their customers and more passenger-oriented. This change promises, more than anything else, to improve the low reputation of public transport and to increase job-satisfaction for those who work in it;

f) The creation of networks of safe and continuous cycle tracks radiating from suburban railway stations and schools and the provision of safe cycle parking merits examination as a lower-cost alternative to providing peak-hour feeder and school bus services;

g) The contracting out of transit and other public services need not result in loss of public control over the quantity or quality of service provided. The service required may be stipulated in contracts. Competition between public and private transport authorities to provide services contributes to efficiency and good service;

h) Opportunities exist to obtain private capital to buy new rolling stock and to finance station modernisation in transit systems. In some cases, it may be possible to use financing mechanisms hitherto confined to the private sector. Such mechanisms have the potential to increase the financial responsibility of transit management;

i) The combination of public opposition to new urban highways and limited resources suggest that new small scale urban roads with low design speeds or roads that are part of traffic management schemes will prove worth investigating;

j) The control of emissions and noise from vehicles has in the past been pursued by blanket measures aimed at all vehicles. Scope also exists for selective actions. Government purchasing policy may be used to reduce emissions from all publicly owned vehicles. Financial inducements may be used to secure the conversion of taxis from diesel to liquid petroleum gas. Licensing schemes may be used to promote the fitting of heavy goods vehicles with hush kits. All these actions point to the possibility of developing specialized vehicles for use in cities.

Part IV

ASSESSMENT OF TECHNICAL CHANGES TO REDUCE AIR POLLUTION AND NOISE EMISSIONS FROM MOTOR VEHICLES

Chapter I

REGULATIONS AND STANDARDS IN OECD COUNTRIES

Regulations on motor vehicle exhaust and noise emissions were developed in most OECD Member countries during the 70s for the protection of public health and the environment. The regulations enforced varied according to different national needs and approaches. At the same time, efforts to harmonize these regulations at international level are being pursued with the aim of avoiding non-tariff barriers to trade and reducing transfrontier pollution and impairment of the environment in general.

Fuel specifications based on the mutual understanding between the automobile industry and the oil companies have existed for a long time. More recently, national authorities have been bringing influence to bear with respect to lead content and in some countries also benzene.

1. REGULATIONS ON EXHAUST EMISSIONS AND LEAD IN GASOLINE

Emission Standards for Cars

Programmes for automotive emission control were progressively elaborated according to local conditions (climate, infrastructure, vehicle population, urban structure, driving conditions, etc.). They began in California and were initiated at Federal level in the United States in 1963. Japan followed in 1966. Canada, Australia and most European countries established control programmes in 1970-72. The US goal was a 90 per cent reduction of exhaust emissions by 1975 as compared with the 1970 automobile emission rate. Other countries set similar targets for new vehicles.

Interest initially focused on emissions of carbon monoxide (CO) as the main concern in urban areas. Later hydrocarbons (HC) were also regulated. The United States regulated both pollutants in 1968 (California in 1966). The EEC countries also adopted regulations concerning those pollutants in 1970 and the ECE countries in 1971. It was not until 1973-74 that control of nitrogen oxides (NO_x) was required in the United States, Canada and Japan. Sweden regulated NO_x in 1976. In the EEC countries NO_x was included in the regulations in 1977. Japan has developed its own driving cycle for testing, whereas Canada, Sweden, Switzerland and Australia have adopted the driving cycle of the US Federal Test Procedure. The ECE (Geneva) test cycle is used by most other European countries. These driving cycles represent the three test procedures used in connection with the different emission regulations applied.

It should be noted that there are so far no regulations on specific pollutants other than CO, HC, NO_x and in the US particulates. Examples of such specific pollutants are aromatics, benzene, aldehydes, etc. (see chapter III.1 for details on pollutants). HC stands for all hydrocarbons without making reference to any specific compound.

1975 models of passenger cars in the United States and Japan were to a large extent equipped with catalytic converters to meet the standards. The use of catalysts necessitated the introduction of unleaded gasoline to avoid poisoning of the active catalyst. Today virtually all passenger cars sold in Japan and the United States (and the majority of cars sold in Canada) are equipped with catalyst and electronic fuel control associated with strict stoichiometric air/fuel ratio (14.5/1) when necessary. This means that more than 40 per cent of all new cars sold in the OECD countries use catalytic converters.

In Europe, Sweden introduced regulations for 1976 models equivalent to the US 1973 regulations.

Figure 1: **TRENDS IN STANDARDS ON AUTOMOBILE EXHAUST EMISSIONS**
(Gasoline Powered)[1]

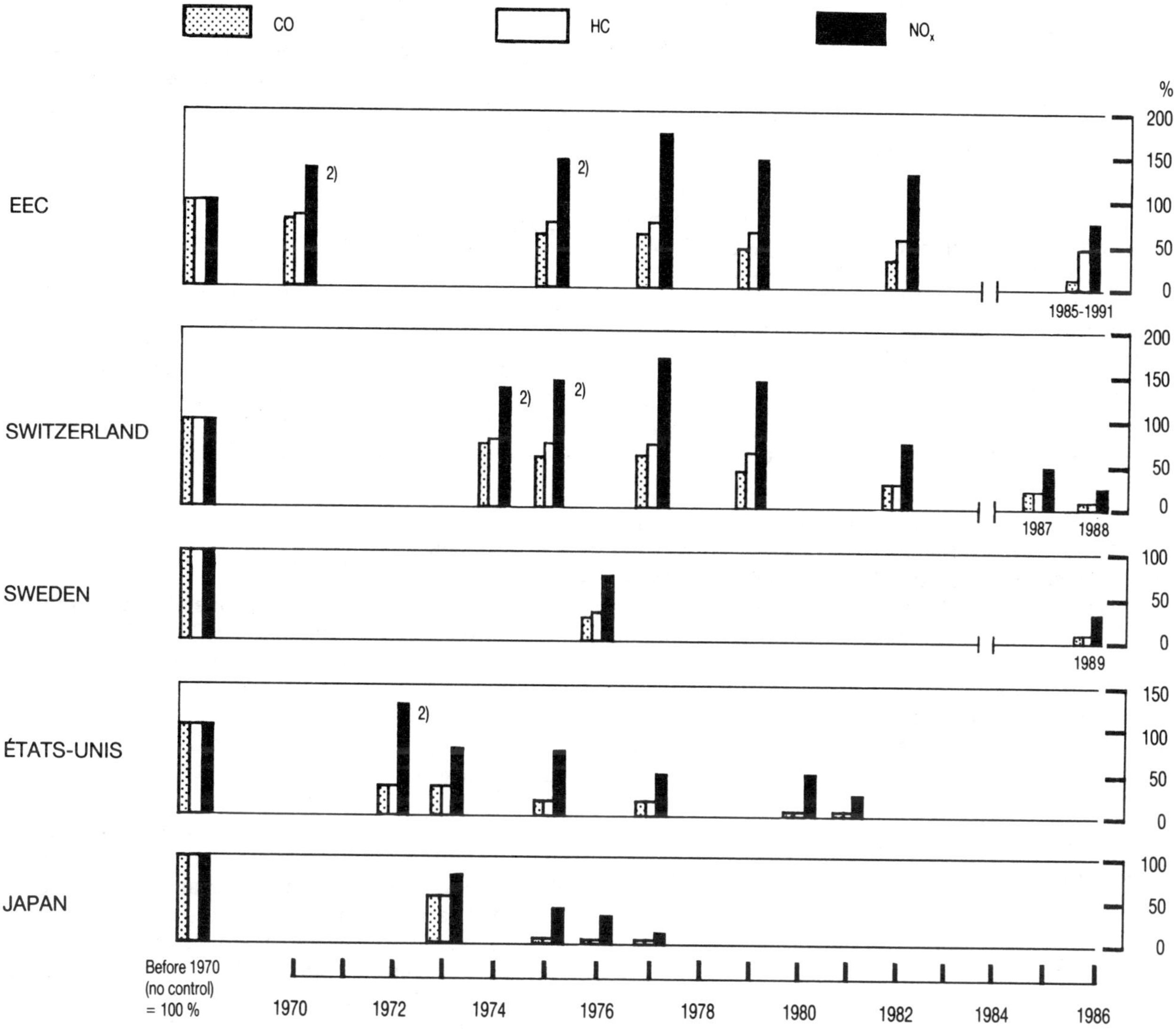

1. Data are not comparable since pre-1970 reference cars were different in levels of pollution and weight across countries.
2. Increase in NO_x due to the absence of regulation.

Switzerland adopted the same standards as Sweden in 1982. ECE-15 regulations were amended in 1977, 1979 and 1982. In 1985, all European regulations can be met without catalysts although more stringent emission standards presently under consideration by the EEC will be met by the use of three-way catalysts for larger cars and possibly by other technologies for medium and small cars (oxydation catalysts or other systems).

The regulations enforced since about 1970 have substantially reduced the allowable level of exhaust emissions from new cars (Figure 1).

In 1979, the OECD study "The cost and effectiveness of automotive exhaust emission control regulation" suggested that Europe should consider the application of evaporative hydrocarbon emission control standards to reduce HC as in the United States and Japan. This provision has not yet been included in any regulations enforced in Europe in 1985.

Much attention is now being paid to emissions of particulates by diesel cars, and particulate standards have been enforced in the United States.

Three different sets of regulations are at present applied to passenger cars in the United States, Japan and Europe (except Sweden and Switzerland). Most European countries observe the ECE/EEC standards, but Sweden and Switzerland have stricter regulations (Tables 1A-1F). Switzerland has decided to enforce stricter emission limits from October 1986 and again from October 1987. Australia recently adopted new regulations, to be enforced by 1986, that are similar to the US Federal regulations of 1975. Canada's regulations are somewhat less stringent than the US 1975 regulations.

Gaseous emissions from the crankcase of passenger cars have been eliminated by means of closed crankcase ventilation, which is mandatory in all OECD countries. Since 1984, closed crankcase ventilation systems have been required on diesel engines without turbocharging in the United States.

Since June 1985, the EEC has attempted to reach an agreement on new EEC emission limits. Different limits apply to different categories of car, depending on piston displacement. The new emission limits will apply to diesel as well as gasoline-fuelled cars (Table 1E and Appendix 1).

The limit values are based on the present European test cycle. For the two vehicle categories with piston displacement of above 1.4 litres, the limit values are liable to possible change in the test cycle due to the addition of non-urban driving sequences.

Exhaust emission standards in some Member countries are shown in Table 1A. The EEC regulations based on ECE procedures 15/03 and 15/04 respectively cannot be compared directly.

Some current exhaust emission regulations have a significant influence on the conditions and performance of new vehicles. Over time, vehicles deteriorate due to wear and insufficient maintenance. Deliberate tampering with emission control equipment also takes place. Devices operating at exhaust manifold level, such as after-burners and catalytic converters, are more exposed to deliberate tampering than emission control measures at combustion level. As a result, emission levels from vehicles in use are often higher and sometimes much higher than the regulatory limits for new vehicles.

Commercial Vehicles

Regulations on gaseous exhaust emissions by trucks and buses have been implemented in the United States and Japan. Several other countries have standards concerning smoke opacity of diesel engine exhausts. There are also ECE regulations concerning smoke and emissions of gaseous components from diesel-fuelled trucks and buses.

Motorcycles

The United States and Europe also have regulations for motorcycles as regards HC anc CO. Different driving cycles are used in testing light and heavy motorcycles.

Lead Content

The lead content of gasoline is regulated in all OECD countries (Table 2). Unleaded gasoline is available in the United States and Japan as a prerequisite to the use of catalytic converters. More than 95 per cent of the gasoline sold in Japan is unleaded, as against only 60 per cent in the United States. Unleaded gasoline is also available in Australia and Canada. The current Canadian exhaust emission standards do not require catalytic converters. However, in 1980 about 70 per cent of the new cars sold in Canada were equipped with catalysts. Unleaded gasoline has recently been introduced on a small scale in several European countries and a decision to introduce unleaded gasoline in the whole EEC area was adopted in 1985 for implementation in 1989. After 1st January 1986, Member countries will be obliged to introduce unleaded fuel on a national scale. The manufacturers are requested that all new vehicles be able to run on unleaded fuel after October 1, 1989. In Switzerland, as from 1st January 1985, only unleaded, regular gasoline may be imported or manufactured; after 1st July 1986 the sale of leaded regular gasoline was prohibited. Unleaded petrol is already

Table 1A. EXHAUST EMISSION STANDARDS OF NEW GASOLINE POWERED AUTOMOBILES

Due to different regulations, values should not be compared

Country	Model year	Test procedure	Emission standards, g/km		
			CO	HC	NO_x
USA[a] weight < 2720 kg	1983 current	USA 1975	2.1	0.25	0.62
Japan[a] (max limits)	1978 current	10-mode	2.7	0.39	0.48
EEC[a]	current[b]		17-33	6-8.7[d]	–
EC[a, e]	1988-91[c]		6-11	1.6-4[d]	0.8-1.5
Australia	1986	USA 1975	9.3	0.9	1.9
Sweden	1976 current	(USA 1973) A10	24.2	2.1	1.9
	1989		2.1	0.25	0.62
Switzerland	1983 current	(USA 1973) A10	24.2	2.1	1.9
	1987	USA 1973	9.3	0.9	1.2
	1988		2.2	0.21	0.62
Canada	current	USA 1975	15.6	1.2	1.9
	1987	USA 1975	2.1	0.25	0.62

a) See more detailed tables.
b) Values vary with vehicle weight.
c) Values vary with vehicle piston displacement.
d) HC + NO_x.
e) "Luxembourg conclusions" of June 1985.

Table 1B. USA: NEW AUTOMOBILE EXHAUST EMISSION CONTROL HISTORY, GASOLINE POWERED AUTOMOBILES

Year	Pollutant standard (g/km)[a] U.S. Federal (CVS-CH)		
	CO	HC	NO_x
Uncontrolled	54	5.4	2.5
1968	32	3.7	3.1
1970	21	2.4	3.1
1972	17	1.9	3.1
1973	17	1.9	1.9
1974	17	1.9	1.9
1975	9.3	0.9	1.9
1977	9.3	0.9	1.2
1980	4.4	0.25	1.2
1983	2.1	0.25	0.6 (0.9)[b]

a) Applicable at 80 000 km.
b) Values in parenthesis indicate applicable standard for 100 000 km durability.

Table IC. JAPAN : NEW AUTOMOBILE EXHAUST EMISSION CONTROL HISTORY, GASOLINE POWERED AUTOMOBILES

Year	Pollutant standard[a]			Measurement unit	Test cycle
	CO	HC	NO_x		
1966	3	–	–	%	4 mode
1969	2.5	–	–	%	4 mode
1973	26.0	3.8	3.0	g/km	10 mode
1975	2.7[b]	0.39	1.6	g/km	11 mode
	85.0	9.5	11.0	g/test	11 mode
1976	2.7	0.39	1.20	g/km	10 mode
	85.0	9.5	9.0	g/test	11 mode
1978	2.7	0.39	0.48	g/km	10 mode
	85.0	9.5	6.0	g/test	11 mode

a) Applicable to all new model vehicles that are greater than 1 000 kg equivalent inertia weight.
b) The figures show the maximum permissible limits of the standards applicable at 30 000 km durability and apply to new model vehicles only.

Table 1D. JAPAN: HISTORY OF PERMISSIBLE LIMITS OF MOTOR VEHICLE EXHAUST EMISSIONS

Fuel	Pollutant	Vehicle	Control	Mode	Application date: New model vehicle	Application date: Existing model vehicle	Limit
Gasoline- or LPG-fueled vehicle	Carbon monoxide (CO)	New vehicle	Control by driving cycle	4-mode	September 1, 1966	September 1, 1967	3.0% for gasoline-fueled ordinary-sized motor vehicle and small-sized motor vehicle
				4-mode	September 1, 1969	January 1, 1970 April 1 1970 **	2.5% for gasoline-fueled ordinary-sized motor vehicle and small-sized motor vehicle **for truck and bus
				4-mode	January 1, 1971		1.5% for LPG-fueled ordinary-sized motor vehicle and small-sized motor vehicle 3.0% for mini-sized motor vehicle
				10-mode	April 1 1973	December 1, 1973	26.0 g/km for gasoline-fueled passenger car, 18.0 g/km for LPG-fueled passenger car (all vehicles except heavy-duty vehicle)
				Gasoline 6-mode			1.6% for gasoline-fueled vehicle, 1.1% for LPG-fueled vehicle (heavy-duty vehicle)
				10-mode	April 1, 1975	December 1, 1975	2.7 g/km for passenger car, 17.0 g/km for truck and bus (all vehicles except heavy-duty vehicle)
				11-mode		(April 1, 1976)	85.0 g/test for passenger car, 130.0 g/test for light-duty vehicle (all vehicles except heavy-duty vehicle)
			Idling		August 1, 1970		4.5%
		Vehicle in use	Idling				5.5%
					October 1, 1972		4.5%
	Hydro-carbon (HC)	New vehicle	Blow-by gas control		September 1, 1970	January 1, 1971	Installation of blow-by gas recirculation device
			Fuel evaporative gas control		July 1, 1972	April 1, 1973	Installation of fuel evaporative emission control device (2.0 g/test)
			Control by driving cycle	10-mode	April 1, 1973	December 1, 1973	3.8 g/km for gasoline-fueled vehicle, 3.2 g/km for LPG-fueled vehicle (all vehicles except heavy-duty vehicle), 22.5 g/km for mini-sized motor vehicle with two-stroke engine
				Gasoline 6-mode			520 ppm for gasoline-fueled vehicle, 440 ppm for LPG-fueled vehicle (heavy-duty vehicle)
				10-mode	April 1, 1975	December 1, 1975 (April 1, 1976)	0.39 g/km for passenger car, 2.7 g/km for truck and bus, 15.0 g/km for truck of mini-sized motor vehicle with two-stroke engine (all vehicles except heavy-duty vehicle)
				11-mode			9.5 g/test for passenger car, 17.0 g/test for truck and bus, 70.0 g/test for truck of mini-sized motor vehicle with two-stroke engine (all vehicles except heavy-duty vehicle)
		Vehicle in use	Device installation		May 1, 1973		Installation of HC/HOx reduction device and adjustment of spark timing
			Idling		January 1, 1975		1,200 ppm for passenger car and bus with four-stroke engine, 7,800 ppm for passenger car and bus with two-stroke engine, 3,300 ppm for passenger car and bus with special structure engine
					June 1, 1975		1,200 ppm for truck with four-stroke engine, 7,800 ppm for truck with two-stroke engine, 3,300 ppm for truck with special structure engine
	Nitrogen oxides (NOx)	New vehicle	Control by driving cycle	10-mode	April 1, 1973	December 1 1973	3.0 g/km (all vehicles except heavy-duty vehicle) 0.5 g/km for mini-sized motor vehicle with two-stroke engine
				Gasoline 6-mode			2,200 ppm for heavy-duty vehicle
				10-mode	April 1, 1975	December 1, 1975 (April 1, 1976)	1.6 g/km for passenger car, 2.3 g/km for truck and bus, 0.5 g/km for mini-sized motor vehicle with two-stroke engine (all vehicles except heavy-duty vehicle)
				11-mode			11.0 g/test for passenger car, 20.0 g/test for truck and bus, 4.0 g/test for mini-sized motor vehicle with two-stroke engine (all vehicles except heavy-duty vehicle)
Gasoline-or LPG-fueled vehicle	NOx	New Vehicle	Control by driving cycle	10-mode	April 1, 1976	March 1, 1977 (March 31 1978)	0.84 g/km for passenger car with EIW of 1 ton or less, 1.2 g/km for passenger car with EIW of more than 1 ton and passenger car of mini-sized motor vehicle with four-stroke engine, 0.5 g/km for mini-sized motor vehicle with two-stroke engine
				11-mode			8.0 g/test for passenger car with EIW of 1 ton or less, 9.0 g/test for passenger car with EIW of more than 1 ton and passenger car of light motor vehicle with four-stroke engine, 4.0 g/test for mini-sized motor vehicle with two-stroke engine
				Gasoline 6-mode	August 1, 1977	April 1,1978	1,850 ppm for heavy-duty vehicle
				10-mode	April 1, 1978 (April 1, 1981)	March 1, 1979 (April 1, 1981)	0.48 g/km for passenger car
				11-mode			6.0 g/test for passenger car
				10-mode	January 1, 1979 (April 1, 1981)	December 1, 1979 (April 1, 1981)	1.4 g/km for truck and bus (light-duty vehicle) 1.6 g/km for truck and bus (medium-duty vehicle and mini-sized motor vehicle)
				11-mode			10 g/test for truck and bus (light-duty vehicle) 11 g/test for truck and bus (medium-duty vehicle and mini-sized motor vehicle)
				Gasoline 6-mode			1,390 ppm for truck and bus (heavy-duty vehicle)
				10-mode	January 1, 1981 (April 1, 1983)	December 1, 1981 (April 1, 1983)	0.84 g/km for truck and bus (light-duty vehicle)
				11-mode			8.0 g/test for truck and bus (light-duty vehicle)
				10-mode	December 1, 1981 (April 1, 1984)	November 1, 1982 (April 1, 1984)	1.26 g/km for truck and bus (medium-duty vehicle)
				11-mode			9.5 g/test for truck and bus (medium-duty vehicle)
				10-mode	January 1, 1982 (April 1, 1984)	December 1, 1982 (April 1, 1984)	1.26 g/km for mini-sized motor vehicle
				11-mode			990 ppm for heavy-duty vehicle
				Gasoline 6-mode			990 ppm for heavy-duty vehicle
		Vehicle in use	Device installation		May 1, 1973		Installation of HC/NOx reduction device and adjustment of spark timing
Diesel-powered vehicle	CO, HC, NOx	New vehicle	Control by driving cycle	Diesel 6-mode	September 1, 1974	April 1, 1975	CO 980 ppm HC 670 ppm NOx 590 ppm (1 000 ppm for direct injection type)
	NOx				August 1, 1977	April 1, 1978	500 ppm (850 ppm for direct injection type)
					(April 1, 1981)	March 1, 1980 (April 1, 1981)	450 ppm (700 ppm for direct injection type)
					January 1, 1982 (April 1, 1984)	December 1, 1982 (April 1, 1984)	390 ppm for IDI passenger car
					October 1, 1982 (April 1, 1984)	September 1, 1983 (April 1, 1984)	390 ppm for IDI vehicle
					August 1983 (April 1, 1985)	July, 1, 1984) (April 1, 1985)	610 ppm for DI vehicle
	CO, HC NOx			10-mode	October 1 1986 (April 1, 1988)	September 1, 1987 (April 1, 1988)	CO: 2.7 g/km HC: 0.62 g/km NOx: 0.98 g/km (EIW of 1,250 kg or less) 1.26 g/km (EIW of more than 1,250 kg) Passenger car with manual transmission
					October 1, 1987 (April 1, 1989)	September 1, 1988 (April 1, 1989)	passenger car with automatic transmission
	Particulates (Diesel smoke)	New vehicle	Full-load test		July 1, 1972		Rate of contamination 50%
			No-load acceleration test		January 1, 1975		

Table 1E. EUROPE : NEW AUTOMOBILE EXHAUST EMISSION CONTROL HISTORY, GASOLINE POWERED AUTOMOBILES

Year[a] and regulation	Pollutant standard[b] (g/km)		
	CO	HC	NO_x
1970 (15)	25 - 55 (100 - 220)[c]	2 - 3.2 (8 - 12.8)[c]	NR[f]
1974 (15-01)	20-44 (80 - 176)[c]	1.7 - 2.7 (6.8 - 10.9)[c]	NR[f]
1976 (15-02)	20 - 44 (80 - 176)[c]	1.7 - 2.7 (6.8 - 10.9)[c]	2.5 - 4 (10 - 16)[c]
1977 (15-03)	16 - 36 (65 - 143)[c]	1.5 - 2.4 (6 - 9.6)[c]	2.1 - 3.4 (8.5-13.6)[c]
1981 (15-04)	17 - 33 (70 - 132)[c]	6 - 8.7 (23.8 - 35.0)[c, d]	
1985 Conclusions CE	6 - 8 - 11 (25 - 30 - 45)[c, e]	1.6 - 2 - 4[d] (6.5-8-15)[c, d, e]	0.8 - 1.5 (3.5-6)[c, e]

a) Year of adoption of regulation by ECE/Geneva, except for the last line concerning the "Luxembourg conclusions" for the European Communities.

b) Varies with vehicle weight (except for 1985 agreement). Dates of actual introduction are given by countries in next table.

c) Figures in parenthesis are the g/test values; test is European test defined by corresponding regulations.

d) Total HC + NO_x.

e) Values vary according to engine size (over 2 litres - 1.4 to 2 litres - under 1.4 litres). Prospective compliance dates are 1988/89, 1991/93, 1990/91.

f) Not regulated.

Table 1F. DATES OF INTRODUCTION OF ECE EXHAUST EMISSION REGULATIONS

Country	Regulation				
	15	15.01	15.02	15.03	15.04
Germany	Sep. 1972	Dec. 1974	Mar. 1977	Mar. 1978	Apr. 1983
France	Oct. 1971	Jan. 1974	Jan. 1977	Jan. 1978	Oct. 1982
United Kingdom	Nov. 1973	Apr. 1977	Apr. 1982	Jan. 1983	Jan. 1985
Italy	Apr. 1973	Jan. 1975	Oct. 1978	Jan. 1982	Jan. 1985
Belgium	Jan. 1973	Jan. 1975	Oct. 1978	Jan. 1984	Jan. 1985
Ireland	Nov. 1973	Jan. 1977	Oct. 1978	Jan. 1984	Jan. 1985
Netherlands	Jan. 1973	Jan. 1975	Oct. 1978	Jan. 1982	Jan. 1985
Spain	–	–	–	Jan. 1983	Jan. 1985
Denmark	Jan. 1973	Jan. 1975	Oct. 1978	Jan. 1982	Jan. 1985

Source: OECD, Environment and Economics, 1986.

Table 2. GASOLINE LEAD CONTENT
IN SOME MEMBER COUNTRIES

Country	Present maximum lead content, g/l	Future maximum lead content, g/l (in effect)
EEC	0.15-0.4	0.013 (voluntary 1986, compulsory Oct. 1, 1989)
Australia	0.4-0.8	0.013 (1985)
Austria	0.15	0.013
Canada		
Unleaded	0.013	
Leaded	0.77	0.29
Finland	0.4	0.15
Japan	0.004	
Spain	0.48-0.65	0.4 (1986)
Sweden	0.15	0.0 (1987)
Switzerland	0.15	0.013 (1986)
United States		
Unleaded	0.013	
Leaded	0.13	0.026 (1986)

available in many countries of the EC; in the Federal Republic of Germany more than 13 000 out of the existing 18 000 petrol stations offer unleaded petrol which has already achieved a considerable share in the petrol market.

Benzene

Restrictions concerning the content of benzene (less than or equal to 5 per cent volume) in gasoline are already enforced in the Federal Republic of Germany, Finland, the Netherlands, Norway, Sweden and Switzerland. The EEC Council has decided to impose a maximum limit of 5 per cent benzene by 1989.

Incentives

Some countries will use financial incentives to reach the goal of reduced exhaust emissions. A financial incentive was provided for in the Federal Republic of Germany as of July 1985. A binding solution was introduced in the light of the decisions taken by the EEC Council meetings on environmental matters held on 21st March 1985 (Brussels) and 26th June 1985 (Luxembourg). Up to the date of compulsory introduction of the European emission norms, the Federal government is promoting the introduction of low-emission cars and the fitting of in-use vehicles so as to achieve relatively low emissions by changing the present annual tax for cars by DM 14.40/100 cm^3 piston displacement. Various tax advantages, depending on the degree of emission reduction, are offered. This incentive scheme provides, among other things, that:

- The maximum tax exemption of up to DM 2 200 may be granted for vehicles with a piston displacement of 1.4 litres and above, and a DM 750 tax exemption for vehicles with a piston displacement below 1.4 litres if the cars concerned are recognised as "low-emission" vehicles (1.4 litres and above) or "relatively low-emission" cars (below 1.4 litres) in accordance with the Luxembourg conclusions of 28th June 1985. For several years no motor vehicle tax has been paid related to piston displacement. This tax advantage will be reduced by 25 per cent in 1987 and by 50 per cent in 1988. Passenger cars with a piston displacement exceeding 2.0 litres are only exempted from motor vehicle tax for a specific period if they are recognised as low-pollution cars up to 30th September 1988;
- For cars with an emission reduction of 50 per cent, classified as "relatively low-emission" vehicles, a permanently reduced motor-vehicle tax on 13.20/100 cm^3 piston displacement will be granted (instead of the present DM 14.40/100 cm^3 piston displacement). For a one-third reduction of emissions due to the fitting of depolluting equipment, this lower rate will be applicable for three years;
- For all other cars without depolluting equipment, a higher tax rate (DM 18.80/100 cm^3) will be payable from 1st January 1986 onward. For new cars with conventional exhaust technology and the corresponding emissions coming onto the road after this date, a DM 21.60 tax will have to be paid.

This means that DM 18.80 is payable if these vehicles come into service for the first time by 31st December 1985, and DM 21.60 after 1st January 1986. For diesel vehicles recognised as "low-emission" vehicles and which came into service for the first time after 1st January 1985, tax exemption will cover only half the period set for gasoline-driven vehicles. The result of these measures was that already more than 4 million cars complied with these emission standards at the end of 1986.

To encourage the use of unleaded petrol in the Federal Republic of Germany, the mineral oil tax charged for unleaded gasoline was reduced by DM 0.02 for the period from 1st April 1985 to 31st December 1985. From 1st January 1986 to 1st April 1987, the tax will be reduced by DM 0.05, between 1st April 1987 and 1st April 1988 the reduction will be DM 0.04 and then until 1st April 1989, the reduction will be DM 0.03. Mineral oil tax for other light fuel oils has been increased by DM 0.02 for the period between 1985 and 1991. At the end of 1986 unleaded petrol had a market share of 18% and leaded regular petrol a share of 30%.

Economic incentives are also introduced by other countries, for example, in Austria, the Netherlands, Sweden and Switzerland. The envisaged system in the Netherlands is a tax reduction for new cars sold of DFL 1700 and 850 (engines with an engine displacement up to 1.4 litre).

2. REGULATIONS ON NOISE EMISSIONS

The OECD Conference on Noise Abatement Policies held in April 1980 concluded that the existing noise emission limits for new cars were too lenient and that technology was available at reasonable costs to make possible, between 1985 and 1990, a reduction of 5 to 10 decibels in the noise emission of new motor vehicles, i.e. to bring it down to 75 dB(A) for motor cars and motor cycles, and 80 dB(A) for trucks and buses. In 1985 these limits were not yet enforced (Table 7).

It should be noted, however, that in October 1986, Switzerland is to adopt two of the OECD conclusions: 75 dB(A) for cars and 80 dB(A) for buses.

Various regulations and test methods apply to noise emissions from motor vehicles. The EEC countries, Japan and the United States have different regulations based on different test procedures. Tests differ by the 'acceleration' concept (partial and full acceleration) and the disposition of the microphonic area.

The first EEC Directive relating to the permissible sound level and the exhaust system of motor vehicles was enacted in 1970 and has been amended several times. The test procedure is based on "full acceleration" test, ISO 362. A reduction of regulatory levels for noise emissions from new vehicles was decided in 1984.

The new EEC values are shown in Table 3. These regulations will be mandatory from October 1988 or October 1989, depending on vehicle category. For vehicles with a maximum permissible mass of over two tonnes designed for off-road use, the limit values are increased by 1 dB(A) if their engine power is less than 150 kW, and by 2 dB(A) if their engine power is equal to or greater than 150 kW.

Table 4 shows noise emission levels in the United States (it should be emphasised that about 6 dB(A) should be added to the emission levels to make them correspond to the European levels, because of the different test procedures).

Buses must meet these standards within an in-use period of two years or 200 000 miles, whichever occurs first. However, this is not tested at any regular vehicle inspections. Buses are tested according to a modified acceleration sound level test procedure, SAE J 366b. Buses equipped with engine brakes are tested according to a specified deceleration test procedure.

In Japan noise emissions are measured at three levels: steady cruising noise, stationary noise and acceleration noise. Procedure for the latter test, TRIAS 20, is similar to the ISO R 362 procedure. Table 5 illustrates noise levels which may not be exceeded by new vehicles measured according to TRIAS 20.

According to these procedures, noise by vehicles in use may not exceed 85 dB(A) (with the exception of acceleration noise). Planned targets under TRIAS 20 are 83 dB(A) for vehicles with a maximum power output of 147 kW, 78 dB(A) for other cars, 75 dB(A) for two-wheeled motor vehicles, and 72 dB(A) for all motor-driven cycles.

Current and future standards for heavy vehicles are shown in Table 6. Here again, there is no tendency towards increased harmonization. Noise standards for various types of motor vehicles are shown in Table 7.

The Netherlands has a voluntary standard for lower noise emissions which can be met by changes to the vehicle after purchase. The future (1989) EEC noise emission standards (84/424) have also been adopted by the UN Economic Commission for Europe (ECE).

Table 3. EEC DIRECTIVE ON NOISE

Vehicle categories	Value expressed in dB(A)
Vehicles intended for the carriage of passengers and equipped with not more than nine seats, including the driver's seat	77[a]
Vehicles intended for the carriage of passengers and equipped with more than nine seats, including the driver's seat, and having a maximum permissible mass of more than 3.5 tonnes and:	
–With an engine power of less than 150 kW	80
–With an engine power not less than 150 kW	83
Vehicles intended for the carriage of passengers and equipped with more than nine seats, including the driver's seat; vehicles intended for the carriage of goods:	
–With a maximum permissible mass not exceeding 2 tonnes	78[a]
–With a maximum permissible mass exceeding 2 tonnes but not exceeding 3.5 tonnes	79[a]
Vehicles intended for the carriage of goods and having a maximum permissible mass exceeding 3.5 tonnes:	
–With an engine power of less than 75 kW	81
–With an engine power of not less than 75 kW but less than 150 kW	83
–With an engine power of not less than 150 kW	84

a) The limit values shall be increased by 1 dB(A) if vehicles are equipped with a direct injection diesel engine. For vehicles with a maximum permissible mass of over two tonnes designed for off-road use, the limit values are increased by 1 dB(A) if their engine power is less than 150 kW and 2 dB(A) if their engine power is equal to or greater than 150 kW.

Table 4. NOISE EMISSION STANDARDS IN THE UNITED STATES

Vehicle	Sound level dB(A)	Date in effect
Passenger cars	No federal regulations State regulations exist	
Medium + heavy trucks (>4.5 tonnes)	83 (89)[a]	1978
	80 (86)[a]	1986
Buses	83 (89)[a]	1979
	80 (86)[a]	1983
Motorcycles	83 (89)[a]	1980
	80 (86)[a]	1982
Mopeds	70 (76)[a]	1980

a) Correspondence with European levels, in brackets.

Table 5. NOISE EMISSION STANDARDS IN JAPAN

Type of vehicle	Engine power (kW)	Weight (tonnes)	Sound level dB(A)	Date in effect
10 passengers	–	–	78 (70)[a]	1982
Trucks, buses	–	≤ 3.5	78 (74)[a]	1984
all wheel-drive motor vehicles		≤ 3.5	78 (74)[a]	1985
id.	≤ 147	> 3.5	83 (78)[a]	1983
id.	> 147	> 3.5	83 (80)[a]	1985
Buses, > 10 passengers	> 147	> 3.5	83 (80)[a]	1984
Two wheeled	(> 250 cc)		75 (74)[a]	1987
id.	(125-250 cc)	–	75 (74)[a]	1985
Motor driven cycles	(50-125 cc)	–	72 (70)[a]	1986
Motor driven cycles	(≤ 50 cc)	–	72 (70)[a]	1984

a) Noise levels within parenthesis refer to steady cruising noise and stationary noise.

Table 6. CURRENT AND FUTURE NOISE EMISSION STANDARDS FOR HEAVY MOTOR VEHICLES WITH A MAXIMUM POWER OUTPUT OF > 147/≤ 147 kW

Country	Standard dB(A)	Regulation	Future standard dB(A)	Implementation	Regulation
Australia	89/87	ADR 28 A			
EEC	88/86	77/212	88/86	1984-85	81/334[a] 84/372[a] 84/424
Finland	91/89				
Japan	83				
Netherlands	85/83	WIR[b]	85/83		Test method acc to 81/334
Norway	88/86	BOK 14			
Sweden	88/86	BOF 33			
Switzerland	86/84	BAV Anhang 4	84/82	1986	
USA	83	EPA Part 205	80	1986	As before

a) Modified test method.
b) Not mandatory.

Table 7. PRESENT AND FUTURE NOISE EMISSION LIMITS FOR MOTOR VEHICLES[a]

Country	Passenger car	Small van (under 3.5t)	Small bus (under 3.5t)	Heavy lorry (under 150 kW)	Large bus (under 150 kW)	Very heavy lorry (over 150 kW)	Very large bus (over 150 kW)	Big motorcycles (over 500 cc)
EEC[b]								
Present	80	81	81	86	82	88	85	86
Future (1988)		78-	78-					
(1995)	77	79	79	83	80	84	83	80
Switzerland								
Present	77	79	79	84	82	86	84	85
Future (Oct. 1986)	75	77	77	82	80	84	82	80
Japan								
Present	78	78	78	83	83	83	83	78
Future (Oct. 1987)								75
United States								
Present	-	-	-	89	86	89	86	86
Future	-	-	-	86	83	86	83	83
Australia								
Present	81	82	82	87	86	89	88	84
OECD Conference proposals (1985-1990)	75	75	75	80	80	80	80	75

a) Measured at 7.50 metres from accelerating vehicle (ISO R362) in dB(A).
b) EEC – European Economic Community: Belgium, Denmark, France, Germany, Greece, Ireland, Italy, Luxembourg, the Netherlands, the United Kingdom; plus, as of 1.1.86, Portugal and Spain.

Chapter II

THE IMPORTANCE OF TEST PROCEDURES

1. RELEVANCE OF TEST PROCEDURES

The previous chapter reviewed the standards adopted by different countries on noise and air pollution from motor vehicles; but these standards are meaningless without uniform, repeatable test procedures by which compliance can be measured. Standards are therefore always associated with a specific test procedure which describes the way the vehicle or engine is to be used, and stipulates sampling and analytical techniques for measuring noise or chemicals or analogs of chemicals in samples of exhaust gas. An ideal test procedure would have the following characteristics:

- It should be representative of the operating conditions that are considered important from an environmental point of view;
- It should be repeatable, accurate, quick and inexpensive;
- It should measure the "pollutants" concerned;
- It should be comprehensive enough to cover several driving modes and prevent the possibility of complying with a standard that will not give the desired overall effect.

In practice, all existing test procedures reflect compromises with regard to the above objectives. Test conditions which may be appropriate for one pollutant or one type of problem may not be appropriate for another.

2. AIR POLLUTION

Light-Duty Vehicle Testing

As time has passed, all the major test procedures for light-duty vehicle exhaust emissions around the world have tended towards the collection of a diluted exhaust gas sample in a small plastic bag by means of a constant volume sampler (CVS). Hydrocarbons (exhaust as well as evaporative) are measured by a flame ionization detector (FID), carbon monoxide by non-dispersive infrared (NDIR) analyzers and nitrogen oxides by chemiluminescence analyzers. These changes have also been incorporated in the ECE 15-04 regulation. The difference still resides in the driving cycle.

The US test cycle was developed to represent urban driving, starting with relatively high-speed suburban driving (max 90 km/h), followed by a lower average speed resembling city driving. This test cycle has been complemented by a fuel economy cycle at medium speed (average 77 km/h). The European driving cycle represents urban driving with a maximum speed of 50 km/h. The first ECE standards included only CO and HC, which at that time were considered to be the principal pollutants. In 1977 NO_x standards were added, but the test cycle remained the same.

In a review of various car manufacturers' studies, Volkswagen concluded that the driving cycle at present used in Europe no longer reflects the average traffic pattern in European cities, although it is still representative of driving conditions in inner city areas. With respect to CO and HC emissions, the difference between the two test cycles is less pronounced and some argue that in fact the ECE cycle is more stringent than the US one for HC and CO. The major difference is with regard to NO_x, as NO_x emissions to a large extent originate from accelerations and from driving at high speed.

Development of an entirely new urban and intercity driving cycle for Europe would be expensive and time consuming. This approach could delay the introduction of effective measures to reduce air pollution. To avoid this problem, Sweden and Switzerland have adopted the US test procedure. Most manufacturers already have the capability to conduct this test; in fact, most have a considerable data base and a high degree of expertise, which is another advantage. Besides, the cycle simulates a reasonable duty cycle which can be expected by most vehicles travelling in modern urbanised areas. The EEC has decided to complement the existing ECE test cycle with a high speed test procedure stating that European driving conditions are different from those in other parts of the world.

The two Japanese driving cycles, 10-mode hot start and 11-mode cold start, are different. The cycles do not try to simulate any specific road route, but are composed of typical Japanese urban transient conditions.

The Importance of Cold Temperatures

All official emissions tests are performed under carefully controlled laboratory conditions in order to minimise variability of test results due to factors such as temperature and humidity. This ensures that approximately the same test results will be obtained wherever or whenever a test is run on a vehicle. Since the tests are run in a laboratory, they are always run at a comfortable room temperature – about 75°F or 20-22°C. However, many of the carbon monoxide problems across Canada, North American and Nordic countries occur at much lower temperatures. Moreover, vehicles tend to emit greater amounts of CO as temperatures are reduced because the engine must be given excess fuel to start up and continue running under cold conditions. Furthermore, certain emission control components, such as the catalytic converter, do not operate effectively until fully warmed up. However, experience has shown that, as CO standards are lowered, emissions tend to be lowered across all temperature ranges at cold start.

Heavy-Duty Vehicle Testing

There are at present two major test procedures for heavy-duty engines, the so called steady state test (9-mode for gasoline trucks and 13-mode for diesel trucks) and the transient test. The transient test was adopted by the US Environmental Protection Agency (EPA) when it adopted stringent HC and CO standards, for several reasons:

- The steady state test was considered unrepresentative of the way trucks are driven in urban areas, since extensive testing over many years in New York and Los Angeles indicated that about 50 per cent of the time trucks are operated in "transient" modes (i.e. accelerations or decelerations) and there are no transient modes on the steady state test;
- The transient test includes a cold start, whereas the steady state test does not;
- The steady state test is more amenable to selective controls than the transient test.

The transient test has recently been modified by the EPA to incorporate certain changes in engine loading, etc., suggested by the truck industry.

At the same time that the United States has been moving away from the steady state test, the ECE has adopted it, but with changes of the weighting factors used in the 13 mode test. There is also a difference in the analytical system for the measured pollutants. The European test procedure gives lower HC emission values and may give slightly higher NO_x emissions than the US counterpart according to data of the Swedish Environmental Protection Board.

3. NOISE

Passenger Vehicles

The first international recommendation pertaining to noise test procedures, ISO R 362, was published in 1964. It was intended to be used for all kinds of motor vehicles in the same manner. The section that has been applied most widely describes a test where the maximum drive-by noise level for full acceleration of the vehicle is determined.

The approach speed before commencing the acceleration was adapted to urban driving conditions. The test was normally carried out in second gear. Since commercial vehicles with more than four gears were included in this rule, it seemed appropriate to test them in third gear, in order to keep them from reaching the engine speed at which maximum power is developed or maximum engine speed permitted by the governor too soon.

During the 60s and 70s, more and more passenger cars were equipped with five manual forward gears. They automatically profited from the third gear testing conditions for noise certification. In some cases a noise level difference or 4 to 5 decibels between test results in second gear and test results in third gear was obtained though normally the difference was 1-2 dB(A). Therefore the rule of carrying out the test in second and third gear was defined, and the mean level between those two gears was postulated for passenger cars with more than four forward gears in ISO 362. ISO 362 was first proposed in 1976, and published in its final form in 1980. It was adopted by ECE in 1980, and by EEC in 1981, with appropriate lead time given to enforcement by the corresponding national authorities.

ISO was also requested to prepare a new test method that more accurately reproduces urban driving conditions. The resulting development of ISO DIS 7188.2, was influenced in part by the fear that further reductions in the legal noise certification limits, according to ISO 362, may not be effective in town driving. This was because the technical problems of engine encapsulation were still far from being resolved. Therefore further reductions of the certification noise limits may have had to be met by design changes specifically tailored to modifying the car's behaviour under the test conditions, with no real benefit in urban driving. Fortunately the necessary technical solutions are available today.

The development of ISO 7188.2 was based on extensive studies of car and driver behaviour in towns for a representative cross-section of the car models available at that time (1976). The proposed method is based on a constant speed test and an acceleration test. The approach speeds tend to be lower than with ISO 362. This can cause problems with background noise at the measuring side and may seriously limit the possibility of promoting quieter cars.

If the method is to be considered in the future, it would have to be complemented by limits applicable to the acceleration test alone, and be based on levels exceeded during only 1 per cent of urban driving time. Also the available specifications for the road surface at the measuring sites are far from being sufficient to ensure consistent results, because this influence will be much more pronounced than for present methods. It is very doubtful that this method can be of any use in promoting the development of quieter vehicles.

Commercial Vehicles

Commercial vehicles were first tested according to the ISO recommendation R 362, and third gear was used. With continuously increasing engine power available, these vehicles accelerated too rapidly and the test method was not representative. This made the test become equivalent to a constant speed condition with reduced load on the engine. To correct this, the standard ISO 362 requires the gear ratio to be increased systematically until the position producing the highest noise level is found. The noise levels measured in this way tend to be 2 to 4 decibels higher than for the earlier method.

In the case of the US test procedure (EPA Part 205), the sound level is measured at double the distance from the vehicle centre line; this results in approximately 6 dB(A) lower levels than the ISO 362 procedure.

Motorcycles

Motorcycles present a special measurement problem, because they comprise a particularly wide range of engine sizes and corresponding engine power, and because both manual gearboxes and automatic gears are available. The original test only distinguished the different types of gears. The development of motorcycles with more powerful engines soon began to emphasize the approach condition of 50 km/h in third gear. For this reason, a Swiss regulation of 1982 specifies that all motorcycles should be tested in second gear, starting with an entry speed of 75 per cent of the speed at which the engine develops its maximum power. It is claimed that this rule has already had an influence on some designs by reducing the maximum engine speed, which is the most effective way of reducing noise levels.

Under the ECE 40 test procedure for motorcycles having a cubic capacity exceeding 175 cm^3 and a gearbox with five gears or more, the motorcycle is tested in second and third gear, the mean value of the two tests being taken as the result. Motor vehicles with smaller engine size, but five gears or more, are tested only in third gear. Irrespective of engine capacity, motorcycles having four gears or less are tested in second gear. The approach speed is 50 km/h.

For motorcycles with automatic gearbox, the approach speed can be 30, 40 and 50 km/h, or 75 per cent of the maximum road speed if that value is lower. The speed producing the highest sound level is chosen.

Mopeds

Full acceleration tests and tests with speed equal to the maximum speed attainable are used.

Chapter III

EXHAUST EMISSION CONTROL TECHNOLOGIES

1. GASOLINE-FUELLED CARS

Before controls were required, engine crankcases were vented directly to the atmosphere. Crankcase emission controls, which basically consist of a closed connection from the crankcase vent port to the intake side of the engine, were introduced on new cars in the early 60s, with the result that today control of these emissions is no longer considered a serious technical concern for natural aspirated engines.

Hydrocarbon evaporative emissions result from distillation of fuel in the carburettor float bowl and evaporation of fuel in the fuel tank. One way of controlling these emissions is to trap them and feed them back into the engine to be burned along with the other fuel.

By far the most difficult emission problems are those related to vehicle exhaust. The following section briefly reviews the combustion factors which most influence emission rates, the critical design variables which can be modified to reduce emissions and, finally, the technologies available for addressing the above problems.

As a basic principle and for the sake of an environmentally-sound strategy, any sort of preventive or curative emission control technology operating respectively at source or as exhaust after treatment should be as far as possible reliable, durable under all driving conditions, tamper-proof, easy to maintain whilst not deteriorating fuel economy.

Combustion and Emissions

Emissions of hydrocarbons (hundreds of different chemical compounds) are largely the result of incomplete fuel combustion. The amounts emitted are primarily related to the air/fuel mixture inducted, the peak temperatures and pressures in each cylinder, combustion chamber geometry and ignition timing.

Nitrogen oxides are generally formed during conditions of high temperature and pressure and excess air (to supply oxygen). Peak temperatures and pressures are affected by a number of engine design and operating variables and, accordingly, so are the concentrations of nitrogen oxides in the exhaust.

Carbon monoxide results from incomplete combustion of the carbon contained in the fuel, and its concentrations are generally governed by complex stoichiometry and equilibrium considerations. The only major engine design or operating variable which seems to affect its concentrations is the air/fuel mixture; the leaner the mixture or the more air per quantity of fuel, the lower the carbon monoxide emission rate.

Finally, lead compounds (and their associated scavengers) are exhausted by an automobile almost directly in proportion to the amounts which are fed into the vehicle.

Engine Modifications

As the above section indicates, certain key engine design variables can cause significant increases or decreases in emissions. Most notable among these are air/fuel ratio and mixture preparation, ignition timing, combustion chamber design and compression ratio.

Air/Fuel Ratio and Mixture Preparation

CO emissions are almost totally dependent on air/fuel ratio, whereas HC and NO_x emission rates can be strongly influenced by other engine design parameters. CO emissions can be dramatically reduced by increasing air/fuel ratio to the lean side of stoichiometric. HC emissions can also be reduced significantly until flame speed becomes so slow that pockets of unburned fuel are exhausted before full combustion occurs, or if extreme misfire occurs. Conversely, NO_x emissions increase as air/fuel mixtures are enleaned up to a maximum point; beyond this point, further enleanment can result in lower NO_x emission rates. To achieve this, mixture preparation and thereby the fuel system must be improved.

Ignition Timing

Ignition timing is the second most important engine control variable affecting "engine out" HC and NO_x from modern engines. When timing is optimised for fuel economy and performance, HC and NO_x emissions are also relatively high (actual values depending, of course, on other engine design variables). When ignition timing is delayed (retarded), peak combustion temperatures tend to be reduced, thereby lowering NO_x and peak thermal efficiency. A 3 per cent decrease of NO_x emissions per degree of initial timing retard, accompanied by a 1 per cent loss in fuel economy, has been reported. The tests were limited to a maximum retard of 5° and apply for city driving only. Excessive retard could, however, cause engine durability problems. By encouraging combustion to continue after the exhaust port is opened, thereby resulting in higher exhaust temperatures, oxidation of unburned hydrocarbons is greater and overall hydrocarbon emissions reduced. On the negative side, fuel consumption is increased.

Compression Ratio and Combustion Chamber Design

Increases in compression ratio lead to improved thermal efficiency and concomitantly increased specific power and reduced specific fuel consumption.

Compression ratios can be linked to combustion chamber shapes and in combination can have a significant impact on emissions. Higher surface to volume ratios will increase the available quench zone and lead to higher hydrocarbon emissions; conversely, more compact shapes such as the hemispherical or pent roof types reduce heat loss, thus increasing maximum temperatures, which tends to increase the formation of NO_x while reducing HC. Further, combustion chamber material, size and specific design such as swirled and cross-flow chambers, associated to spark plug location, can have an impact on emissions and fuel economy. In general, because of higher thermal conductivity, aluminium cylinder heads lead to lower combustion temperatures and therefore lower NO_x rates, but at the expense of increased HC emissions. Since the length of the flame path has a strong influence on engine detonation and therefore fuel octane requirement, larger combustion chambers which can lower HC emissions tend to be used only with lower compression ratios.

Intake Charge Dilution by Exhaust Gas Recirculation (EGR)

Charge dilution of homogeneous charge engines by excess air and by exhaust gas recirculation has been used for many years. Recirculating a portion of the exhaust gas back into the incoming air/fuel mixture (EGR), thereby lowering peak cycle temperature, is now frequently used as a technique for lowering NO_x.

On conventional engines, the use of excess air alone seems to cause relatively small NO_x reductions. However, when EGR is incorporated, substantially higher NO_x reductions have been demonstrated.

Fuel consumption can be increased, maintained, or decreased, depending on the type of engine and EGR-system used.

The first-generation systems recirculated exhaust gas in approximately inverse proportion to engine load. Such systems can significantly impair performance and fuel economy. Venturi vacuum and sonic systems electronically guided can yield flows that increase with engine load. These are the most advanced systems and provide the least impact on driveability. The latest technique for improving dilution tolerance is to increase the burn rate or flame speed of the airfuel charge.

Electronics

Modifications in spark timing must be closely co-ordinated with air/fuel ratio changes and degrees of EGR unless significant fuel economy or performance penalties result from emissions reductions, or NO_x emissions increase as CO goes down. In addition, controls which can be much more selective, depending on engine load or speed, have been found beneficial in preventing widespread adverse impacts.

To address these problems, electronics have begun to replace more traditional mechanical controls. For example, electronic control of ignition timing has demonstrated an ability to optimise timing under all engine conditions and has the added advantage of reduced maintenance and improved durability as compared with mechanical systems. When coupled with electronic control of EGR, it has been demonstrated that NO_x emissions can be reduced with no fuel economy penalty and, in some cases, with an improvement.

With electronic controls, it is possible to control critical engine parameters resulting in much lower "engine out" emission levels prior to any exhaust aftertreatment.

Exhaust Aftertreatment

The approaches which receive close scrutiny when tighter exhaust emission standards (especially hydrocarbons or nitrogen oxides) are considered are exhaust aftertreatment devices such as catalytic converters and thermal reactors. Three main catalytic systems are used today. The three-way catalyst is currently the most common and is sometimes combined with an oxidation catalyst. An electronic closed loop system is required to control the air/fuel mixture at strict stoichiometric. Normally the catalyst is efficient when reaching a temperature of about 225 °C.

The combination of a reduction catalyst to reduce NO_x emissions and an oxidation catalyst to take care of HC and CO emissions has also been used. Normally it is necessary to provide excess air before the oxidation catalyst. A more fuel-efficient possibility is the combination of an oxidation catalyst with an effective EGR system to reduce NO_x emissions.

The utilisation of catalyst systems should be contemplated together with an integrated optimisation of the engine-exhaust emission system.

Oxidation Catalysts

An oxidation catalyst will oxidize almost all the HC and CO in the exhaust stream. In general, monolith systems lend themselves to reduced size and weight, whereas pelleted systems tend to be slightly less expensive.

Starting in 1975, catalysts were placed on upwards of 80 per cent of all new cars sold in the United States, and by 1981 they were being placed on 100 per cent of new cars. In Japan and Canada, oxidation catalysts are also widely used to meet emission standards. From 1986 onwards, they will be required on most new cars in Australia.

Three-Way Catalysts

Three-way catalysts (so called because of their ability to lower HC, CO and NO_x levels simultaneously) were first introduced in the United States in 1977 by Volvo and subsequently widely used when the US NO_x standard was made more stringent, 0.6 g/km. It is necessary to control air/fuel mixtures much more precisely than for oxidation catalyst systems. As a result, three-way management systems have indirectly fostered improved air/fuel management systems, such as advanced carburettors and throttle body fuel injection systems, as well as closed-loop electronic controls of fuel metering. A three-way catalyst combined with a closed-loop system operates at stoichiometric air/fuel ratio to effectively reduce pollutants.

Three-way catalyst systems are also sensitive to the use of leaded gasoline. An occasional tankful of leaded gasoline will have a small but lasting cumulative effect on the level of emitted pollutants.

Features of Catalyst Systems

The current standard for exhaust hycrocarbon emissions in most countries reflects reductions in total hydrocarbons. However, since catalytic converters tend to selectively oxidize the more reactive hydrocarbons more easily than methane, a greater proportion of the hydrocarbon species which participate in the photochemical reactions leading to smog will be reduced by catalysts.

Aldehydes are the most prevalent oxygenated organic species in gasoline engine exhaust and tend to be highly photochemically reactive and to contribute directly to eye irritation. Aldehydes are effectively reduced by catalysts.

Emissions of polycyclic organic matter (POM) are of particular concern because of the well-established direct carcinogenic effects of, for instance, certain specific PAH compounds which have been detected in vehicle exhaust. PAH emissions from gasoline-powered cars are reduced substantially by controls designed to reduce hydrocarbons and carbon monoxide, but catalytic converters can almost eliminate them.

The three-way catalyst system will reduce not only HC, CO and NO_x, but also unregulated exhaust emission components as shown in Figure 2, where a comparison is made between two cars designed for the Swedish market and two others for the US market (three-way catalysts). An oxidation catalyst will reduce the same components with the exception of NO_x.

A catalyst is, by definition, always unaltered. However, the catalyst could degrade in use over a lifetime. The efficiency of the catalyst is affected by misfuelling, tampering, etc. To minimize misfuelling, measures could be taken to assure that the consumer does not have to pay more for unleaded fuel than for leaded.

Thermal Reactors

Thermal reactors are used to promote oxidation of CO and HC emitted from the engine. A major problem with these systems is the difficulty in maintaining exhaust temperatures sufficiently high to promote combustion. Measures to increase exhaust temperatures, such as retarded ignition, richer air/fuel ratios or valve timing delays, result in significantly increased fuel consumption.

A hybrid reactor concept has been reported to be capable of lowering HC and CO emissions to extremely low levels. In combination with the use of EGR, this system has reportedly also achieved 0.6 g/km NO_x. The concept involves a turbulent flow system, port liners, and a thermal reactor.

Advanced Combustion Techniques

Modification of the basic combustion process is proceeding along several fronts in work by a number of engine manufacturers and research organisations. Summarised below are the major approaches receiving serious consideration.

Figure 2: **EXHAUST EMISSION MEASUREMENTS ACCORDING TO THE US FTP 1975**

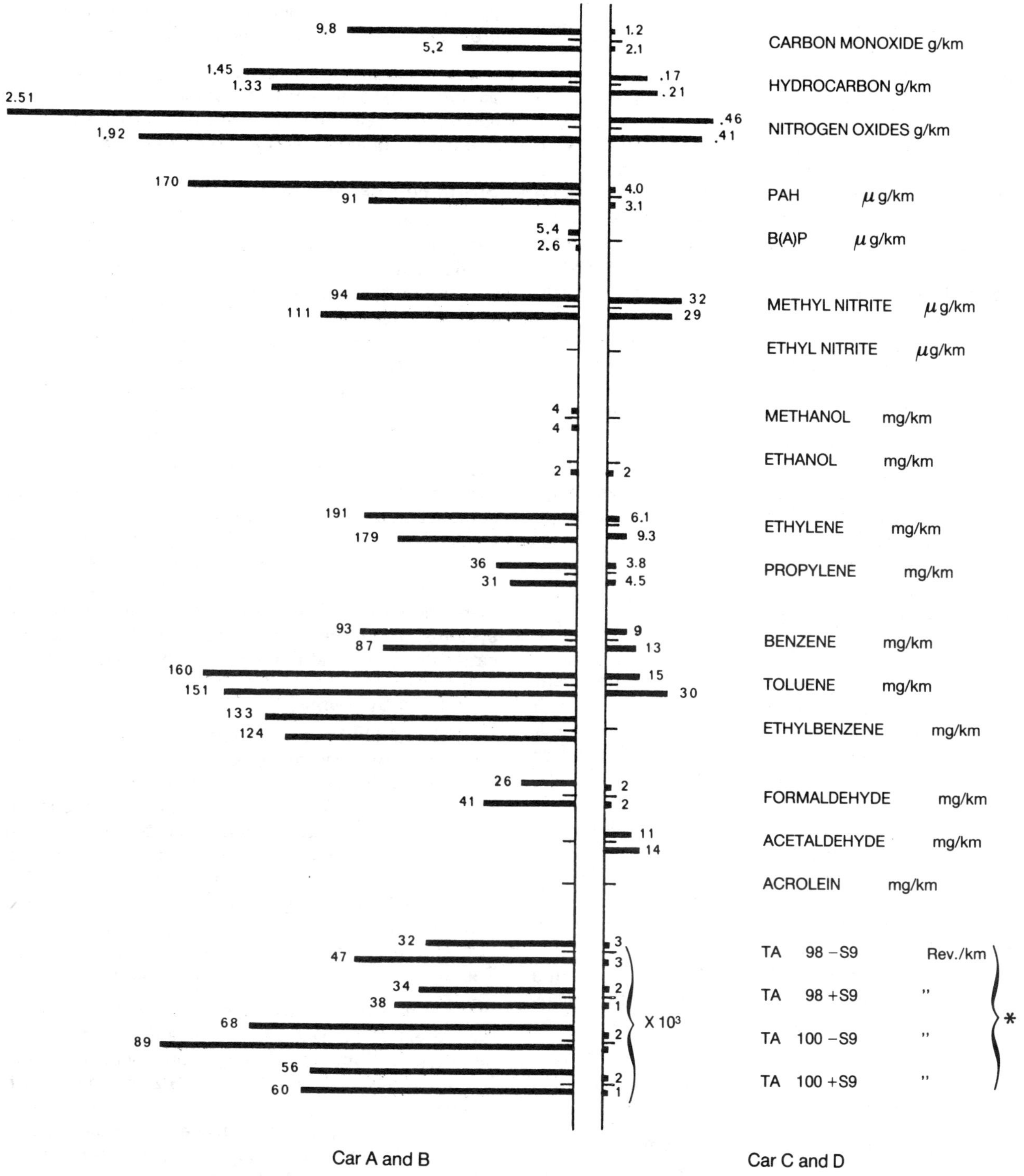

* Measurements of mutagenicity (Ames' test) on particulate fraction of exhaust.

Note: Cars A and B are designed for the Swedish market (without catalysts) whereas cars C and D are designed for the US market and equipped with three-way catalyst system and electronic fuel injection. (Ethyl nitrite and acrolein can sometimes be detected in exhaust emissions though not in these tests. Acet-aldehyde was found in exhaust from the catalyst equipped car but not from the car without catalyst. There is currently no explanation for this).

Source : Motor Vehicles and Cleaner Air, Swedish Government Committee on Automotive Air Pollution, 1983.

High-Compression Lean-Burn Engines

An alternative which could achieve lower emission levels with leaded gasoline and with potentially good fuel economy is the high-compression, lean-burn engine. By designing combustion chambers with great turbulence to promote mixing, compression ratios as high as 13:1 and air/fuel ratios in the range of 20:1 have been demonstrated without detonation. Such systems have also demonstrated very good fuel economy: about 20 per cent better than from more conventional engines. In addition, CO emissions are very low and NO_x emissions are lower than from conventionally controlled engines without catalysts. However, because exhaust temperatures are low and a high amount of quenching occurs, HC emissions tend to be quite high and have so far proved resistant to control. Furthermore, high-compression lean-burn engines require premium grade gasoline, very precise carburation and mixture control, as well as electronic ignition systems.

Manufacturers and research organisations around the world have been working intensively with such systems. The major impediment remains the high hydrocarbon emission rate, which does not appear amenable to solution without catalytic aftertreatment and unleaded gasoline.

Some recent data from the Netherlands are available. Three concepts have been studied:

- Carburetted engine with 15-20 per cent EGR, oxidation catalyst and "pulsair" to supply the amount of oxygen needed, approximate stoichiometric air/fuel ratio (typical for the Japanese or the US markets);
- Lean-burn engine with mechanical fuel injection, electronic ignition, 3-5 per cent EGR and oxidation catalyst;
- Lean-burn engine with electronic fuel injection, controlled ignition timing and fuel supply (i.e. "Engine Management") and oxidation catalyst.

Vehicle 3 is running without EGR, leaner and at a higher compression ratio than vehicle 2. Both engines have compact combustion chambers.

The vehicles equipped with engines 2 and 3 have been optimised for low fuel consumption and low emissions respectively.

When optimised for low fuel consumption, a gain in fuel efficiency of 12-20 per cent was reached over ECE and FTP driving cycles and somewhat less at higher speed. HC emissions were almost double, compared with a standard vehicle, and NO_x was slightly higher. When optimised for low exhaust emissions, fuel efficiency was down, but still some 10 per cent better than the standard vehicle. In an additional optimisation programme the lean burn plus oxidation catalyst vehicle showed the potential to meet the US 1983 equivalent emission levels at virtually the same fuel economy level as the economy optimised vehicle. Realisation of this concept in mass production still requires a major development effort.

Recently Toyota introduced a car meeting the Japanese exhaust emission standards and, at the same time, giving a 10 per cent better fuel economy. The car is equipped with an oxidation catalyst.

Stratified Charge Engines

In general, a stratified charge engine provides a controlled variation of air/fuel ratios within the combustion chamber – rich mixtures near the spark plug to initiate combustion, with the remainder, the largest portion of the charge, very lean. Potential advantages are lower emissions of all three regulated pollutants and low fuel consumption. In addition, stratified charge engines can be designed to use a wide variety of fuels.

The only production stratified charge engine is the Honda CVCC, which contains a prechamber where ignition of a fuel-rich mixture takes place. The resulting combustion continues into the main chamber, where a weak mixture is ignited. This engine produces substantially lower CO and NO_x emissions than more conventional engines, without the need for exhaust aftertreatment; however, HC emissions are similar to normal systems. Therefore, if tight control of HC is needed, catalysts or thermal reactors may be needed.

Fast-Burn Systems

The fast burn uses a homogeneous mixture, fast burn being intended to increase the lean ignition limit and thereby decrease NO_x emissions and, at the same time, increase EGR tolerance. More rapid combustion of the air/fuel mixture is promoted by reducing the flame travel distance. Thus end gas reaction time is lowered; concomitantly, engine octane requirements are reduced. Reliable ignition has to be provided by a sufficiently powerful ignition, and rapid combustion by strong turbulence of the charge and/or dual ignition. The system may achieve low NO_x emissions.

Several techniques have been used to increase burn rate, including increased swirl and squish, shorter flame paths, and multiple ignition sources. Nissan Motors has developed the NAPS-Z engine, which combines a fast-burn combustion system and a large-flow EGR system to achieve low exhaust emissions and high fuel efficiency. The EGR improves fuel efficiency due to a reduction in pump losses.

Relationship between Emission Control and Energy Conservation

Design of a modern passenger car involves a series of compromises or choices between traditional performance, cost, fuel consumption and emissions.

Experience to date has demonstrated that, with any given set of emission standards, it is possible to design and build vehicles emphasizing fuel economy and/or performance. It is also apparent that even without emission standards, vehicles can be built and sold with wide divergence in fuel economy and emissions; emission requirements reflect one additional constraint on the design. With or without further emission controls, very substantial improvements in fuel economy are possible, using existing technologies, albeit at a cost. It is this latter factor, cost (and not emission control), which appears to be the limiting or constraining factor in achieving any ultimate fuel economy level.

Many technologies which exist today to improve fuel economy – for example, advanced air/fuel management systems such as fuel injection, electronic control of spark timing, advanced choke systems, improved transmissions, etc. – can also result in significant exhaust emission benefits. In fact, some of the advances were developed as a direct result of tight emission control requirements.

The Ministry of Environment of Canada performed a comparison in which 1980 model continental European cars were compared with 1979-1982 model North American cars on the ECE "three-mode" fuel consumption test. In general, the vehicles sold in North America, whether of European, Japanese or US origin, showed equal or better fuel consumption than their European-sold counterparts. These results are especially significant in that the comparison is between "North American production automobiles tested in a government laboratory with data provided by manufacturers on European homologation prototypes".

As part of the EEC ERGA project [Evolution of Regulations, Global Approach (ERGA) to motor vehicles], the EEC Group of Car Manufacturers (CCMC) conducted a comparison of the emissions and fuel economy of vehicles designed for the European, Swedish and US markets. The results are summarised below:

PERCENTAGE CHANGE RELATIVE TO EUROPEAN COUNTERPARTS
Measured according to ECE 15-04

	United States	Sweden
Hydrocarbons	−85	−17
Carbon Monoxide	−76	+2
Nitrogen Oxides	−84	−35
City Fuel Consumption	+7	+14
90 km/h Fuel Consumption	+7	+10
120 km/h Fuel Consumption	+7	+7
Power	−7	−3
Acceleration 0-100 km/h	+11	+5
Cost	+11	+3

With regard to emissions, the US vehicles were significantly cleaner on average, while the Swedish vehicles were also better, except for CO. The US cars averaged about 7 per cent poorer fuel consumption, while the Swedish vehicles were somewhat worse. The US vehicles showed the poorest performance, with their Swedish counterparts about half-way between the US and European cars. The US cars were most expensive, with the Swedish cars only slightly more expensive than the European cars. It is important to note that the emission and fuel economy measurements were all based on the ECE test procedure.

A more careful look at the data, however, indicates that the differences between cars were in some cases greater than the differences between the groups. With regard to emissions, the US cars were always cleaner – usually by a substantial margin – and the costs were always greater. However, with regard to city fuel consumption, out of thirteen cars, four US cars were superior to their European counterparts (one car was actually 22 per cent better). Some US models were superior at 90 and 120 km/h as well. Performance was also superior on some of the US models.

A careful review of this data indicates that the selection of technology by individual manufacturers determines to what extent a fuel consumption penalty is associated with tight emissions standards. Also, the tighter the emissions standards are, the more likely it is that the better technology will be used.

Current experience indicates that vehicles may achieve very low exhaust emission levels for hydrocarbons, carbon monoxide and nitrogen oxides, alongside good fuel savings. A recent comparison between fuel consumption in IEA countries (members of the International Energy Agency) reveals that there need not be any fuel economy penalties due to more advanced emission control systems used in, for instance, Japan and the United States (Table 8). Comparison is based on cars of the same weight category.

The extent to which a fuel economy penalty is associated with compliance with emissions standards is controlled by any given manufacturer's choice of emission control system. With more sophisticated (and more costly) forms of emission control, fuel economy penalty can be minimised. On the other hand, with less optimised (and cheaper) systems of the type employed by manufacturers on pre-1975 cars in the United States, fuel economy penalties as high as 10 per cent are not unusual.

Cost of Emission Controls

Over several years, a series of studies has been conducted in the United States in an effort to arrive at reasonable estimates of the costs of various emissions

Table 8. COMPARISON OF AVERAGE FUEL CONSUMPTION LEVELS (URBAN CYCLE)[a] OF THE THREE TOP SELLING MODELS IN 1982 BY WEIGHT CATEGORY (l/100 km)

Country	800 kg	801-1 000 kg	1 001-1 200 kg	1 200 kg
Germany	7.6	9.1	10.3	11.9
Italy	7.3	8.2	11.3	8.8
Japan	6.1	6.7	8.1	10.9
United Kingdom	7.9	9.8	10.5	13.6
United States	6.6 (7.4)[b]	7.3 (8.2)[b]	9.5 (10.6)[b]	11.0 (12.3)[b]

a) Values are drawn from the urban fuel consumption test procedures used in each country.
b) Figures within parenthesis for the United States have been adjusted to the ECE test procedure.
Source: IEA, 1984.

standards. Through these studies, a cost model has evolved, which can be used to arrive at estimates of the initial cost paid by consumers to comply with the US emission standards. The cost estimates are based on an analysis of the retail price equivalent of each component in the emission control systems used in gasoline-fuelled cars. Two types of data are used in the analysis: components (hardware) used in the emission control system of each new car are determined, and price estimates are applied to each component. The list of components on each car was obtained from the Application for Certification submitted to the US EPA by automobile manufacturers.

Table 9. NEW CAR PRICE INCREASES AS A FUNCTION OF EMISSION STANDARDS

In 1981 US dollars

Model year	HC/CO/NO_x g/km	Initial cost increase (dollars)
1968-69	5.9/50.8/–	30
1970-71	3.9/33.3/–	50
1972	3.0/28.8/–	70
1973-74	3.0/28.0/3.1	100
1975-76	1.5/15.0/3.1	150
1977-79	1.5/15.0/2.0	175
1980	0.41/7.0/2.0	225
1981	0.41/3.4/1.0	350

Source: Studies by US EPA, 1981.

Prices and price estimates were obtained from three sources: a study conducted for EPA; a price survey of dealer parts departments; and direct request to the manufacturers for parts price information.

Based on the above, new car price increases as a function of various emissions standards are estimated in Table 9. For the sake of uniformity, all emissions standards are based on the US 1975 test procedure along with the US compliance programme.

Another cost estimate has been undertaken in Sweden: going from present Swedish standards (comparable to US 1973) to meet US standards of 1983 would increase the price of a new car by about $500 (1981 price level), according to the Swedish Government Committee on Automotive Air Pollution. This includes additional cost for components, such as catalytic converter and control system, including, for example, fuel injection and electronic fuel metering. There are variations in the cost estimate from $300 to $1 000. Extra service cost was estimated to $10 per year, including increased cost for the new system as well as decreased cost because of improved engine-oil and spark-plug life due to the use of unleaded gasoline.

Together with change in fuel consumption and the supply of unleaded fuel, the extra cost per year and car was estimated to be $50-110.

Within the EEC ERGA work, comparisons were made between various exhaust emission control systems. A current (1983) conventional engine designed to comply with ECE-15.03 standards was used as a base-line.

High-compression lean-burn engines designed to meet ECE-15.04 standards would show a fuel economy gain of 4-15 per cent and result in an increased vehicle cost of 5 to 9 per cent. The latter figure includes an EGR system. To meet more stringent standards for HC, an oxidation catalyst would be necessary.

For engines with conventional compression ratio, the use of an oxidation catalyst and EGR would entail a fuel penalty of 8-12 per cent, of which 6 per cent refers to decreased compression ratio due to the use of RON 92 gasoline instead of RON 98. The additional cost would be 3-15 per cent of vehicle cost.

ERGA has also concluded that a three-way catalyst system would give consumption penalties of -5 per cent to +16 per cent (6 per cent attributable to low octane gasoline) and cost penalties between 4.4 per cent and 22 per cent, the highest relative cost increase being for small cars. However, other data presented earlier would lead to different cost penalties. The conclusion is rather that there is a wide range of cost estimates.

2. DIESEL-FUELLED CARS

In recent years there has been a trend towards diesel-equipped vehicles for private cars and all categories of commercial vehicles. While the energy advantages of the diesel are unquestioned, there is concern over the environmental consequences of increased dieselisation. Although inherently cleaner than gasoline engines from the standpoint of carbon monoxide (CO) and evaporative hydrocarbons (HC), diesels produce more aldehydes, sulphur oxides (because of the higher sulphur content in diesel fuel than in gasoline), polyaromatic hydrocarbons, and noise (see chapter IV for noise). However, most passenger car diesel engines emit less NO_x than their gasoline-fuelled counterparts. Offensive smoke and odour emissions are also a problem. Most importantly, however, uncontrolled diesel engines emit approximately 30 to 70 times more particulate than current gasoline-fuelled engines equipped with catalytic converters, and approximately ten times more than current gasoline engines without catalyst.

Combustion Technology

Two major approaches exist for meeting tight light-duty diesel particulate standards: engine modifications to lower engine out emission levels, and trap-oxidizers and their associated regeneration systems. Engine modifications include changes in combustion chamber design, fuel injection timing and spray pattern, turbocharging, and the use of exhaust gas recirculation. Using these techniques, average particulate emissions in the United States have been reduced from a mean of approximately 0.4 g/km in 1980 to about 0.2 g/km (based on US certification data). These reductions are even more remarkable in that they occurred simultaneously with a lowering of NO_x emission levels from 0.12 to under 0.09 g/km. This is significant because there is a trade-off between certain NO_x control techniques and particulate controls. Further particulate controls appear possible through greater use of electronically controlled fuel injection, which is currently under rapid development. However, a more thorough engine development is needed to achieve a considerable reduction of emission.

NO_x Control Techniques

EGR reduces combustion temperatures and thereby NO_x emissions. In the short term, use of first generation systems which employ constant EGR can also lead to increased particulate emissions. There is also concern about increased engine wear. However, in the longer term, electronically modulated EGR systems, combined with careful control of fuel injection timing should minimize or even eliminate any trade-offs.

Exhaust Aftertreatment

Exhaust aftertreatment methods include traps, trap oxidizers, and catalysts. Trap oxidizer prototype systems have shown themselves capable of 70 to 90 per cent reductions from engine out particulate emissions rates and, with proper regeneration, the ability to achieve these rates for high mileage. Three types of trap oxidizer systems show promise for commercial development:

- Ceramic monolith trap/burner regeneration system;
- Catalyzed wire mesh trap/regeneration by HC and CO enrichment of exhaust; and
- Ceramic monolith trap/self regeneration by means of fuel additives.

The regeneration systems require more development and, particularly, high mileage tests.

The US EPA estimated at the time it adopted the 0.12 g/km in 1980 that trap systems would average from $138 to $164 per vehicle over the first five model years; engine modifications were estimated to cost about $10 per vehicle. In 1982, the State of

California concluded that engine modifications should not increase the price of new cars at all, since most current models already achieve 0.25 g/km, but that trap systems could cost from $115-450 per car. Another study estimated $200-550 initial price increases.

EPA estimated no fuel penalty to be associated with either engine modifications or trap oxidizer systems. California estimated no additional cost for an estimated small and insignificant fuel economy penalty.

While EPA estimated that trap oxidizers would require maintenance at about five years of age, costing about $30 per car, it also estimated maintenance savings due to the reduced need for mufflers and resonators and the more durable exhaust pipe, at a saving of $80 per car, or a net saving of $50 per car.

3. TRUCKS AND BUSES

Trucks are shown to be a very important source of NO_x, smoke emissions, particulates and noise (see chapter IV for noise).

Stringent emission standards for heavy-duty vehicles equipped with diesel engines have not been developed as rapidly as for gasoline-powered light-duty vehicles. Therefore the development of control technologies for trucks and buses began later. However, more attention has lately been given to these categories of vehicles. Recently the US EPA set new regulations for light- and heavy-duty trucks and buses regarding NO_x and particulates. These standards will emphasize the need for new, efficient technology.

NO_x Control Technology

NO_x control techniques likely to be available in the near future include variable injection timing and pressure, charge cooling, especially when turbo charging is used, and possibly exhaust gas recirculation. Retarding injection timing, while a well-known method of reducing NO_x formation, can lead to increases in fuel consumption, particulate and hydrocarbon emissions. These problems can be mitigated to some extent by varying the injection timing with engine load or speed. If coupled with electronic controls, it appears that NO_x emissions could be reduced significantly, with a simultaneous improvement in fuel economy; however, the fuel economy increase could be even greater with electronic controls if NO_x control was not a concern. Optimizing all factors influencing combustion can lead to reduction of NO_x up to 30-40 per cent without loss in fuel economy.

To reduce fuel consumption and exhaust emissions in city buses with a stop-and-go driving pattern, new systems are being developed, for example, to store brake energy in pressure accumulators later to be used for acceleration, etc.

Control of Smoke and Particulates

Smoke emissions from diesel engines are regulated in several countries. Smoke results when there is an excess amount of fuel available for combustion, and this is most likely to occur under high engine load conditions, such as acceleration and engine lugging, when the engine needs additional fuel for power. Failure to clean or replace a dirty air cleaner may produce high smoke emissions. Vehicle operation can also be important. Selection of the proper transmission gear, according to engine load conditions, moderate accelerations, and strict respect of maximum vehicle loading, can minimize smoke emissions. The development of turbo charged engines has led to a reduction of particulate emissions, such as smoke emissions.

Particulate standards of 0.88 g/kWh (0.6 g/bhph) will be enforced by the US EPA in 1988. Ultimately (by 1991 and 1994 for buses and heavy trucks respectively), 0.14 g/kWh will be met. Control technologies are similar to those discussed for light-duty vehicles. Engine modifications include changes in combustion chamber design, fuel injection timing and spray pattern, turbocharging, and use of exhaust gas recirculation. Further particulate controls appear possible through greater use of electronically controlled fuel injection, currently under rapid development. Using such a system, signals proportional to fuel rate and piston advance position are measured by sensors and are electronically processed by the electronic control system to determine the optimum fuel rate and timing.

Exhaust Aftertreatment

Exhaust aftertreatment methods include traps, trap oxidizers, and oxidation catalysts of similar types as used for light vehicles. However, much less experience has been acquired. Catalysts will not solve the NO_x problem.

More stringent standards have been adopted in the United States for gasoline trucks up to 7 000 kg, starting 1987. This regulation will probably require the use of oxidation catalysts.

4. TWO-WHEELED VEHICLES

Two-wheeled vehicles, including motorcycles are responsible for a relatively small fraction of the total mileage in most countries and have therefore tended to receive minimal attention from an air pollution control standpoint. However, as cars and other sources achieve tighter emission standards, the relative pollution contribution from motorcycles increases. For example, it has been estimated that, per mile driven, uncontrolled motorcycles emit 22 times as much hydrocarbons and 10 times as much carbon monoxide as automobiles controlled to US 1978 levels. In addition, the contribution of motorcycles to certain local problems can be significant. Finally, some air quality problems are so severe that all reasonable controls of all sources will be necessary to achieve acceptable air quality levels.

Technologies available to control emissions from two-wheeled vehicles are the same as those available to other Otto cycle powered engines. Refining the fairly simple type of carburettors used would significantly reduce HC, CO and smoke emissions. Recently, the State of California concluded that even catalytic converters are technologically feasible for these engines.

Chapter IV

NOISE EMISSION CONTROL TECHNOLOGIES

1. VEHICLES AS NOISE SOURCES

The noise produced by motor vehicles consists mainly of propulsion noise and tyre/road noise. The propulsion noise is caused by noise radiation from the following sources:

- Engine block;
- Exhaust system;
- Cooling system;
- Air intake;
- Power train (transmission).

When the driving speed of a vehicle is not too high, for example within a city, the propulsion noise generally defines the overall noise of the vehicle. The noise certification procedures for vehicles are mainly aimed at measuring this characteristic. The engine speed and the power required are the primary variables controlling this noise. For equal power and speed, diesel engines typically exhibit a higher noise level.

The tyre/road noise level depends on the road surface, the tyre tread characteristics and the speed of the vehicle. At high driving speeds, such as used on a motorway, the tyre/road noise will determine the overall noise level of passenger cars and of many commercial vehicles. At a greater distance from the road, behind some shielding or inside a building, the tyre/road noise may be less dominant. Recently it has become evident that the road surface can have a significant influence on the overall noise level, including propulsion noise. In the case of porous (drainage-type) surfaces, the overall noise level is lower than for conventional asphalt or concrete roads.

The relative contribution of different vehicle types to the overall noise impact can be determined by roadside measurements in everyday traffic. This has been done recently in Germany for a large sample of vehicles under urban driving conditions. The greatest mean levels which were measured at 7.5 m are caused by heavy commercial vehicles with more than 147 kW engine power. Commercial vehicles in the power range below 147 kW cause mean levels in the range of 80 to 83 dB(A). Buses were found to behave like commercial vehicles of equal engine power. Light commercial vehicles using diesel engines with indirect fuel injection produced a mean sound level of 78 dB(A), which is about 2 dB(A) lower than was found for the same class with direct fuel injection. For all types of commercial vehicles and buses the spread of measured sound levels comprising 90 per cent of all values was of the order of 12 dB(A) [+6 dB(A)].

The results found for two-wheeled vehicles show a mean value of 78 dB(A) for regular motorcycles, and of 73 dB(A) for mopeds. In this vehicle group the spread covering 90 per cent of all measured levels is particularly large and extends to 17 dB(A) [+8.5 dB(A)]. This means that some motorcycle noise levels were equal to the most noisy commercial vehicles with engine powers greater than 200 kW.

The category of passenger cars gave a mean level of 73 dB(A) for gasoline engines, and 74 dB(A) for diesel engines. The total spread for 90 per cent of the measured levels was 10 to 12 dB(A).

The above results are based on more than 100 000 measurements taken at 45 different measuring sites. This means that not only the characteristics of the vehicles, but also the behaviour of the drivers and the road surface and traffic conditions were included in the survey. Corresponding data for long-distance traffic on main roads and on motorways is not at present available.

2. PASSENGER VEHICLES

A large number of approved passenger cars exhibit lower noise levels than 80 dB(A) based on the ISO 362. About 40 per cent are below 77 dB(A) and about 20 per cent do not exceed 75 dB(A). These results are influenced by the fact that some cars are five-gear cars tested in third gear. Automatic transmissions also give lower peak noise levels.

Several comprehensive studies have been carried out recently on methods for reducing the exterior noise levels of motor vehicles. They include data on some experimental cars, where considerable noise reductions were achieved. The most successful approaches include the following methods (however, the figures quoted cannot be added to give the overall effect):

- Redesign of the engine for lower engine speeds and greater displacement. This can reduce the engine noise levels by up to 6 dB(A);
- Redesign of the engine structure and configuration can reduce levels by 4 to 8 dB(A), but this measure will need more development time;
- Engine encapsulation can reduce engine noise by as much as 6 to 8 dB(A). Where complete enclosure is not feasible, shielding measures can achieve reductions up to 3 dB(A).

These measures generally do not increase fuel consumption, they cause only a slight increase in vehicle weight, and the cost of the vehicles is likely to be increased by 4 to 10 per cent of the retail price for an overall reduction of the vehicle noise level of 5 dB(A), based on the test method ISO R 362 or ISO 362.

Since only positive results concerning this kind of redesign are usually reported, it must be assumed that not all attempts have been successful, and that not all cars existing today lend themselves to these modifications.

Encapsulation will increase weight, but to a degree which will have only a marginal effect on fuel consumption, about 0.4 per cent per dB(A). It has been estimated that the weight increases by 5-10 kg per dB(A) unit reduction.

Encapsulation could increase fuel consumption, due to increased cooling requirement, or decrease it due to improved aerodynamics, better thermal efficiency of the engine and improved warm-up system. A Norwegian report states that the net effect of encapsulation with a noise reduction of 5-7 dB(A) is an improved fuel economy of 3-5 per cent. Some servicing penalties could occur. The use of thermal or catalytic converters to reduce air pollution could create heat problems when combined with encapsulation.

Gasoline engines are mostly optimised for the greatest possible power output, whereas diesel engines are often optimised for low fuel consumption and low maintenance cost. This has led to an increasing interest in diesel-powered passenger cars, although these are inherently more noisy, and have the yet unsolved problem of high noise levels immediately after starting a cold engine and generally at idling speeds. The proposed use of fuel-efficient, direct-injection diesel engines will further increase the noise levels up to 3 decibels. Compared to gasoline engines, the noise level could then be about 5-8 dB(A) higher. There are newly designed pre-chamber diesel powered passenger cars featuring between 71 and 75 dB(A), depending on type of transmission.

Turbocharging of gasoline and diesel cars will normally increase the noise level if measured during an acceleration test. However, some direct-injected diesel engines would benefit from turbocharging.

Exhaust noise can be reduced by about 5 dB(A) by improved design and position of the muffler. Defective exhaust systems are a significant source of noise. As for emission control, this highlights the importance of an inspection maintenance strategy.

Cars and Road/Tyre Noise

In the field of road/tyre noise, substantial research work has been carried out, and is still in progress. The modern designs of tread patterns have proved to be rather close to the optimum technology known to date, so that no break-through seems to be in sight. Work on the quality of the materials used still promises some improvements. As regards the overall shape of tyres, it is known that narrow tyres are substantially quieter. Unfortunately a recent research project has shown that high-powered cars are of necessity increasingly equipped with wide tyres, which can cause rolling noise to be up to 6 dB(A) higher than the average level for similar vehicles. This is an argument for the introduction of some kind of tyre-noise certification, but there is no international consensus yet on the methods to be used. However, it is important that no sacrifices be made as to existing tyre/road adhesion qualities.

Impact of Driving Habits on Noise

Driving habits have a very important impact on noise, as well as on fuel consumption. Two different driving styles can produce differences in vehicle noise levels of 4-6 dB(A) and a large difference in fuel consumption. It has been estimated that the average noise level can be reduced by 1-2 dB(A) for every litre of fuel saved per 100 km of urban driving by tighter and more strictly enforced speed limits. Generally, smooth driving reduces noise emissions and especially noise peaks.

Cost of Noise Reductions

The more recent cost estimates originate from the EEC ERGA Group on Noise (Table 10).

Noise reductions of 3 dB(A) from 80 dB(A) according to ISO R 362 would increase the cost of the car by 1-4 per cent. Reductions of 5 dB(A) could cost between 2-10 per cent of the vehicle cost. For most vehicles, however, the cost will be about 2-3 per cent.

In certain cases maintenance and repair costs may increase by about 1 per cent per dB(A) gained. A reduction of 5 dB(A) would increase operating cost per kilometre by about 2 per cent.

Additional weight caused by encapsulation or shielding could have an effect on taxation, as some countries (Denmark, the Netherlands and Sweden) impose annual car tax according to vehicle weight, and others (Japan and Portugal) use combinations of engine size and vehicle weight, while France uses taxation combining engine size and transmission ratio.

Table 10. ECONOMIC EFFECTS OF MORE STRINGENT NOISE EMISSION STANDARDS FOR CARS IN EEC COMPARED TO PRESENT LIMIT 80 dB(A)

EEC ERGA report

Proposed limit dB(A)	Increase in vehicle cost %	Increase in operating cost %	Variation in fuel consumption %	Lead time Years
78	0.5-2.5	2	1.6	2-5
77	1-4	3	2.4	3-7
75	2-10	5	2-5	5

Source: EEC, 1983.

3. TRUCKS AND BUSES

The propulsion noise from heavy vehicles is composed of noise from the engine, exhaust system, cooling system, air intake system and the power train, with the noise level decreasing in that order.

In a number of countries, commercial vehicles have been modified to provide experimental evidence and practical experience with low-noise versions. The noise reductions achieved have been very substantial, often reaching overall noise levels similar to current passenger vehicles. The methods employed usually excluded any change in engine design.

The current trend in the development of commercial vehicles is towards the use of diesel engines with turbocharging and intercooling of the air needed for combustion. This approach is favourable for noise reduction, but substantial improvements will still require extensive shielding around engines, or complete enclosures. The difficulties encountered are great, since thermal cooling in the order of magnitude of the mechanical power produced is also required, and the maximum permissible temperatures must be observed.

A future standard of maximum 80 dB(A) for heavy vehicles was recommended by the OECD Conference on Noise Abatement Policies in 1980, but is not yet implemented. Combustion is a significant noise source of diesel engines. Turbo-charging can reduce the noise level up to 3 dB(A). The use of intercooling may again increase the noise level by 1 dB(A). However, intercooling normally leads to decreased NO_x emissions.

Shielding of the engine combined with, for example, vibrational damping could reduce noise by up to 3 dB(A). Total enclosure or encapsulation of the engine compartment could entail a noise reduction of 8-13 dB(A).

One marketed truck with complete enclosure, the 7.5 t Magirus-Deutz, reaches a noise level of 77 dB(A) according to ISO R 362. This entails an extra weight of about 100 kg.

Various research projects in Europe on "quiet vehicles" are under way, showing that 80 dB(A), according to ISO 362, may be achieved with measures on the engine, encapsulation and improved muffler systems.

A US programme has also verified that heavy-duty trucks can reach 78 dB(A) according to ISO R 362. Noise control was achieved by partial engine and transmission enclosures and exhaust silencing systems. European trucks might have difficulties incorporating some of the US noise reduction solutions, due to the more limited space.

The feasibility of air-cooled diesel engines with encapsulation has been demonstrated in mass production, whereas water-cooled engines lend themselves less readily to this treatment due to the increased need for cooling air.

The design of exhaust muffler is normally a compromise between volume and back pressure increase due to flow resistance. Very efficient exhaust silencers have been demonstrated.

Complete engine encapsulation in buses is quite common. This is particularly suitable for buses with rear engines. Urban buses with encapsulated engines marketed in Europe show noise levels of 77 to 82 dB(A) according to ISO 362. In Germany, 90 per cent of all new buses registered now have encapsulated engines.

The market for commercial vehicles has traditionally been characterised by fierce competition that fully utilizes all legal specifications for the dimensions and weights of the vehicle components. For this reason it can easily become prohibitive to add even 1 per cent to the weight, or anything at all to the overall dimensions of a vehicle as it exists today. The transition from experimental quiet vehicles to regular production would be facilitated if certification requirements could be modified to exclude weight – and/or size – increases that are clearly due to noise reduction measures.

A special noise source that occurs only on commercial vehicles is the brake noise due to braking operations with the engine, and air release noise from pneumatic brakes. Some noise certification regulations already take these sources into account, but they should still be given general recognition. It is clear that this type of noise will become more important as noise from other sources in vehicles is reduced.

Cost of Noise Reductions

For trucks with an engine power of less than 150 kW, the 80 dB(A) target can be reached with an extra vehicle cost of 5-6 per cent. For heavy vehicles, a noise reduction from 88 to 83 dB(A) would increase vehicle cost by the same proportion. These estimates originate from the work within EEC, ERGA-Noise (Table 11).

Maintenance cost would increase by about 0.6 to 1 per cent per dB(A) gained. Total operating cost would rise by approximately 1-2 per cent, depending on the type of vehicle.

Table 11. ECONOMIC EFFECTS OF TIGHTER NOISE EMISSION STANDARDS FOR COMMERCIAL VEHICLES IN THE EEC COUNTRIES

Vehicle type	Present limit dB(A)	Proposed limit dB(A)	Variation in cost of vehicle %	Variation in operating cost %	Lead time Years
Urban buses	82	80	2-3.0	1.5	3-5
Coaches	85	80	5	1.5	5
Small commercial	81	79	5	2.0	2-5
(up to 3.5 t)		77	5	3.0	5
Heavy vehicles (over 3.5 t)		84	5	2.0[a]	3-5
< 75 kW	86	80	5	6.0[a]	4-8
		83	4	0.8[a]	3-8
75-150 kW	86	80	5	1.2[a]	5
		86	2.5-5.0		2-5
> 150 kW	88	83	5-10.0	1.3-1.6[a]	6

a) If encapsulation is necessary.
Source: EEC, 1983.

Heavy Vehicles and Road/Tyre Noise

Another serious problem exists in the field of road/tyre noise for some commercial vehicles. Although tread patterns with much improved noise characteristics have been developed for commercial vehicles, these cannot be used in the case of off-road vehicles, such as trucks that serve building sites. In this case only the introduction of speed limits based on the characteristics of the tyres could lead to an improvement. The available knowledge of tyre characteristics is probably sufficient to allow an adequate selection and some international rules for this purpose.

The same problem occurs once again for all kinds of commercial vehicles that use retreaded tyres. These tyres often cause the road/tyre noise of commercial vehicles to be more than 6 decibels higher than with the corresponding new tyres, largely because the tread patterns do not correspond to the latest designs. Since efforts are already being made with respect to controlling the safety aspects of retreaded tyres, this could well be extended on an international level to include noise characteristics. This could best be done as mentioned above, by specifying the maximum permissible speed on the road, and by providing clear markings that can be easily controlled by police organisations (such as with the use of spiked tyres on passenger cars).

Classification of Heavy Vehicles

In the case of commercial vehicles, the area of operation and the time of day for operating the vehicles will not be the same for all types. This means that the power of the engine (at present used to classify vehicles) is not the only valid criterion. Another approach could be to create two distinct classes according to noise emission. The general class could then be restricted to vehicles for long-haul operations and probably also off-road operations during the daytime. The second, low-noise class would comprise all the vehicles that should preferably be used in noise-sensitive periods and areas. This distinction can be made particularly effective, if the required characteristics can be defined by an internationally recognised, separate class for vehicle certification.

4. MOTORCYCLES

The most important means of reducing motorcycle noise are based on engine design. The attractiveness of this type of vehicle to the user lies in the capability for fast acceleration. The optimum engine speed for this is characterised by maximum available torque. Since noise reduction requires lower engine speeds, the only promising policy seems to be a certification method that controls the engine speed range concerned. This approach has brought some results, and would be far more effective if it were adopted on an international level.

The technology for exhaust silencer systems is available. They merely have the disadvantage of a slightly reduced power-to-weight ratio and increased cost.

It must be pointed out that high-powered motorcycle models are to be regarded as sports equipment rather than as a regular means of transportation. Therefore power restrictions in favour of the environmental protection of a far greater number of persons than are represented by the owners of these vehicles can be considered. There is no real reason why motorcycles should be allowed to make as much noise as the largest commercial vehicles carrying considerable payloads.

In addition, care must be taken to force manufacturers to use design principles that make later manipulations and modifications of these vehicles difficult or impossible. Motorcycles show the greatest range of sound levels found in real traffic, and a major part of this is probably due to modifications effected by their owners.

In the United States, the EPA has estimated the cost increase per engine when decreasing the noise emission level from 86 dB(A), according to SAE J 331 a, to 83, 80 and 78 dB(A). This increase amounts to 0.3 per cent, 2.0 per cent and 6.6 per cent, respectively.

5. MOPEDS

In this class of vehicle, remarkable progress in noise reduction has already been achieved. Continued improvement can be ensured by making design specifications part of the certification conditions. One example is the requirement of a centrifugal clutch precluding any engine acceleration while the vehicle is stationary.

A general requirement is the use of well-defined and identifiable component parts that neither need nor allow adjustments. The best product is one with a minimum number of separate parts, so that later modifications of the vehicle by the owner become difficult or impossible.

6. ADDITIONAL MEANS OF REDUCING NOISE FROM MOTOR VEHICLES

Road Surfaces

Studies on road/tyre noise have shown that the road surface itself can be an important parameter. It has been known for a long time that very rough road surfaces, such as cobbled roads, cause an increased noise level and should be replaced by asphalt roads in cities or residential areas. Some planning authorities working on new concepts of residential streets may need to be reminded of this.

In addition, certain types of asphalt surfaces classified as drainage surfaces, because of their porous structure, have been found to have excellent acoustic absorption characteristics. This already leads to a reduction of motor vehicle noise of the order of 2 to 4 dB(A) for stationary vehicles with the engine running. In the case of moving traffic, both engine noise and road/tyre noise can be reduced by 3 to 6 dB(A). Resurfacing a section of motorway with a drainage-type surface of only 4 cm thickness has reduced roadside noise levels by 3-4 dB(A); this corresponds to a reduction of traffic volume from 100 per cent to 45-50 per cent. This improvement can be applied locally at short notice, and is especially interesting in cities. There it could probably be used as an acoustical compensation for traffic concentrations on main streets. These methods need additional research before they can be applied on a large scale.

Traffic Control

Accelerating vehicles, at traffic intersections, for example, give rise to substantial noise emissions. The irregular traffic flow is in some areas improved by "green waves" and "fly overs" at cross-roads. Further improvements could be made, for example, by making traffic lights more easily visible at a distance, or even providing traffic information electronically.

Barring noisy vehicles, particularly heavy commercial vehicles and motorcycles, from sensitive areas could improve the situation. For example, their use could be prohibited at weekends, on public holidays, and/or during the night in residential and recreational areas. This would also reduce local air pollution. Quiet vehicles could be allowed, since this would be an incentive for their construction and use.

Chapter V

NEW VEHICLE SYSTEMS AND ALTERNATIVE POWERPLANTS

1. BACKGROUND

Over the last few decades there has been considerable interest in alternative engines which would replace the conventional Otto cycle, because of superior fuel economy characteristics, inherently low emissions, superior performance or some combination of the above.

Brayton

Also known as the gas turbine, this is a continuous-burning engine in which the hot gases produced by the burning air/fuel mixture are expanded through a turbine to provide power. These engines have the potential to provide excellent fuel savings, low emissions and high adaptability to different fuels; however, initial costs could be significantly greater than for Otto cycle engines, and manufacturability will be complex. Torque and response characteristics do not meet modern road vehicle requirements. Ceramic technology will be a critical element of this engine as it emerges.

Stirling

This continuous combustion engine transfers heat from the burning air/fuel mixture to a separate closed system containing a non-condensible working fluid. In producing power, the working fluid is alternatively cooled during compression and heated during expansion. The design of the engine also provides for recycling most of the heat energy left in the working gas after expansion. This engine has appeared very promising for many years because of its potentially high fuel efficiency. It should also be easily adaptable to various alternative fuels. Once again, however, high costs have been a major stumbling block. Low emissions could be obtained, depending on the fuel used.

Rankine

Since the best working fluid appears to be water, these engines are also frequently referred to as steam engines. The working fluid is vaporised and superheated in a boiler, expanded to produce power, and then condensed back to a liquid for re-use. This engine, while offering the same potentially low emissions and good fuel adaptability as the Brayton and Stirling engines, offers inferior fuel savings and is therefore unlikely to emerge in the future.

Electric

Electric engines consist of a system to direct electrical energy from rechargeable batteries through an electric motor to propel a car. To go beyond their current limited applications in short range vehicles will require a major breakthrough in battery technology. Furthermore, their pollution characteristics are dependent on those of the electricity-generating facility.

2. CONCLUSIONS

While there are many attractive features in alternative powerplants, their widespread commercialisation during this decade appears unlikely. Work is continuing, and it may be that emerging materials, such as ceramics, will reduce their cost and increase the likelihood of their use during the next ten years.

Chapter VI

FUEL MODIFICATIONS: UNLEADED GASOLINES AND OXYGENATES

1. FUEL QUALITIES

During the past two decades, a large share of petroleum refinery industry investment was focused on increasing the yield of gasoline from the crude oils processed, increasing the octane number of gasoline to satisfy engine compression ratio increases and lowering the sulphur content of fuel oils. Among the major effects in Europe are a substantial increase in the available "cracking" capacity and an excess refinery capacity. Concurrently, the use of lead additives is being severely curtailed or eliminated by government regulation, and this further increases the demand for higher octane. In response to this pressure on lead the use of high octane alcohols and ethers is increasing in Europe as well as in the US. However, oxygenates still play a minor role as a transportation fuel.

Gasoline demand appears to have peaked in most major industrial countries, although a trend towards increased consumption has been apparent recently in some countries. Major new investments are also required to accommodate the processing of heavier crudes and the likely decline in residual fuel demand.

2. UNLEADED FUEL

Background

Lead is the cheapest way of raising the octane level of gasoline and has been used since 1922. A major impediment to the use of lead in gasoline, even after it was found to improve gasoline octane quality, was the very significant build-up of deposits in the combustion chamber and on spark plugs, which adversely affected durability. To relieve these problems, lead scavengers were added to gasoline to encourage greater volatility in the lead combustion by-products so they would be exhausted from the vehicle. These scavengers, which continue to be used today with leaded gasoline, contribute to increased vehicle maintenance, for example, less durable exhaust emission systems.

Impact of Lead Reductions on Vehicle Maintenance

The cost savings associated with maintenance reductions from unleaded gasoline could be significant. Expressed as 1980 Canadian cents per litre, the results of the principal studies on maintenance cost savings from unleaded gasoline are:

Wagner (American Oil Co.)	1971	1.4 c/l
Gray and Azhari (Am. Oil Co.)	1972	2.1 c/l
Pahnke and Bettoney (DuPont)	1972	0.3 c/l
Adams (Ethyl Corp.)	1972	0.4 c/l
Environment Canada	1979	1.2 c/l

The following savings would result if unleaded gasoline were used instead of leaded gasoline:

	Leaded	Unleaded
Spark plug changes	Every year	Every other year
Oil changes and filter	Twice/year	One/year
Muffler replacements	Twice/5 years	One/5 years
Exhaust pipe replacements	One/5 years	None

Overall maintenance savings from unleaded fuel are estimated to average about C$38 per year; for a car averaging 10 litres per 100 km fuel consumption, this is equivalent to 2.4 cents per litre of gasoline for 16 000 km yearly driving.

Overall Energy Consequences of Lead Reduction

The required octane level for finished gasoline is achieved through the use of lead and/or by refinery processing. If the concentration of lead is reduced, either fuel octane levels will go down or the octane must be replaced by increasing processing severity or the use of a substitute octane booster. Increased processing severity operation will result in additional energy consumption and less gasoline per barrel of crude oil. This increases the amount of crude oil required by refiners and also increases their refining costs.

Decreased octane levels usually result in decreased fuel economy of the vehicle, due to the need for lower compression ratio. This is estimated to result in approximately 1 per cent weight increase in gasoline consumption for each unit reduction in octane number.

CONCAWE (the EEC oil companies organisation) has recently estimated the optimum octane number for unleaded gasoline when minimising energy consumption in the vehicle and the refinery, regarded as one system. With RON/94.5 and MON/84.5 the total extra energy required in comparison with 0.4 g lead/l is 44 tonnes of crude oil for each 1 000 tonnes of gasoline. Cost optimum is supposed to be one octane unit lower and would result in a cost increase of $19 tonne (-1.4 cents/l) of gasoline as compared with the base case.

Energy requirement and cost increase at higher octane levels for a single-grade unleaded gasoline. Energy requirement would also increase with lower octane levels. The use of two grades, 92 RON/82 MON (25 per cent) and 96 RON/86 MON (75 per cent), would result in a slightly higher cost than the single-grade case above.

The content of aromatics and benzene in gasoline is estimated to increase, particularly in a high octane unleaded gasoline.

Current vehicles in Europe are mainly made for premium grade gasoline. According to the EEC ERGA Group, almost 90 per cent of the 239 different engines from EEC manufacturers are high-compression engines, so that vehicles need gasoline of high octane numbers. For 1982-produced engine types, about 50 per cent of the total production is believed to be suitable to run on 97/98 RON unleaded gasoline, whereas 14 per cent could use 92 RON unleaded gasoline.

The EEC ERGA project concluded that fuel consumption is likely to increase by 1 per cent to 1.5 per cent (weight) when the octane number is decreased by one unit. However, engines with new combustion techniques, such as the fast-burn system, are not unduly sensitive to octane numbers.

The cost of a "typical" medium sized European car (1.6 l, 200 000 units/annum) running on RON 97/98 and redesigned to run on RON 92 without a loss in fuel saving would increase by about 1 per cent. If RON 94 gasoline could be used, the extra cost would be less than 1 per cent.

ERGA estimates the total investment cost for the automotive industry within the European Community to be $640 million (1983) for the RON 92/MON 82 unleaded gasoline, less ($430 million) for the RON 94/MON 84 case and $230 million for the two-grade system RON 92 and RON 96. Corresponding investment figures for the oil industry are estimated at $1.5-2.2, 2.1-3.2 and 2.3-3.8 billion. Distribution costs are not included and may vary, depending on current system, whether an unleaded quality would replace a leaded, etc. The extra cost for the consumer was estimated at approximately $22 per year and per car in all three cases.

Most US unleaded gasoline is at 92 RON/82 MON, but a premium grade unleaded gasoline, 94-96 RON/86 MON, is also available. The premium accounts for about 15 per cent of all gasoline. The situation in the United States and Europe is slightly different. In the United States, large amounts of leaded regular gasoline are consumed by gasoline-powered trucks. However, use of lead will have decreased to 0.026 g/l by 1986. Moreover, in the United States, the share of gasoline amounts to 42 per cent of total crude oil consumption, as compared with about 20 per cent in Europe. The high degree of conversion necessitates the use of light, high octane components such as alkylates and polymer gasoline.

Japan has a regular grade of unleaded gasoline which accounts for about 97 per cent of all gasoline sold. Recently an unleaded premium, 98 RON/86 MON, was introduced.

The elimination of lead from gasoline in the United States (with the introduction of 91 octane unleaded gasoline) is estimated to result in approximately 20-40 000 barrels per day of excess oil consumption or approximately 0.003 per cent of the 14 million barrels per day which would otherwise be consumed. The total cost of eliminating the addition of lead is about 0.5 cent/l unleaded gasoline.

A 1976 General Motors study of vehicles designed to meet 1977 US emission standards concluded that a 2-3 per cent penalty would be likely to result from going from 91 to 100 RON. An earlier study by Sun Oil found "no significant economic optimum in the range of 91-98 RON". An Amoco Oil Co. study found very little to change in this conclusion, even with different refinery gasoline-to-distillate ratios or fuel saving improvement estimates:

VEHICLE MILES TRAVELLED PER BARREL OF CRUDE

Fuel economy improvement % per octane	RM/2 pool[a] octane	RON pool[b]	Gasoline/distillate ratio			
			1.6	1.3	1.0	0/7
1	86	89	520	530	543	557
1	88	91-92	521	532	545	557
1	90	95	522	532	545	558
1	92	97-98	514	528	540	553
2	86	89	515	526	540	554
2	88	91-92	525	535	548	560
2	90	95	533	542	555	566
2	92	97-98	533	546	556	566

a) RM = RON + MON.
b) Estimated RON to coincide with RM/2 listed.
Source: Automotive Fuels - Refinery, Energy and Economics, Amoco Oil, 1980.

These data show that more miles per barrel of crude are likely as the gasoline-to-distillate ratio goes down (due to higher efficiency of diesel engines and higher efficiency in the refinery, representative of the European refinery situation) and as the percentage fuel-saving improvement per octane increases, but that for any given petrol-to-distillate ratio there is very little to be gained from an increase to 97-98 RON.

Retaining high-octane, i.e. 97/98 RON fuel, as a single grade without lead is not thought to be financially feasible in a foreseeable timeframe.

Gasoline of 91 RON has certain advantages to both the auto manufacturers and the petroleum industry. From the auto industry standpoint, the availability of 91 RON fuel has already been established in the other major automobile markets around the world – Canada, Japan, the United States and (very recently) Australia. Therefore only very minor changes would be needed in vehicles which are, in many cases, already being mass produced. For the oil industry, least investment will be needed to produce 91 RON petrol and refinery energy penalties will be minimised. However, total energy consumption is likely to increase. Low octane fuels are in conflict with the goal of vehicles with low fuel consumption; that is why most European manufacturers require 95/96 RON fuels.

3. FUEL EXTENDERS

Some of the increased cost and energy penalty which might be associated with the elimination of lead in gasoline can be reduced by the use of high octane components, such as methyl tertiary butyl ether (MTBE), tertiary butyl alcohol (TBA), or other alcohols. Alcohols and ethers are currently blended in gasoline in the United States and Europe.

Methyl Tertiary Butyl Ether (MTBE)

MTBE is produced commercially by the reaction of isobutylene and methanol. MTBE has proved to be an excellent blending component for gasoline because its research and motor octanes of 119 and 101 respectively are higher than other major blending components such as toluene, reformate and alkylate. The specific blending octane of MTBE is dependent on the properties of the base fuel. In general, the MTBE blending value decreases as the octane value of the base stocks increases and as its own concentration increases.

MTBE exhibits only small water tolerance problems and is miscible in all quantities with gasoline.

Methanol, Ethanol and Tertiary Butyl Alcohol (TBA)

Methanol is currently used in blends with gasoline. Because of water sensitivity, methanol is normally used in conjunction with TBA, isopropanol or other higher alcohols, usually in the proportion 1:1. Gasoline blends containing methanol and higher alcohols are marketed in the United States with a maximum oxygenate content of about 9.5 per cent (methanol/TBA: 9.5 per cent, ethanol 10 per cent, TBA 16 per cent). In Europe, oxygenates are used particularly in the Federal Republic of Germany, normally at a concentration of 5 per cent or less of alcohols (methanol/TBA).

Ethanol, normally 10 per cent, has been used as a blending agent in the United States for quite some time, due to tax subsidies.

Auto manufacturers in Europe have indicated that blended gasolines up to 10 per cent oxygenates are feasible, provided methanol does not exceed 3 per cent of the total fuel (because of water tolerance and materials problems when vehicles are not designed for higher methanol concentrations). A directive for a fuel specification including low levels of oxygenates in gasoline has been agreed upon within the European Community.

Alcohols are currently available on a limited scale. Methanol is the only alcohol that could be cost-competitive with petroleum products; it can be produced from natural gas, coal and biomass.

A Discussion of Octane and Other Fuel Properties

Present methods for measuring research octane number (RON) and motor octane number (MON) are less valid for oxygenate containing gasoline, particularly when methanol is used.

Even with the proper RON and MON values, the effects of alcohols and ethers have not been fully evaluated. Practical experience indicates that engine performance, when running on a blend, might be different from what would be expected from the values of RON and MON. The road octane number (Road ON) is also influenced. An addition of 10 per cent ethanol in gasoline was shown to give a small but beneficial effect on Road ON, independent of laboratory octane rating. An investigation with European cars gave the opposite effect. The formulation of the alcohol/gasoline blend is important, and MON is the governing factor. Obviously the conventional rating of fuels in terms of RON and MON does not reveal the entire effect of oxygenates as gasoline extenders.

The true values of some of these components on an energy basis are sometimes difficult to establish because they depend very much on the particular refinery configuration and crude oil composition.

Studies have shown savings in the range of 0.5-1.0 tonne crude for each tonne of methanol or ethanol when used as blends (i.e. about 15 per cent alcohol) with gasoline in engines optimised for that fuel. This means that alcohol, on an energy basis, would be "worth" as much as gasoline or more. At present the production cost of methanol from natural gas is only slightly higher than gasoline on an energy basis, whereas methanol based on other feedstocks is more expensive, as are higher alcohols and ethers.

Alcohols and ethers influence other fuel properties such as volatility, material compatibility and water sensitivity. Their effect also depends on the composition of the base gasoline. For example, a gasoline high in aromatics and blended with alcohols will show increased volatility, more severe material problems, but less water sensitivity than a gasoline with less aromatics.

Impact of Oxygenate Blending on Emissions

The addition to gasoline of oxygenates (low-level blends of approximately 6 per cent oxygenates or less) will alter the stoichiometric air/fuel ratio as compared with pure gasoline. The leaner mixture may either reduce or increase the level of pollutants in the exhaust gas, depending on the carburettor setting. The leaning-out effect, provided the carburettor setting is unchanged, may reduce emissions of CO and HC. If the mixture becomes too lean, HC emissions could increase considerably due to misfiring. For vehicles equipped with catalytic converters and closed loop systems, the problem is less significant, as the air/fuel ratio is controlled.

The available data on exhaust emissions when using low-level blends refer to vehicles with catalytic converters. The impact on the emission of CO, HC and NO_x seems to be negligible. There is, however, a tendency towards increased evaporative emissions.

Gasoline containing 15 per cent methanol has been demonstrated in Germany and the Nordic countries in cars adapted to that fuel, which is not intended for use in vehicles designed solely for gasoline. Exhaust emissions of CO, HC and NO_x are reported to be about the same as for gasoline-powered vehicles. An optimisation of the engine for this fuel could result in lower CO and NO_x emissions and lower fuel consumption compared with its gasoline-powered counterpart. Aldehyde emissions tend to increase when alcohol-containing fuels are used, although a vehicle equipped with catalysts will give only small amounts of formaldehyde, regardless of fuel.

4. ALTERNATIVE FUELS

During the last decade petroleum supply disruptions and cost increases have accelerated interest in alternative fuels for motor vehicles. The need for these fuels, especially liquid fuels suitable for internal combustion engines, is of the highest priority for both developing areas and the industrial countries. In 1976, nearly 67 per cent of total commercial energy consumption in developing countries consisted of petroleum and refined products (51 per cent in the industrial countries). While about half this consumption might be replaceable by other non-liquid sources for the generation of electricity or the provision of mechanical energy, there is at present no viable alternative to liquid fuels in most of the transport sector. Such fuels can be produced from a number of sources, including coal, oil shale, natural gas, uranium and biomass. While synthetic gasoline, synthetic diesel fuel, methanol and ethanol are all possible, most investigators have concluded that the alcohols – ethanol and methanol – appear most promising during the next twenty years and probably beyond.

Alcohol Fuels

A spark ignition engine requires several changes to operate satisfactorily on pure alcohol. Basic engine changes include increasing the compression ratio, enlarging carburettor jets, and adjusting engine timing. The greatest concerns are related to lubrication, cold starts, and aldehyde emissions in the exhaust. The problem with cold start can be solved by using a separate gasoline or LPG starting system, or by adding a volatile component to the alcohol. The introduction of pure ethanol vehicles in Brazil and their demonstration in Germany and California have shown that suitable materials for designing and building vehicles for both alcohols exist.

Pure alcohol engines will allow high compression. Together with other fuel properties, an increased thermal efficiency of 15-20 per cent could be achieved.

With regard to diesel engine operation on neat alcohols, most current interest is focused on the so-called spark-assisted diesel and, more recently, on the two-stroke diesel. A spark-assisted methanol-fuelled diesel bus engine demonstrated equal-to-diesel energy consumption, reduced NO_x emissions, no smoke (accompanied by low particulate emissions), adequate cold starting and good performance.

Similar results have been obtained with a dual fuel injection system with diesel serving as the pilot fuel that ignites first. The concept has been demonstrated in trucks and buses. Methanol supplies about 80 per cent of the required energy input.

Emission Characteristics of Pure Alcohol Vehicles

The use of neat alcohol engines will result in exhaust emissions with only a few components as compared with gasoline. Aromatic hydrocarbons (including benzene) are not formed, and PAH emissions are very low. The characteristic emission components are carbon monoxide, unburned alcohol, nitrogen oxides and aldehydes. Engines for neat methanol tend to have low emissions of CO, NO_x and unburned fuel and can be used together with catalysts. Durability of the catalyst systems remains to be studied. Evaporative emissions are low.

Aldehyde emissions, however, can be four to eight times higher than for gasoline vehicles. These compounds tend to be highly photochemically reactive and to contribute directly to eye irritation. Aldehydes can be effectively reduced by catalysts, as has been shown in tests in the United States.

Emission characteristics of the alcohol-fuelled diesel engines are good. They feature low emissions of NO_x, PAH and particulates. Both concepts can be used together with an oxidation catalyst which effectively reduces the unburned fuel and aldehydes. The spark-ignited methanol engine shows virtually no particulate emissions and lower noise emissions than its diesel counterpart.

Liquefied Petroleum Gas (LPG)

LPG has many attractive features as an automotive fuel. Because it is a gas, mixture distribution tends to be inherently good. It is also compatible with most vehicle materials and can be readily used on many existing vehicles with only minor modifications. However, its widespread use is hampered by the practical difficulties associated with its use. ECE is preparing a regulation concerning safe installation and use of LPG. LPG must be stored in containers that cut into space for people and luggage. There are about 5 000 LPG retail outlets in Europe, a large proportion of them associated with ordinary gasoline stations. There are slightly more than one million LPG-powered vehicles in Europe, most of them in Italy and the Netherlands. Tax incentives to compensate the consumer for the conversion cost are normally necessary.

LPG vehicles are usually equipped with two fuel systems to permit the use of gasoline as well as LPG, because of the incomplete distribution network. From an environmental point of view this might result in more air pollution than necessary, because of compromises in design. Vehicles optimised for LPG have the potential of being low-emission vehicles. Vehicles with add-on equipment for LPG usually show low CO emissions and fairly low HC emissions, whereas NO_x emissions tend to be high. The HC emissions contain hardly any aromatics and the PAH emissions are low.

Heavy diesel vehicles can be converted to run on LPG by changing to a spark ignition system. This will lead to increased fuel consumption but give lower noise levels and improved exhaust emissions.

Compressed Natural Gas (CNG)

CNG as an automotive fuel has many of the same attractive features as LPG. Because it is a gas, mixture distribution tends to be inherently good. Also, it is compatible with most vehicle materials and can be readily used on many existing vehicles with only minor modifications. However, its widespread use is hindered by the practical difficulties associated with its use. CNG must be stored in heavy containers which would have to use trunk space and add extra weight to the vehicule. At present there is no network for distributing it comparable to that for gasoline, nor is there likely to be in the near future. CNG could, however, be used for fleets where vehicles can be refuelled on company premises from a large supply and stay fairly close to the central fuelling area, since driving range is limited compared with gasoline.

CNG entails lower CO emissions, harmless HC emissions, little PAH, unchanged or lower NO_x and higher formaldehyde emissions compared with gasoline. To reach US 83 exhaust emission requirements, catalysts would be needed. In Italy there are about 300 000 CNG-fuelled vehicles, and the use of CNG is promoted in some countries, particularly in New Zealand and Canada. Prerequisites for increased use are a price of about 50 per cent that of gasoline, other economic incentives to compensate for the cost of the add-on equipment and changes in infrastructure.

Chapter VII

COMPLIANCE WITH STANDARDS

1. MANUFACTURER-DIRECTED APPROACHES

Exhaust Emissions

The major manufacturer-directed elements of the compliance programme include certification, assembly line testing, recall and warranties. The advantage of the certification programme is that it can influence vehicle design prior to mass production. However, the certification process must, as a practical matter, deal with certification cars (sometimes almost hand-made) in an artificial environment (e.g. very careful maintenance, perfect driving conditions with well-trained drivers using ideal roads, on dynamometers, etc.). As a result, one cannot say with a great deal of confidence that cars which pass certification will inevitably perform well in use.

The current US and Japanese standards are based on certification of engine families. The Swedish standards are based on the premise that most of the control measures are implemented by car manufacturers in accordance with specified procedures, the authorities operating a system of random checks on the results produced by the manufacturers.

The EEC standards are based on ECE Regulation 15, under the terms of which each type of vehicle is approved individually after testing by the authorities. The regulation system is based on the mutual approval of type tests between the countries using the regulations, control activities being shared by the countries involved.

Switzerland and Sweden are currently co-operating in this area, having adopted the same standards for 1983 and subsequent models.

The Switzerland 87 standards are based on the same administration model as the currently valid Swedish standards, and it may be assumed that their introduction would limit the choice of models, at least initially.

Assembly line testing provides an additional check on mass-produced vehicles to ensure that the designs found adequate in the certification phase are satisfactorily translated into production, and that quality assurance on the assembly line is sufficient to provide reasonable certainty that cars in use will meet standards.

The major advantage of this programme over certification is that it measures emissions from "real" production cars.

Conformity of production could be checked by selecting and testing a random sample of a given car model after the vehicles have been delivered to the consumers. If vehicles are found not to comply with standards, the certificate of conformity could be recalled. This procedure is practised in Sweden.

The EEC rules make provision for follow-up testing; however, effective measures are difficult to implement in practice. Even if test results made it clear that standards were not being complied with, the means of taking effective action would be limited. No instance has yet been recorded in which this type of testing has resulted in the withdrawal of exhaust emission certification.

The Switzerland 87 standards are based on the same regulation system as that presently used in Sweden. Marketing of cars that do not meet the standards can be stopped by withdrawal of certification for the particular type of car. The manufacturer's responsibility for sub-standard cars already sold is not defined in the same manner as in the United States and elsewhere.

The authorities can stipulate that a certain proportion of the cars produced in a particular plant must be inspected, the number of test vehicles being determined in proportion to the production output and in accordance with specified rules. The vehicle group represented by the tested cars is approved if no more than 40 per cent of the tested cars fail the test. If not approved, the original certification may be recalled, temporarily or permanently.

The recall programme in the United States and the programme for conformity of production in Sweden measures emissions from "real" cars driven by actual consumers in the "real" world and is perhaps the best test of how well manufacturers have designed and built durable emission controls. However, when a class of vehicles is subject to recall, air quality is already potentially being degraded by high-emitting cars. Further, in many cases, cars which need remedial action are not brought in for repairs by their owners (only about 55 per cent of the vehicles eligible for emission recalls have been tendered by their owners) leaving a substantial number of high-emitting cars on the road. As emissions standards have become more stringent, manufacturers have also started to allege that they are unable to find means of bringing cars up to standard. In addition, mandatory recalls are only possible when a "substantial number" of cars in a class or category are found to be below standard, which may preclude recalls of infrequent but gross failures. Finally, repair of vehicles when they are already in the hands of consumers may be the most expensive of the options.

Warranty programmes are the last potentially important step in the process. They can help ease consumers' burden when saddled with "gross" emitters but are effective only if States proceed with inspection and maintenance programmes, since vehicles in use do deteriorate with time.

Noise Emissions

Test vehicles for type approval are used in the United States, Japan and Europe. More elaborate compliance programmes such as assembly line testing or conformity-of-production testing are not known to be used to check noise emission standards.

2. INSPECTION AND MAINTENANCE PROGRAMMES FOR IN-USE MOTOR VEHICLES

Exhaust Emissions

It is virtually impossible to check vehicles in use for full compliance with emission rules because the complete compliance tests tend to be complex, time-consuming and expensive. Appropriate tests have been developed which can be used to check the condition of vehicles in use. In several programmes with different designs and stringencies around the world, carbon monoxide is measured while the car is idling. This is the case on a yearly basis in Switzerland, Sweden, West Germany and parts of the United States. In 1986 the Netherlands will introduce periodic in-service testing in 1986 for cars more than three years old. In the United States, many State and local jurisdictions have been required to implement inspection and maintenance programmes as a means of complying with Federal air quality goals. Hydrocarbon emissions at idling are included in the Switzerland 87 and the current US standards. A more advanced test is used in California, the car being loaded by being driven at constant speed on a simplified chassis dynamometer – a procedure which also enables nitrogen oxide emissions to be measured.

Compliance with emission standards by in-use cars is ultimately dependent upon vehicles being properly maintained and adjusted. Inspection and maintenance programmes will encourage vehicle owners to keep their cars in a good state of repair, the service industry to do the maintenance properly and the manufacturer to make vehicles more serviceable and durable.

When more stringent standards are applied, vehicle maintenance will become increasingly important. For example, a catalyst out of operation could lead to emissions 400-800 per cent higher than with converters working properly.

Experience in some States in the United States and some European countries indicates that the idle test is a quick and simple test procedure and is, in most cases, effective in identifying those vehicles which are polluting excessively. In Portland, Oregon, the idle test fails approximately 35 per cent of all cars and identifies 80 per cent of CO and HC emissions in excess of Federal standards. The average CO and HC emission levels of vehicles which failed are two to three times higher than those of passed cars. Most vehicles needed only minor adjustments or replacement of inexpensive parts to comply with standards.

The inspection and maintenance programme in Washington State showed a cost of $140 for the removal of one tonne of carbon monoxide and hydrocarbon emissions in 1982. It has been estimated that the average repair cost to pass a retest was $48 for the approximately 20 per cent of vehicles which failed the initial test. Complying with the short test standards also implies a great potential for compliance with the FTP emission levels for which the vehicle family was once certified.

Experience with heavy diesel engines in Sweden indicates that these maintain their original emission levels in a completely different manner from, for example, gasoline-fuelled cars. Even after covering 700 000 km, the emission levels are roughly the same as for a new engine, with the exception of the hydrocarbon concentration, which does show a certain (though limited) increase due to engine wear, etc.

Consequently, routine inspections designed to monitor stricter emission control standards for heavy vehicles could probably be based mainly on the method of smoke measurement used at present. This would have to be complemented by the random subjection of new vehicles to full-scale emission testing to ensure that production line models comply with the relevant emission standards. However, there are considerable difficulties in establishing a simple, cheap and meaningful smoke test for in-service tests. This subject is being reconsidered by ECE.

The need for inspection and maintenance programmes for heavy-duty vehicles could increase substantially if these vehicles were subjected to more stringent emission regulation. Current standard methods of carrying out complete emission testing for certification assume that the engine is run on a test bed. An engine test using the complete vehicle can be carried out to a satisfactory degree of accuracy on a chassis dynamometer. Since this method would be considerably less expensive as a basis for random inspection, it would appear to be the most appropriate choice in this context.

Noise Emissions

Regular vehicle inspection as currently carried out comprises no measurement of noise emissions. This is mainly due to the lack of reliable and inexpensive test methods.

An international standard, ISO 513 O, has been issued for control measurements designed for vehicles in use. Due to technical difficulties, however, it is not currently used.

Vehicle inspection could be designed to cover mufflers in the near future and, later on, the encapsulation system and engine noise baffles that might be needed with stricter standards, provided that a control measurement technique is developed.

Chapter VIII

CONCLUSIONS

1. GENERAL CONCLUSIONS CONCERNING AIR AND NOISE POLLUTION

Different sets of regulations concerning air and noise pollution exist in the various OECD countries. Increased international co-operation when developing new emission standards will be beneficial to avoid placing a heavy burden on the industry, to facilitate international trade and to avoid transfrontier pollution. However, particular national needs concerning the environment, such as those due to climate, type and characteristics of the vehicle population, driving conditions, etc., would have to be taken into account. Within this framework the implications for international trade and agreements should be considered.

New emission standards should be developed with not only new vehicles in mind. Vehicles in use deteriorate over time with respect to the emission of pollutants and noise. Stress ought to be laid on the maintenance and repair of vehicles in use. Maintaining the vehicle according to the manufacturer's specifications is the best way to slow down significantly the degradation factor affecting the emission and noise performance of the vehicle in use. Environmental benefits would be reaped by having regulations for vehicles in use as well as for new vehicles. For reasons of costs and practicality, however, regulations for vehicles in use should be simplified as compared with those for test procedure for new vehicles.

Because of the long average lifetime of vehicles in use, the environmental impact of new regulations will be noticeable only after some considerable time. There is also a trend towards increased average lifetime for cars. For these reasons, tighter emission regulation should be enforced where necessary as soon as possible in order to reach desired environmental goals. Taking this into account and to provide car manufacturers with sufficient lead-time, decisions concerning new regulations should be taken without unnecessary delay.

Improvements concerning air and noise emissions will not take place without the enforcement of regulations which should specify certain maximum emission levels without stipulating the use of any particular technology. The latter would have to be left to the market.

Proven technology exists to reduce emissions of pollutants and noise and to improve the environment without conflicts between noise and air pollution abatement. Significant improvements in fuel economy have already been made. Work continues on further improvements to emission control technology and to achieve simultaneous advances in emission control and fuel saving. Such technology can be implemented at acceptable costs, provided sufficient lead time is allowed, in which case costs should be marginal, provided that time is used for developing and incorporating new technology in new vehicles.

Test procedures are important tools to ensure that current regulations result in the desired effect on the environment. Test procedures are needed for new vehicles as well as for vehicles in use.

Test procedures for certification of new vehicles should be designed in such a way that they are representative of the operating conditions that are considered important from an environmental point of view. Otherwise vehicles might be made to comply with a standard that will not give the desired environmental effect.

Simplified test procedures for vehicles in use should be utilized. It is important that such procedures should be inexpensive, rapid and easy to apply.

To ensure that vehicles on the road maintain the ability to produce only low air and noise emissions, programmes for controlling production vehicles, durability requirements and vehicles in use should be implemented. Conformity of production tests is a good way of making certain that vehicles sold comply with standards.

To encourage durable technical solutions, special durability tests should be implemented. Regular tests of vehicles in use will entail improved maintenance and thereby durability. These regular tests could be useful even if the simplified test procedure does not represent a wide range of operating conditions, and could be incorporated in an extended inspection and maintenance programme.

Special low-pollution and quieter vehicles are desirable in sensitive areas, like residential or leisure areas, and for particular purposes. Economic and other incentives could be used to encourage the development and use of such vehicles.

The behaviour of drivers is an important factor, especially where noise is concerned. It could be improved by information programmes emphasising the links between driving habits, fuel consumption and noise and air pollution, as well as safety.

2. AIR POLLUTION

Within OECD there are at present three main sets of different regulations and test procedures (the United States, Japan, Europe), and this sometimes makes it difficult to compare emission standards. The United States and Japan have more stringent exhaust emission standards than the European countries. At the beginning of 1988 the EC countries will also introduce more stringent standards. These standards are already applied on a voluntary basis using tax incentives in some countries. It should however be noted that Switzerland, Austria and Sweden have adopted emission standards as stringent as the current standards in the United States.

The test procedures used in the United States, Japan, Sweden and Switzerland were developed to reflect urban and suburban driving. The procedure used in the ECE/EEC was developed to represent urban conditions. With regard to NO_x emissions, high speed and accelerations are of great importance. Test procedures reflecting these conditions should therefore be used.

Advanced technologies are available to reduce pollution by gasoline-fuelled cars. Similar technologies for diesel cars are, however, less advanced. Today almost all cars sold in the United States and Japan are equipped with catalytic converters. This means that more than 40 per cent of the cars sold within OECD are already equipped with catalytic converters to reduce exhaust emissions. There is a range of estimates as to the extra cost for cars of various models equipped with a catalytic system, for example, in the range of $250 to 750 or a 4-22 per cent increase in the cost of the vehicle concerned. Other advanced technologies, such as lean-burn combustion, are being developed.

Trucks, buses and motorcycles have not received as much attention as cars. Their importance is increasing, so that more stringent standards may be needed and are, in fact, being introduced in some countries. Trucks are particularly important as regards NO_x emissions, and buses contribute to air pollution in central city areas.

The goals of low emissions and low energy consumption are not incompatible. Certain technologies to reduce emissions have improved fuel savings by cars to some extent.

Unleaded fuel permits the use of catalytic converters to reduce air pollution of regulated, as well as of some currently unregulated, pollutants. The use of unleaded fuel could reduce maintenance costs, whereas the use of catalytic converters and additional components may slightly increase service costs. The use of unleaded fuel is also desirable because of the effects on health of lead and scavengers.

Unleaded gasoline is available today in the United States and Japan and was introduced in several European countries in 1985. It will be generally available in the EEC area in 1989. Unleaded fuel entails an extra cost of about $0.5-1.50 per litre, depending on required octane numbers and refinery configuration. Low octane numbers would minimise crude consumption in refineries, but would increase fuel consumption in cars.

The use of leaded fuel in automobiles equipped with catalytic converters impairs the function of the catalyst and can significantly increase exhaust emissions. Incentives such as a lower price for the consumer of unleaded, as compared with leaded fuel, would be helpful in preventing misfuelling. This could be achieved through tax incentives.

Subject to certain engine and fuel system modifications, alternative fuels, such as alcohols and gaseous fuels, could entail environmental advantages as well as improved fuel efficiency and security of supply. Low-level oxygenate gasoline blends are currently being used in the United States and some European countries to improve octane numbers.

Possible disadvantages, such as increased evaporative emissions, could occur. It is important to limit the amount of oxygenates to what is technically feasible. Work on fuel specifications should continue, taking this point into consideration.

3. NOISE POLLUTION

The goal set at the OECD Conference on Noise Abatement Policies in 1980 (80 dB(A) for heavy vehicles and 75 dB(A) for cars and motorcycles) had not yet been achieved in 1985. (Values refer to "full acceleration test" as in ISO 362, the most commonly used test procedure).

There are possibilities to enforce more stringent regulations without increased fuel consumption or air pollution as required technology exists and has been proven in both experimental heavy vehicles and a limited number of heavy vehicles on the road.

It is most important to reduce noise emissions from buses, trucks and motorcycles as they are responsible for the peak noise emissions. The 80 dB(A) goal could be met by all but the heaviest vehicles for an extra vehicle cost of 5 per cent or less.

With more stringent regulations there is a greater need for appropriate test procedures for both new vehicles and vehicles in use. Currently no entirely satisfactory assembly line, durability or conformity of production tests exist. To keep up maintenance and ensure that enacted regulations are met, inexpensive and rapid test procedures would have to be developed for vehicles in use.

Noise emissions from the tyre/road interaction is of special importance for traffic outside city centres. Technologies exist to achieve further reduction of this noise without safety constraints. Attention should be directed toward tyres of commercial vehicles and particularly recapped tyres. Porous road surfaces promise substantial noise reductions for traffic noise both in cities and on high-speed roads. Such road surfaces should be used where there is a definite noise problem. Their development is very important, because they reduce the emissions of new vehicles as well as all vehicles in use at the same time.

Restricting noisy vehicles from sensitive areas could provide an incentive for the development and use of quiet vehicles. The introduction and use of quiet vehicles could be encouraged by economic and other incentives.

Low frequency sound should be emphasized more as a noise emission of increasing concern.

Appendix 1

ENVIRONMENTAL POLICY MEASURES OF THE EUROPEAN COMMUNITIES IN THE FIELD OF LEGISLATION GOVERNING CAR EXHAUST EMISSIONS

The starting point of the voluntary phase of legislation concerning the introduction of low-pollutant cars in Europe was 1st July 1985. Since that date Member States have been allowed to grant tax relief (graded according to cubic capacity) for low-pollutant cars already complying with standards to be applied starting October 1988.

On 1st October 1988 these standards will be phased in on a mandatory basis.

The Directive on Lead-Free Petrol was passed making it mandatory, starting October 1989, for countries to provide for a system of lead-free petrol filling stations covering their whole territory.

For the different categories of cars, the following dates of application and exhaust emission standards were determined:

1. Cars with a cubic capacity of more than 2 litres:

   For new models: 1 October 1988;
   For new cars: 1 October 1989.

   25 g carbon monoxide (CO)/Euro-test; 6.5 g hydrocarbons (HC) and nitric oxides (NO_X)/test as aggregate value; however, the amount of NO_X in the aggregate value may not exceed 3.5 g/Euro-test.
   For diesel-driven cars with a cubic capacity of more than 2 litres, limit values for medium-sized cars shall be applicable.

2. Cars with a cubic capacity ranging from 1.4 to 2 litres (medium-sized cars):

   For new models: 1 October 1991;
   For new cars: 1 October 1993.

   30 g CO/test; 8 g HC + NO_x/test.

3. Cars with a cubic capacity of less than 1.4 litres (small cars):

   First stage: For new models: 1 October 1990;
   For new cars: 1 October 1991.

   45 g CO/test; 15 g HC+NO_x/test as aggregate value; however, the amount of NO_x in the aggregate value may not exceed 6 g/test.

   Second stage: Determination of more stringent limit values which shall become applicable on a mandatory basis by 1992 at the latest, for all new models, and by 1993 for all new cars.

These limit values mean that cars with a cubic capacity of more than 1.4 litres shall, as a rule, need a catalytic converter; specifically, larger cars with a capacity of more than 2 litres need a closed-loop three-way catalytic converter, whilst cars of the medium-sized category need partly a closed-loop and partly an open-loop three-way catalytic converter. In accordance with the present state-of-the-art technology, the so-called lean-burn engine also needs a catalytic converter in order to comply with the limit values fixed, i.e. an oxidation catalyst.

The limit values for gaseous emissions fall within the range of values which the Commission determined for measuring results in the Euro-test concerning those cars which comply with US standards.

Whereas modern diesel-driven cars do not have any problems complying with the limit values fixed for gaseous emissions, they do have a problem with particulate emissions, in comparison with cars with spark-ignition engines. Negotiations on limit values for particulate emissions are still under way.

REFERENCES

1. *Better Towns with Less Traffic*, OECD, Paris, 1975.
2. *The Automobile and the Environment*, OECD, MIT Press, Cambridge, 1978.
3. *Urban Transport and the Environment*, OECD, Paris, 3 volumes, 1979.
4. *The Cost and Effectiveness of Automobile Exhaust Emission Regulations*, OECD, Paris, 1979.
5. *Photochemical Smog – Contribution of Volatile Organic Compounds*, OECD, Paris, 1982.
6. *Report from a Workshop on Polycyclic Aromatic Hydrocarbons*, OECD, Paris, 1983.
7. *Long-Term Outlook for the World Automobile Industry*, OECD, Paris, 1983.
8. *Impacts of Heavy Freight Vehicles*, OECD, Paris, 1983.
9. *Environment and Economics*, OECD, Paris, 1985.
10. *The State of the Environment 1985*, OECD, Paris, 1985.
11. *Compendium of Environmental Data 1987*, OECD, Paris, 1987.
12. *Report of Toxic Substances in the Atmosphere-Benzene*, OECD, Paris, 1985.
13. *Environmental Effects of Automotive Transportation*, OECD, Paris, 1986.
14. *Reducing Noise in OECD Countries*, OECD, Paris, 1978.
15. *Noise Abatement Policies*, OECD, Paris, 1980.
16. *Fighting Noise*, OECD, Paris, 1986.

LIST OF THE MEMBERS OF THE AD HOC GROUP ON TRANSPORT AND THE ENVIRONMENT

CHAIRMAN: **Mr. P. FORTON**

AUSTRALIA	Mr. G. McALPINE
BELGIUM	Mr. J. BEYLOOS Mr. P. FORTON
CANADA	Mr. J. HOLLINS Mr. A. STONE
DENMARK	Mr. L. LARSEN Mr. O. MUNSTER Mr. S. SCHMIDT
FINLAND	Mr. R. HAKANEN Mr. J. NYRHILA
FRANCE	Mr. P. BAR Mr. B. DEROUBAIX Mr. B. DURAND Ms. A. EYSSARTIER Ms. A. LE FLOCH Mr. Y. LE GOFF Mr. B. LEQUIME Mr. L. ROPARS
GERMANY	Ms. U. DALDRUP Mr. W. HULSMANN Mr. H. KEITER Mr. K. RIBBECK Mr. H. SCHULZ
GREECE	Ms. V. SOTIRIADOU Mr. E. VASILAKOS
ITALY	Mr. S. CASADIO Mr. G. DEGIORGIS Mr. G. L'OCCASO KRIEGERN Mr. C. LOMONACO Mr. G. PUGLISI
JAPAN	Mr. Y. HIRAYAMA Mr. H. KAJIWARA Mr. H. KOYANAGI Mr. T. MATSUMURA Mr. N. OZAWA Mr. H. TAKAGI Mr. T. TAKEUCHI
NETHERLANDS	Mr. R. BOEREK Mr. BRAAKENBURG Mr. W. HOOGENDOORN Mr. M. JANSSENS Mr. S. JITTA Mr. R. LANSMAN
NORWAY	Mr. P. DOVLE Mr. L. LANDRO
PORTUGAL	Mr. G. CANCIO MARTINS
SWEDEN	Ms. B. BERTILSSON Mr. G. FRIBERG Mr. J. KARLSSON Mr. B. KOHLMARK
SWITZERLAND	Mr. J. AQUARONE Mr. A. CLERC Mr. E. RATHE Mr. F. RIEHL Mr. R. ROTHEN Mr. G. VERDAN
TURKEY	Mr. A. KIZIL Mr. K. TEPEDELEN
UNITED STATES	Mr. G. HAWTHORN
CEC	Mr. E. MACKINLAY Mr. MARK Mr. H. SCHMIDT-OHLENDORF
YUGOSLAVIA	Ms. M. ZLATIC

OECD SECRETARIAT

Mr. A. ALEXANDRE
Mr. C. AVEROUS

Consultants: Mr. T. BENDIXSON, Ms. B. BERTILSSON, Mr. K. HIROOKA, Mr. A. KANAFANI, Ms. M. LINSTER, Mr. T. MAY, Mr. E. RATHE, Mr. G. VERDAN, Mr. M. WALSH

WHERE TO OBTAIN OECD PUBLICATIONS
OÙ OBTENIR LES PUBLICATIONS DE L'OCDE

ARGENTINA - ARGENTINE
Carlos Hirsch S.R.L.,
Florida 165, 4° Piso,
(Galeria Guemes) 1333 Buenos Aires
Tel. 33.1787.2391 y 30.7122

AUSTRALIA - AUSTRALIE
D.A. Book (Aust.) Pty. Ltd.
11-13 Station Street (P.O. Box 163)
Mitcham, Vic. 3132 Tel. (03) 873 4411

AUSTRIA - AUTRICHE
OECD Publications and Information Centre,
4 Simrockstrasse,
5300 Bonn (Germany) Tel. (0228) 21.60.45
Gerold & Co., Graben 31, Wien 1 Tel. 52.22.35

BELGIUM - BELGIQUE
Jean de Lannoy,
avenue du Roi 202
B-1060 Bruxelles Tel. (02) 538.51.69

CANADA
Renouf Publishing Company Ltd/
Éditions Renouf Ltée,
1294 Algoma Road, Ottawa, Ont. K1B 3W8
Tel: (613) 741-4333
Toll Free/Sans Frais:
Ontario, Quebec, Maritimes:
1-800-267-1805
Western Canada, Newfoundland:
1-800-267-1826
Stores/Magasins:
61 rue Sparks St., Ottawa, Ont. K1P 5A6
Tel: (613) 238-8985
211 rue Yonge St., Toronto, Ont. M5B 1M4
Tel: (416) 363-3171

DENMARK - DANEMARK
Munksgaard Export and Subscription Service
35, Nørre Søgade, DK-1370 København K
Tel. +45.1.12.85.70

FINLAND - FINLANDE
Akateeminen Kirjakauppa,
Keskuskatu 1, 00100 Helsinki 10 Tel. 0.12141

FRANCE
OCDE/OECD
Mail Orders/Commandes par correspondance :
2, rue André-Pascal,
75775 Paris Cedex 16
Tel. (1) 45.24.82.00
Bookshop/Librairie : 33, rue Octave-Feuillet
75016 Paris
Tel. (1) 45.24.81.67 or/ou (1) 45.24.81.81
Librairie de l'Université,
12*a*, rue Nazareth,
13602 Aix-en-Provence Tel. 42.26.18.08

GERMANY - ALLEMAGNE
OECD Publications and Information Centre,
4 Simrockstrasse,
5300 Bonn Tel. (0228) 21.60.45

GREECE - GRÈCE
Librairie Kauffmann,
28, rue du Stade, 105 64 Athens Tel. 322.21.60

HONG KONG
Government Information Services,
Publications (Sales) Office,
Information Services Department
No. 1, Battery Path, Central

ICELAND - ISLANDE
Snæbjörn Jónsson & Co., h.f.,
Hafnarstræti 4 & 9,
P.O.B. 1131 – Reykjavik
Tel. 13133/14281/11936

INDIA - INDE
Oxford Book and Stationery Co.,
Scindia House, New Delhi 110001
Tel. 331.5896/5308
17 Park St., Calcutta 700016 Tel. 240832

INDONESIA - INDONÉSIE
Pdii-Lipi, P.O. Box 3065/JKT.Jakarta
Tel. 583467

IRELAND - IRLANDE
TDC Publishers - Library Suppliers,
12 North Frederick Street, Dublin 1
Tel. 744835-749677

ITALY - ITALIE
Libreria Commissionaria Sansoni,
Via Lamarmora 45, 50121 Firenze
Tel. 579751/584468
Via Bartolini 29, 20155 Milano Tel. 365083
Editrice e Libreria Herder,
Piazza Montecitorio 120, 00186 Roma
Tel. 6794628
Libreria Hœpli,
Via Hœpli 5, 20121 Milano Tel. 865446
Libreria Scientifica
Dott. Lucio de Biasio "Aeiou"
Via Meravigli 16, 20123 Milano Tel. 807679
Libreria Lattes,
Via Garibaldi 3, 10122 Torino Tel. 519274
La diffusione delle edizioni OCSE è inoltre assicurata dalle migliori librerie nelle città più importanti.

JAPAN - JAPON
OECD Publications and Information Centre,
Landic Akasaka Bldg., 2-3-4 Akasaka,
Minato-ku, Tokyo 107 Tel. 586.2016

KOREA - CORÉE
Kyobo Book Centre Co. Ltd.
P.O.Box: Kwang Hwa Moon 1658,
Seoul Tel. (REP) 730.78.91

LEBANON - LIBAN
Documenta Scientifica/Redico,
Edison Building, Bliss St.,
P.O.B. 5641, Beirut Tel. 354429-344425

MALAYSIA/SINGAPORE - MALAISIE/SINGAPOUR
University of Malaya Co-operative Bookshop Ltd.,
7 Lrg 51A/227A, Petaling Jaya
Malaysia Tel. 7565000/7565425
Information Publications Pte Ltd
Pei-Fu Industrial Building,
24 New Industrial Road No. 02-06
Singapore 1953 Tel. 2831786, 2831798

NETHERLANDS - PAYS-BAS
SDU Uitgeverij
Christoffel Plantijnstraat 2
Postbus 20014
2500 EA's-Gravenhage Tel. 070-789911
Voor bestellingen: Tel. 070-789880

NEW ZEALAND - NOUVELLE-ZÉLANDE
Government Printing Office Bookshops:
Auckland: Retail Bookshop, 25 Rutland Stseet,
Mail Orders, 85 Beach Road
Private Bag C.P.O.
Hamilton: Retail: Ward Street,
Mail Orders, P.O. Box 857
Wellington: Retail, Mulgrave Street, (Head Office)
Cubacade World Trade Centre,
Mail Orders, Private Bag
Christchurch: Retail, 159 Hereford Street,
Mail Orders, Private Bag
Dunedin: Retail, Princes Street,
Mail Orders, P.O. Box 1104

NORWAY - NORVÈGE
Tanum-Karl Johan
Karl Johans gate 43, Oslo 1
PB 1177 Sentrum, 0107 Oslo 1Tel. (02) 42.93.10

PAKISTAN
Mirza Book Agency
65 Shahrah Quaid-E-Azam, Lahore 3 Tel. 66839

PHILIPPINES
I.J. Sagun Enterprises, Inc.
P.O. Box 4322 CPO Manila
Tel. 695-1946, 922-9495

PORTUGAL
Livraria Portugal,
Rua do Carmo 70-74, 1117 Lisboa Codex
Tel. 360582/3

SINGAPORE/MALAYSIA - SINGAPOUR/MALAISIE
See "Malaysia/Singapor". Voir «Malaisie/Singapour»

SPAIN - ESPAGNE
Mundi-Prensa Libros, S.A.,
Castelló 37, Apartado 1223, Madrid-28001
Tel. 431.33.99
Libreria Bosch, Ronda Universidad 11,
Barcelona 7 Tel. 317.53.08/317.53.58

SWEDEN - SUÈDE
AB CE Fritzes Kungl. Hovbokhandel,
Box 16356, S 103 27 STH,
Regeringsgatan 12,
DS Stockholm Tel. (08) 23.89.00
Subscription Agency/Abonnements:
Wennergren-Williams AB,
Box 30004, S104 25 Stockholm Tel. (08)54.12.00

SWITZERLAND - SUISSE
OECD Publications and Information Centre,
4 Simrockstrasse,
5300 Bonn (Germany) Tel. (0228) 21.60.45
Librairie Payot,
6 rue Grenus, 1211 Genève 11
Tel. (022) 31.89.50
United Nations Bookshop/
Librairie des Nations-Unies
Palais des Nations,
1211 – Geneva 10
Tel. 022-34-60-11 (ext. 48 72)

TAIWAN - FORMOSE
Good Faith Worldwide Int'l Co., Ltd.
9th floor, No. 118, Sec.2
Chung Hsiao E. Road
Taipei Tel. 391.7396/391.7397

THAILAND - THAILANDE
Suksit Siam Co., Ltd.,
1715 Rama IV Rd.,
Samyam Bangkok 5 Tel. 2511630
INDEX Book Promotion & Service Ltd.
59/6 Soi Lang Suan, Ploenchit Road
Patjumamwan, Bangkok 10500
Tel. 250-1919, 252-1066

TURKEY - TURQUIE
Kültur Yayinlari Is-Türk Ltd. Sti.
Atatürk Bulvari No: 191/Kat. 21
Kavaklidere/Ankara Tel. 25.07.60
Dolmabahce Cad. No: 29
Besiktas/Istanbul Tel. 160.71.88

UNITED KINGDOM - ROYAUME-UNI
H.M. Stationery Office,
Postal orders only: (01)211-5656
P.O.B. 276, London SW8 5DT
Telephone orders: (01) 622.3316, or
Personal callers:
49 High Holborn, London WC1V 6HB
Branches at: Belfast, Birmingham,
Bristol, Edinburgh, Manchester

UNITED STATES - ÉTATS-UNIS
OECD Publications and Information Centre,
2001 L Street, N.W., Suite 700,
Washington, D.C. 20036 - 4095
Tel. (202) 785.6323

VENEZUELA
Libreria del Este,
Avda F. Miranda 52, Aptdo. 60337,
Edificio Galipan, Caracas 106
Tel. 32.23.01/33.26.04/31.58.38

YUGOSLAVIA - YOUGOSLAVIE
Jugoslovenska Knjiga, Knez Mihajlova 2,
P.O.B. 36, Beograd Tel. 621.992

Orders and inquiries from countries where Distributors have not yet been appointed should be sent to:
OECD, Publications Service, 2, rue André-Pascal, 75775 PARIS CEDEX 16.

Les commandes provenant de pays où l'OCDE n'a pas encore désigné de distributeur peuvent être adressées à :
OCDE, Service des Publications. 2. rue André-Pascal, 75775 PARIS CEDEX 16.

71556-02-1988

OECD PUBLICATIONS, 2, rue André-Pascal, 75775 PARIS CEDEX 16 - No. 44269 1988
PRINTED IN FRANCE
(97 88 01 1) ISBN 92-64-13045-4